The Future of Consumer Society

The Future of Consumer Society

Prospects for Sustainability in the New Economy

Maurie J. Cohen

OXFORD
UNIVERSITY PRESS

OXFORD
UNIVERSITY PRESS

Great Clarendon Street, Oxford, OX2 6DP,
United Kingdom

Oxford University Press is a department of the University of Oxford.
It furthers the University's objective of excellence in research, scholarship,
and education by publishing worldwide. Oxford is a registered trade mark of
Oxford University Press in the UK and in certain other countries

Published in the United States of America by Oxford University Press
198 Madison Avenue, New York, NY 10016, United States of America

British Library Cataloguing in Publication Data
Data available

Library of Congress Control Number: 2016938015

ISBN 978-0-19-876855-5

Printed in Great Britain by
Clays Ltd, St Ives plc

Preface

It may seem unwarranted—perhaps even bizarre—to devote an entire book to the future of consumer society. A casual glance around would appear to suggest that consumerism is securely entrenched in the United States and other affluent countries. The shopping malls are packed with a seemingly inexhaustible array of come-hither splendors with new bedazzling offerings arriving every day. We are continually surrounded by alluring promotional inducements celebrating the virtues of a world of limitless goods. Moreover, television, which has long been a powerful tool for impelling mass consumption, has, in its most recent incarnation, become untethered and completely portable. Numerous Internet platforms now deliver a relentless stream of marketing appeals to handheld and conveniently mobile devices. Most indications are that consumer society as a dominant system of social organization is more deeply and extensively rooted than ever before. Its most ardent proponents assert that a consumption-driven economy, supercharged with abundant product choice and ample consumer credit, is the height of human achievement.

Given these circumstances, it is not difficult to understand that our political priorities have moved in a similar direction. Government officials loudly champion the importance—indeed the absolute necessity—of economic growth premised on more rapid and expansive turnover of retail inventories. To do otherwise, it is axiomatically stated, is to risk dispatch into oblivion. When consumer society shows any sign of faltering, policymakers avidly rush to the rescue with new and evermore innovative subventions. Trapped by contemporary logic, activists and other visionaries of social change have had great difficulty seeing beyond the strictures of extant conditions.

The point of departure for this book is that the last several hundred years of Anglo-European history have been marked by three distinct, but inevitably overlapping and ultimately persistent, systems of social organization. Premodern society was structured in accordance with an agrarian logic and provisioning practices were determined by agricultural modes of production and consumption. As the Industrial Revolution began to gather momentum in the later part of the eighteenth century, agrarianism was supplanted by a new underlying rationale predicated on manufacturing and its allied activities. Large numbers of people were uprooted from the countryside and forced to remake their lives in burgeoning, fetid cities. Predominant lifestyles arranged largely around subsistence agriculture gradually dissipated as former farmers were increasingly absorbed by the expanding industrial economy. These new arrangements required most workers to sell their labor in exchange for a wage and to use the proceeds to purchase the rudiments with which to maintain themselves.

The acquisition of advanced training, especially in engineering or other professional pursuits like accounting and law, provided a pathway out of industrial poverty and more fortunate laborers elevated their status sufficiently to join the ranks of a growing middle class. During the second half of the nineteenth century, the first recognizable department stores were established and these early "palaces of consumption" quickly became destinations that offered new and unparalleled opportunities for both leisurely diversion and material acquisition. A powerful feedback response developed whereby the enlarging manufacture of consumer goods gave rise to widening opportunities to appropriate them.

Initially during the 1930s, and more intently in the decades following World War II, consumer society began to solidify into a robust and highly resilient assemblage of social practices and cultural sensibilities that in due course supplanted the preexisting order of industrial production. This progression was actively augmented by government policies that raised working incomes, provided for retirement pensions, and enabled construction of new transportation infrastructure and housing alternatives. It was further abetted by demographic trends that delivered an expanding cohort of alacritous consumers at the same time that technologies to enable the mass distribution of goods were reaching commercial scalability.

While commentators like Vance Packard, John Kenneth Galbraith, and Rachel Carson cast a discerning and critical eye on these unfolding routines, it was not until the 1970s that serious questions about the durability of consumer society began to surface. The onset in the United States of economic conditions of so-called stagflation (the troubling combination of elevated unemployment and high inflation), in part prompted by curtailment of international oil flows in the wake of the 1973 Yom Kippur War between Israel and its neighbors, sapped the capacity of consumers to keep the stock turning over. Austerity converged with the radical politics still resonant from the prior decade and prompted a wave of defiance to prevalent consumerist lifestyles. Ultimately, this resistance proved fleeting and by the early 1980s consumer exuberance was again fashionable, aided to a large degree by relaxation of regulatory controls on financial markets. More permissive lending practices and the popularization of readily available consumer credit effectively re-energized enthusiasm for consumption. These developments combined with heightened fixation on social status and cultural distinction in an era of increasing income inequality to further the transition to a system of social organization premised on consumerism.

We are again reaching a point where the prospects for consumer society are once more becoming a subject of topical debate. If we dig below the spectacle that surrounds prevalent and widely lauded lifestyles, we find that the foundations of consumerist lifestyles are becoming shaky and less reliable. To expose these underpinnings, it is first necessary to acknowledge that consumerism is the manifestation of a certain set of social circumstances that have been vigorously amplified to achieve a set of predetermined outcomes. More pointedly, consumer society has been engineered to ameliorate the fundamental problem of industrial overproduction and there is nothing inexorable about its perpetuation.

As industrialism evolved during the nineteenth century and the scale of production expanded to previously unprecedented proportions, it became apparent that affluent consumers could be relied on to absorb only a fraction of the goods spilling out of manufactories of the day. In other words, the pace of production increased much faster than consumption capacity. In contemporary terms, the economy suffered from the interlinked conundrum of surplus production and insufficient demand. To avoid the accumulation of unsold output it was necessary to expand consumer markets by making it possible for widening circles of workers to acquire the fruits of their own labor. While significant headway was made addressing this dilemma (primarily through raising wages and decreasing retail prices), it has never been completely resolved. Even today, producers are regularly compelled to devise more inventive ways to ensure the profitable sale of increasing volumes of goods. We can conceive of this imbalance as the paradox of ever-increasing productivity.

Another way out of this trap calls for reducing working hours and dampening the propensity to generate excess production. Various strategies to this end have been pursued in Europe in recent decades including generous time off for extended vacations and parental leave, as well as opportunities for job-sharing and early retirement. While there is a common tendency to view these interventions as the result of unrestrained paternalism, a more hardheaded interpretation is that it is simply sound economic and social policy to more equitably distribute employment among workers and to restrain tendencies toward overproduction.

The United States has encountered this same fork in the road on several occasions: first in the 1920s, again in the 1950s, and once more during the 1970s. In each instance, the branch toward less work and more leisure was purposefully not taken. The reasons for repeatedly throttling national capacity to consume in order to keep up with expanding production are, of course, complicated, but all of the usual suspects have played their part: shortsighted policymakers, avaricious corporations, and imprudent labor unions. There are now indications that this recurrent design flaw is emerging yet again and calling into question the durability of consumer society.

This book examines several expressions of this problem—the emergence of contingent employment practices as embodied in the putative "sharing economy," the quest for more personally rewarding forms of provisioning inherent in the so-called Maker Movement, and the desire by some producers and consumers to valorize goods with reputed local provenance. The volume also examines what may be the greatest threat of all to consumer society, namely the likelihood that a new generation of digital technologies will further undermine the livelihoods of working- and middle-class households and drastically degrade their ability to continue to uphold their consumption obligations.

* * *

Claims of transition and movement toward a new system of social organization have been in the air for some time. In 1984, Michael Piore and Charles Sabel argued in their seminal book, *The Second Industrial Divide*, that the era of large integrated manufacturing was ending and was being replaced by configurations of nimble firms congregated in vibrant industrial districts and able to respond promptly to dynamic changes in fashion and consumer demand through "flexible specialization."[1] An especially celebrated exemplar was the northern Italian region of Emilia-Romagna, home to dozens of small knitwear manufacturers producing stylish, high-value garments for international markets. This work triggered a wave of interest (that continues until today) in "post-industrialism" and the related concept of "post-Fordism" became familiar across a wide range of the social sciences. A decade later, Stanley Aronowitz and William DiFazio and Jeremy Rifkin provocatively announced that customary opportunities for labor were disappearing and we faced a future without work.[2] These two themes—socio-industrial transformation and the disappearance of jobs—have recently acquired contemporary salience due to a new wave of efficiency-driven changes in the organization of production and the commercial advent of novel digital technologies.[3]

At the same time, public misgivings have emerged in some quarters about the high ecological costs of consumerist lifestyles. Environmentalists and others have, of course, been drawing attention since the nineteenth century to the voracious demand, in terms of both energy and raw materials, necessary to maintain economies organized around resource throughput. The debate reached a certain tipping point in 1992 when at the United Nations Conference on Environment and Development in Rio de Janeiro, 172 nations (including 108 heads of state) convened to endorse the notion that "the major cause of the continued deterioration of the global environment is the unsustainable pattern of consumption and production." In the three decades since this historic event, the risks that consumerist lifestyles impose on the biosphere have only grown more acute. These threats center not only on anthropogenic climate change, but also include increasing water scarcity in many regions, soil degradation, and toxicity as well as more ordinary and long-standing concerns arising from air and water pollution. This situation has prompted development of a research and policy agenda organized around the idea of *sustainable consumption* which seeks to reduce resource utilization while enabling a growing number of people around the world to lead good and dignified lives.

Separate from the need to pursue more sustainable consumption, there are a number of developments that prompt skepticism about the ability of consumer society to hold up in the future. These issues include demographic change, growing income inequality, economic stagnation, and political fractiousness, which are simultaneously combining to erode the enabling conditions that give rise to consumerist lifestyles. While uncertainties surrounding this array of factors are variously acknowledged, there seems to be little recognition of how integral they are to reproducing our predominant system of social organization. This under-appreciation, I argue, stems from inadequate comprehension of transitional dynamics and how, from a prospective vantage point, it can be extremely difficult to discern either the trajectory along which we are proceeding or the eventual destination of our journey.

The truth of the matter is that we will likely need to learn to live, perhaps for some time, with considerable ambiguity. It is useful to keep in mind that the decline of agrarianism and the subsequent rise of industrialism was by no means straightforward and seamless. More readily tangible evidence of the disarray that accompanies societal transformation, and the inevitable incompleteness of any transition, is provided by the abandoned hulks that still stand in many former industrial districts and the dispirited people that often occupy proximate areas. This book seeks to provide a clear-eyed appraisal of the extremely challenging circumstances in which we now find ourselves.

* * *

My own biography is evocative of this narrative about the unremitting entrenchment and gradual dissolution of consumer society in the United States. After being expelled by the Czar's paramilitaries from the Pale of Settlement (part of present-day Ukraine), my paternal grandfather passed through Ellis Island and in subsequent years sponsored the arrival of several dozen relatives. My father came to the country as a young child, attended Harvard for a spell, and during the 1930s enlisted his two brothers to open a retail housewares business in Newark, New Jersey, which was at the time a humming industrial center within sight of New York City. Dubbing their enterprise Imperial Outfitters (a vainglorious name that by most accounts derives from a lucky bet on a horse), they sold a wide assortment of merchandise to customers who were just developing a taste for consumer society.

Their business model was not particularly innovative, but it did help to resolve an endemic predicament of the early years of mass consumption, notably how to distribute goods before consumer credit became widely and easily available. Imperial Outfitters traded in refrigerators, washing machines, radios, televisions, furniture, bedsheets, window curtains, slip-covers, cutlery, dinnerware, and much more, all on an installment-payment basis. The business was located in a three-story building on Newark's major commercial thoroughfare with a showroom at street level and administrative offices on the two upper floors. It was, though, not walk-in customers that Imperial Outfitters primarily sought to attract. Its mainstay clientele lived either in immigrant enclaves in the manufacturing cities of northern New Jersey or dwindling agricultural hamlets scattered across the rest of the state and had—due to insuperable language, cultural, or geographic barriers—little recourse to other retail options.

Housebound women longing for modern conveniences relied on Imperial Outfitters salesmen who would arrive each week in road-battered sedans that doubled as roving showrooms. The commercial strategy relied on these intrepid road warriors peddling a continuous stream of home furnishings, appliances, and other household accoutrements. Customers would make a nominal down payment and then commit to weekly cash installments to satisfy the remaining cost. Imperial Outfitters kept its prices relatively high to compensate for the large number of delinquent accounts and the inevitability of deadbeats who vanished without leaving a forwarding address.

Saturday was always a big day on the sales routes because paychecks came at the end of the workweek and everyone felt a bit flush. The primary task, of course, was to ensure that customers booked a new purchase before the prior deliveries had been completely paid off, thus ensuring a continuously revolving debt. Given that most Imperial Outfitters' regulars had no access to alternative sources of credit, it was only the least adept salesmen who let people off the hook.

Throughout the early postwar period, my father and his brothers achieved reasonable commercial success. The business became a family enterprise. One uncle managed the stockroom, an aunt kept the accounts, and various cousins suffered the misfortune of conscription as summer employees. My mother started working at Imperial Outfitters as a student fresh out of high school and quickly developed a fearsome reputation for chasing down overdue accounts and exhorting recalcitrant shipping agents to maintain punishing delivery schedules. This story, though, has a predictable ending.

By the 1960s, increasing automobile ownership had begun to break down consumer isolation, new highways opened up vast suburban hinterlands and property developers built warehouse-sized shopping malls, and, most importantly, consumer credit became readily accessible and rendered installment plans obsolete. A new retail landscape was rapidly coming into view and it did not include affable salesmen with catalogs and payment books. This marketplace also had little use for the homespun radio advertisements—complete with studio vocalists singing breezy jingles—that my father commissioned and aired on local radio stations. Demise during the following decade came through a sequence of spasmodic contractions, but in due course Imperial Outfitters, and numberless other businesses like it that played pivotal roles in the transition to mass consumer society, disappeared from the scene.

* * *

This book, in many respects, is the result of a collective journey. Ironically enough, the seeds for this project were cast in 2013 while I was a member of a study commission convened by the China Council for International Cooperation on Environment and Development. Our report sought to contribute to a discussion taking place in China at the time on how to more effectively manage the environmental dimensions of the country's relentless transition toward consumption-driven life-styles. I am grateful for the invitation to contribute to the work of the commission and the opportunity to collaborate with Michael Kuhndt, Helio Mattar, Oksana Mont, and Patrick Schroeder. I also had the timely occasion to present some preliminary ideas on a transition beyond consumer society at a stimulating conference on modernization theories organized by Chuanqi He of the China Center for Modernization Research at the Chinese Academy of Sciences.

Critical to both the conception and completion of this book has been ongoing work with colleagues on the Executive Board of the Sustainable Consumption Research and Action and Initiative (SCORAI). Launched in 2008 as a humble effort to create a network of North American researchers interested in absolute reductions in energy and material consumption, SCORAI has become an accidental success story of completely unexpected proportions. From an informal meeting around a conference table in Boston, the initiative has swelled in size to include today more than 800 academics, policymakers, and activists and to spawn affiliated networks in Europe, China, and Israel. My appreciation to Jeffrey Barber, Halina Szejnwald Brown, John Stutz, Philip Vergragt, and, more recently, Emily Huddart-Kennedy, for their tireless support and valued friendship.

I have also benefited from affiliation with the Tellus Institute and the colleagues that assemble under its organizational umbrella. In an academic world that these days is too often caught in the grip of instrumental credentialism, unalloyed careerism, and political opportunism, the Tellus Institute is a cherished sanctuary for unconstrained thought and action.

I am especially appreciative of the support of Paul Raskin, Richard Rosen, John Stutz, Alan White, and James Goldstein.

An early draft of Chapter 3 on the sharing economy was written during the fall of 2014 while I was a visiting researcher at the Sustainable Consumption Institute at the University of Manchester. My thanks to Dale Southerton and Andy McMeekin for facilitating these arrangements and to SCI for convening a seminar that allowed me to discuss this work at a very preliminary stage. I additionally had the good fortune to receive a visiting fellowship from the Research Institute for Humanity and Nature in Japan. Steven McGreevy was a wonderful host and I would have never survived without the generous assistance of Yuko Matsuoka and Haruka Shinkura. Though the book discusses the case of Japan in only very cursory terms, the country has shaped my understanding of the evolutionary arc of consumer society in important ways.

Chapter 6 focuses on how a new generation of digital technologies is likely to upend demand for human labor in coming decades and contribute to significant disruption of established consumption practices. This work was supported by a Lewis O. Kelso Fellowship from the School of Labor Relations and Management at Rutgers University. I owe a huge debt to Joseph Blasi for encouraging me to consider how cooperatives and broad-based stock ownership might help to relieve some of the distress of the pending transition beyond consumer society and to Laura Hanson Schlachter for getting me up to speed on labor-union sponsorship of worker cooperatives.

During the extended period that this book was under development, I had the opportunity to present portions of its gestating contents at the Stockholm School of Economics, Chalmers University of Technology, Vienna University of Economics and Business, the University of Borås, the Garrison Institute, and the Tellus Institute as well as at workshops and conferences at Utrecht University, Fordham Law School, Renmin University, Shanghai University, Kingston University London, and Fudan University. My heartfelt thanks to the organizers of these events and the participants for their serious engagement and thoughtful questions.

This book has also benefited from valuable discussions with several extremely perceptive and engaging students including Karin Dobernig, Jeanine Cava Rogers, and Esthi Zipori. The prior description of Imperial Outfitters is partly based on the reflections of Ronald Cohen and Diane Cohen and borrows shamelessly from a furtive family memoir.

Several publications over the last few years prompted me to begin to synthesize the large body of literature encompassed by this book. The volume draws on cogitations that first appeared in *Futures*, the *Great Transition Initiative*, and the *Green European Journal* and chapters that I contributed to books including the *Handbook of Research on Sustainable Consumption* (edited by Lucia Reisch and John Thøgersen) and *Global Modernization Review: New Discoveries and Theories Revisited* (edited by Chuanqi He and Alberto Martinelli). Preliminary efforts to flesh out some of the ideas in this volume also appeared as postings to the blog affiliated with the journal *Sustainability: Science, Practice, and Policy*. Thanks to Amy Forrester and Ethan Goffman for help on this front. Early consideration of the notion of multi-stakeholder cooperativism that I discuss in Chapter 6 was first published in a contribution that I wrote for the website *Shareable*. Its founder and editor Neal Gorenflo originally brought this concept to my attention and I appreciate his willingness to make space for my thoughts on the subject when they were at a rudimentary stage of development.

At Oxford University Press, Adam Swallow was an early champion of this book when it was little more than a proposal and Aimee Wright and Alex Guyver were extremely helpful in shepherding the project to completion. Susan Frampton and Hayley Buckley scrupulously copyedited the manuscript and Premkumar Kaliamoorthi effectively managed production of this volume.

Moving for a moment from the human to the canine world, I owe a large debt of gratitude to Ruby, a Border collie-Labrador mix, who allowed me to accompany her on daily rambles through the woods down the road from my house. Indeed, sections of this text were conceived while hiking the trails and various passages were initially scribbled in a notebook while my dog patiently stalked her next squirrel. If not for Ruby's insistence to get out every morning, this book would not have seen the light of day.

Finally, my wife, Patricia, has strived tenaciously to encourage me to think about consumer society through a sociological lens but bears no responsibility for my obstinacy and overall inadequate performance as a student. Jeremy, Alexander, and Lydia have endured a distracted father for longer than is reasonable and I dedicate this book to them.

Princeton, New Jersey
March 2016

Contents

List of Figures

1

Introduction

It is both poignant and historically significant that one of the more dramatic, if now largely forgotten, moments of the Cold War occurred not in a crisis room but in the more mundane confines of a suburban house. The setting was the kitchen of an archetypal late-1950s American home temporarily built in Moscow's Sokolniki Park for a trade and cultural exhibition. In this improbable venue, the American Vice-President Richard Nixon and the Soviet Premier Nikita Khrushchev engaged in a spontaneous and vigorous face-off while their aides anxiously scurried around agonizing over how to forestall the political consequences. Journalists afterward dubbed the impromptu clash the "kitchen debate."

The animated discussion occurred at a pivotal juncture in the increasingly fraught relationship between the two superpowers. Four years had passed since previous high-level engagement at the Geneva Summit in 1955 and two years after the Soviet Union had successfully launched its Sputnik satellite. In the days leading up to Nixon's trip, the US Congress took preemptive action, provocatively proclaiming "Captive Nations Week" which encouraged Americans to pray for "peoples enslaved by the Soviet Union."[1] The U-2 crisis involving the interception of an American spy plane in Soviet airspace in 1960 would erupt a few months later, followed the next year by construction of the Berlin Wall.

The repartee between the two leaders covered a broad range of combustible issues, including the rocketry capabilities of their respective countries, the contrasting virtues of communism and capitalism, and the prospects of war and peace. However, because of the backdrop, they could not escape talking about consumer goods. At one point early in the exchange, Nixon gestured toward a glittering screen and asserted that "this television is one of the most advanced developments in communication that we have ... There are some instances where you may be ahead of us, for example, in the development of the thrust of your rockets for the investigation of outer space; there may be some instances in which we are ahead of you—in color television, for instance . . . Wait till you see the picture." The American vice-president then steered Khrushchev over to another part of the exhibit and intoned, "I want to show you this kitchen. It is like those of our houses in California." Nixon then described the electronic controls on the washing machine, observing, "This is the newest model. This is the kind which is built in thousands of units for direct installation in the houses . . . What we want to do is make easier the life of our housewives." He continued to lecture the Soviet Premier, remarking that the house accommodating the kitchen "could be built for $14,000 and that most veterans had bought houses for between $10,000 and $15,000 . . . Let me give you an example you can appreciate . . . [A]ny steelworker could buy this house. They earn $3 an hour. The house costs about $100 a month to buy on a contract running 25 to 30 years."

Perhaps feeling defensive, Khrushchev responded, "We have steelworkers and we have peasants who also can afford to spend $14,000 for a house" and further observed that the American residence would likely last for only twenty years, a construction strategy conceived to ensure that builders could sell replacements without having to wait an unduly long time.[2] Nixon, rarely one to concede a debating point, retorted that it would be ludicrous to build more durable homes because after two decades most Americans would want a different house with a newly updated kitchen. Khrushchev, though, was unconvinced. In the Soviet Union, he noted, "We build firmly. We build for our children and grandchildren." Then shifting subjects and turning toward Nixon, he proceeded to pose a question that was emblematic of deeper and more pervasive mutual misunderstanding, "Don't you have a machine that puts food into the mouth and pushes it down? Many things you've shown us are interesting, but they are not needed in life. They have no useful purpose. They are merely gadgets." After offering an apology, hoping that he had not spoken offensively, Khrushchev declared that "all you have to do to get a house is to be born in the Soviet Union. You are entitled to housing. I was born in the Soviet Union. So I have a right to a house. In America, if you don't have a dollar—you have the right to choose between sleeping in a house or on the pavement. Yet you say that we are slaves of communism."

Despite his reservations about the imputed advantages of obsolescence and contrived demand, Khrushchev evinced an irrepressible interest in the washing machine. Nixon found himself compelled to expound, "To us, diversity, the right to choose, the fact that we have 1,000 builders building 1,000 different houses, is the most important thing... We have many different manufacturers and many different kinds of washing machines so that the housewives have a choice... Would it not be better to compete in the relative merits of washing machines than in the strength of rockets?"

And so it went, for an hour, with the debate racing from jazz music (the two men both expressed little appreciation for the genre) to foreign affairs to military deployment and then back to the appliances displayed before them. At the end of the spirited tour, the two leaders festively shared a cold Pepsi.[3]

Throughout the extended encounter, Khrushchev was simultaneously bombastic and ebullient. Nixon, in contrast to his often dour public demeanor, demonstrated himself to be an enthusiastic salesman of the consumer lifestyle. And this was just the beginning. During the following decades, the juggernaut of American mass consumption steadily gathered momentum and scale under the tacit guidance of a broad consortium of marketers, public policymakers, and product designers. The Soviet system, by comparison, struggled—and in some cases muscularly resisted—to provide people with opportunities to acquire similar contrivances.[4] History has unambiguously demonstrated that consumption-impelled capitalism—measured in terms of both longevity and efficacy—was the superior model.[5]

For three-quarters of a century, consumerism has been at the center of an economic system that in terms of ensuring political stability has few rivals.[6] A prescient Henry Ford gleaned its essential virtue in 1914 when he brashly announced that he would pay his factory workers five dollars per day. The trailblazing carmaker recognized that purchase of the vehicles rolling off his assembly lines required that prospective buyers have sufficient discretionary cash. In other words, employees were also customers and managerial strategies that drove down household incomes were bound to be counterproductive over the longer run. Because Ford was ahead of his time, and certainly more forward-thinking and sagacious than many of his fellow captains in industry, he was reviled for bidding up wages and for drawing attention to the penurious living conditions of the working man.[7]

Though it would take the Great Depression, the New Deal, and two world wars before Ford's insight became accepted wisdom, by the 1950s few people in the United States (or indeed within the expanding circle of countries under its influence) questioned the interdependence between workers' incomes and consumers' expenditures. To be sure, tensions existed with, on one hand, management trying to keep wages from rising too quickly and, on the other hand, labor unions arguing that salaries needed to be bid up, but everyone ultimately recognized that rising paychecks were the source of future profits. The politics of the day reflected this understanding and policymakers, more or less regardless of ideological hue, committed themselves to apportioning the proceeds of economic growth on a generally equitable basis.[8] The economist Paul Krugman expands on this observation when he writes that:

It turns out that the middle-class society we used to have didn't evolve as a result of impersonal market forces—it was created by political action, and in a brief period of time. America was still a very unequal society in 1940, but by 1950 it had been transformed by a dramatic reduction in income disparities . . . How did this happen? Part of the answer is direct government intervention, especially during World War II, when government wage-setting authority was used to narrow gaps between the best paid and worst paid. Part of it, surely, was a sharp increase in unionization. Part of it was the full-employment economy of the war years, which created very strong demand for workers and empowered them to seek higher pay.[9]

This situation persisted until the 1970s when economic anxiety and political disarray (ironically prompted in no small part by former Vice-President Nixon and the ill-fated Watergate imbroglio) began to cast doubt on the continued viability of the familiar economic model.[10] President Jimmy Carter sought to put his finger, maladroitly and not without consequence for his political fortunes, on the sources of this discomfort when he reproved the nation in a speech on energy policy during the summer of 1979:

In a nation that was proud of hard work, strong families, close-knit communities, and our faith in God, too many of us now tend to worship self-indulgence and consumption. Human identity is no longer defined by what one does, but by what one owns. But we've discovered that owning things and consuming things does not satisfy our longing for meaning. We've learned that piling up material goods cannot fill the emptiness of lives which have no confidence or purpose.[11]

However, the American public was not in the mood for self-improvement, certainly not of the sort that the White House had in mind, and this diagnosis was roundly rejected.[12] Far more uplifting was the sunny optimism that Ronald Reagan exuded when he confidently announced that it was "morning in America."[13] This alternative interpretation did not call for forsaking mass consumption but rather for doubling down on its promising allure. Once elected, the new president and his perspicacious advisors pressed forward an agenda that lowered taxes, disabled government oversight, deregulated financial markets, liberalized international trade, and projected a more pugnacious foreign policy.[14]

This multi-pronged strategy provided a kind of macroeconomic defibrillation, jolting the system and reviving the decaying underpinnings of American consumer society. A torrent of inexpensive consumer goods flowed into the country and banks unloosened a complementary deluge of accessible credit.[15] The combined effect of these changes was to put more money into the pockets of consumers (with wealthier consumers receiving a proportionately larger infusion) and to open up new opportunities for households to expand consumerist lifestyles.[16]

While the binge lasted few consumers devoted much attention to the factors that had enabled the headlong rush or gave extended thought to the problems that in due course would ensue. An even smaller number noticed that the federal government in the United States was slowly but steadily losing its enthusiasm for investing and subsidizing activities that had long been pivotal to creating the preconditions for consumer society in previous decades and enabling them to persist over time.[17]

As is now widely recognized, the contradictions engendered by an incapacitated government and a rampant financial industry eventually came to a head in 2008.[18] Large numbers of homeowners in the United States lost their property, banks were dissolved or forced to merge with competitors, and investigations were launched to assign blame. Most people caught up in the throes of the breakdown were disinclined to zoom out to see the larger picture and to do so was in many circles regarded as impertinent or at the very least unhelpful. The undisclosed truth was that the foundations of American consumer society had been eroding for some time.[19] Though the 1970s are remembered as a decade of difficult economic problems—high unemployment, spiraling inflation, skyrocketing energy prices, steeply rising interest rates—it was also a period when several trends that had been strongly auspicious for consumer society first began to shift into reverse. Most portentously, forty years of progress reducing income inequality started to ebb as the earnings of the richest Americans began to diverge from those at the bottom of the earnings scale.[20] A remarkable achievement was that this drift was largely kept off the political agenda until the post-financial crisis Occupy Movement thrust it forward from its disheveled encampment within sight of Wall Street.[21]

This is a useful point to make clear that consumer society is not an immutable historical outcome. Rather, as the economist Walter Rostow recognized more than a half century ago, this system of social organization is the outgrowth of a progression that began with agriculture, transitioned to industrial production, and matured with mass consumption.[22] However, successful navigation of these developmental stages is by no means ineluctable and, in the American case, is the result of a convergence of several propitious processes that initially floated, and have long buoyed, consumerist lifestyles in the country. As this once providential arc begins to bend in a less favorable direction, the future of consumer society becomes increasingly contestable. Let us take a brief look at how demographics, household economics, consumer culture, and global resource availability initially expedited mass consumption and how the reversal of formerly favorable conditions is now undermining the reproduction of familiar routines.

First, the large population cohort born in the United States during the aftermath of World War II triggered a "demographic dividend."[23] The impact of this "baby-boom" generation is reflected in the median age in the country which attained its post-1945 nadir of 28.3 years in 1970, has since risen to 38.0 years today, and is expected to reach 41.7 years by 2050. The households into which the baby boomers were born launched during the 1950s the first truly mass wave of suburbanization and large-scale acquisition of consumer products.[24] Now, as this generation retires, its preferences are shifting dramatically toward smaller homes, fewer goods, and more healthcare services and these changes are having pronounced impacts on provisioning practices in many communities across the country.[25]

Second, household-income dynamics are changing. Robust industrial employment and relatively progressive taxation policies in the United States in the years following World War II steadily and more or less continuously lifted wages across the board, a process that fueled broad participation in the expanding consumer society.[26] Median household income peaked at just under $57,843 in 1999 (in 2014 dollars) but declined to approximately $52,605 over the next decade. While easy consumer credit cushioned some of the impacts precipitated by these developments, access to this source of funds also contributed to rising levels of household indebtedness, bankruptcy, and foreclosure, especially among the poor.[27]

Third, the baby boomers were the first generation of Americans to be immersed from birth in a culture premised on and organized around mass consumption.[28] At the center of this system of social organization has been the suburban house which has both constituted and enabled lifestyles founded on consumerist commitments. As members of this demographic cohort reach retirement age, the costs and inconveniences of outsized houses, with their needs for extensive upkeep and maintenance, are being reassessed. At the same time, their children—the so-called echo boomers—evince diminished interest in this lifestyle. Discerning the extent to which this is a genuine value shift versus a post hoc justification due to challenging economic and occupational circumstances is methodologically difficult. There is though little question that changes in the opportunity structure of the labor market, the implementation of more stringent underwriting requirements for mortgages, and the burden of overwhelming student loans have made the purchase of a home of envisaged size and comfort a daunting undertaking.[29]

In terms of the second most significant consumer purchase, a personal car, evolving practices of both baby boomers and echo boomers are contributing to changes in automobile ownership and use.[30] Members of the millennial generation especially are buying fewer cars, driving less, and using more public transportation.[31] These changes in mobility practices are partly reflected in increasing preference for more "livable" communities and the tendency is contributing to a historically significant process of reurbanization.[32]

Finally, the global system faces several types of resource scarcity, ranging from shortages of precious metals to insufficient fresh water in highly populated regions.[33] Recent attention has also centered on "peak oil," the point at which global production reaches its zenith and then declines.[34] Despite an apparent surfeit of oil at present, with prices at record lows and seemingly limitless supplies, we may nonetheless be nearing this historic juncture. According to geologist Colin Campbell, we are consuming four barrels of oil for each one newly identified.[35] While deep-water drilling, hydraulic fracturing (fracking), and the exploitation of tar sands and other nonconventional sources are picking up some of the slack, the era of readily exploitable supplies appears to be waning. In the near-term future, if we do not successfully transition away from fossil fuels (a problem only made more urgent by climate change), we will need to pursue more expensive (and environmentally harmful) sources. Meanwhile, over the medium to long term, demand will continue to grow—albeit more slowly than anticipated a few years ago—in China, India, and emerging markets in the global South.[36] Increasing prices will over time pose pronounced difficulties for the United States, which has not appreciably improved its energy efficiency or made adequate headway expanding renewable sources of supply.[37] Ultimately, inexpensive oil has encouraged profligacy and waste, and significant price increases will in due course have profound repercussions on American consumer society.[38]

So the primary question pursued by this book boils down to the following: Can American consumer society persist as the preconditions that have enabled mass consumption as a system of social organization continue to dissipate? More specifically, over the next few decades the United States will become a country that is older, less affluent on average, and more urban. In addition, important resources—most notably fossil fuels—are likely to become less readily available and more expensive due to a combination of increasing scarcity and global competition. We may be able to ameliorate the adverse impacts of some of these developments through the deployment of inventive technologies, but it is improbable that such interventions will confer more than partial solutions.[39]

The precursors of early adjustment to these circumstances are starting to become apparent and it is the task of this volume to identify them and to assess their efficacy. Even a quick look about brings forth evidence of nascent developments that signal adjustments to new constraining and enabling factors. With respect to how we meet our nutritional requirements, there is vibrant interest in alternative agro-food networks as households restructure their provisioning practices to favor local and more healthful alternatives.[40] At the same time, employment insecurity and downward pressure on household income are pushing a growing number of households into food poverty which creates dependency on substandard and exploitative vendors as well as, in the extreme, reliance on overstretched charitable organizations.[41] There is furthermore little question that purchasing routines are changing as the Internet becomes an increasingly common venue for food purchases. Some retail experts have already begun to predict the demise of the familiar supermarket, a change that would have ramifying impacts across the entire retail landscape.[42]

The slow pace of top-down-driven change in shifting energy systems toward renewable sources of supply has prompted an increasing number of individuals, and whole neighborhoods, to embark on grassroots efforts to create their own alternatives. So-called community-energy initiatives are proliferating and these distributed production arrangements represent an incipient challenge to the large centralized utility companies that have been critical to the development and diffusion of consumer society.[43]

Cutting across and newly animating these consumption domains are several insurgent social movements. These are not civil mobilizations in the customary sense of campaigns that target the political sphere and appeal to government for intervention through legislation or other action. They are instead assemblages engaged in decentralized and typically impromptu projects joined together into wider networks, often facilitated by the Internet.[44] These multifarious and oftentimes messy activities are focused on designing more livable communities, formulating plans to facilitate transitions beyond fossil fuels, fostering new modes of economic exchange, teaching and learning artisanal skills, and encouraging reductions in working hours and more family-friendly employment policies.[45] Advocates involved in these issues do not typically frame their activities in terms of seeking to transcend contemporary consumer society, but their efforts to develop alternatives to current consumerist lifestyles are implicit in these projects.

At the same time, more threatening storm clouds are forming. The pending commercial diffusion of a new generation of digital technologies promises to reduce—perhaps significantly—the availability of jobs. While employment instability, and even protracted idleness, have been a standard feature of working-class lives, the large-scale diffusion of robotics and artificial intelligence platforms, is apt to displace workers regardless of education, experience, or socioeconomic standing. Transformations in consumption will reflect these changes in work. For too long, visions of the future have failed to consider the essential inseparability of production and consumption and an objective of this study is to bridge this persistent divide.

Consideration of all of these developments in a book of modest size is clearly an impossible mission. Yet, there is unmistakable overlap and mutual dependency across many of these emergent processes. The strategy that I employ is to trace out in Chapter 2 the rationale for invoking consumer society as an analytically useful concept and to marshal the various social innovations outlined earlier into a manageable framework. I explore in the following chapters how three unfolding trends are altering prevalent understandings of what it means to live in a consumer society—the sharing economy (Chapter 3), the Maker Movement (Chapter 4), and the localization of economies (Chapter 5). The first two pursuits have achieved a degree of public visibility over the last few years though critical questions have been posed regarding their scalability as well as their effectiveness as sustainability strategies. With respect to economic localization, efforts to formulate viable ways to proximately reintegrate consumption and production have achieved modest institutionalization, but the overall project is fraught with contradictions and many of the details are still being actively negotiated. Chapter 6 adopts a different vantage point and focuses more directly on how technology is likely to disrupt the need for human labor and, as a consequence, further undermine the increasingly fragile superstructure on which consumer society relies. Chapter 7 provides a concluding discussion that assesses the prospects of consumer society and considers what may transpire as consumerism continues to lose its coherence.

There are a few other issues that warrant consideration before bringing this introduction to a close. First, it must be acknowledged that the notion of consumer society is something of an academic conceit. Treating our activities as consumers in distinct and exclusive terms defies everyday experience because they are, of course, seamlessly connected to our lives as parents, community members, and, perhaps most importantly, workers. Both research and policy programs tend to reify the aforementioned impression by failing to consider the ways in which, for example, the arrangements inherent in a consumer society are inextricably reliant on—and interdependent with—the organization of labor markets. This characterization holds for a vast swath of the social sciences, and most certainly has been the case among researchers in consumer studies and allied fields.[46] It is tempting to try to correct this problem by alleging a causal connection, one that suggests it is conditions in the realm of work that are preeminent because employment provides the financial means with which to consume. However, this deterministic logic can readily be turned on its head: consumption, because it dictates what is produced, is the source of revenue for firms, and thus, income for workers. A more appropriate conceptual view is to regard the relationship as a mutually reinforcing feedback loop where the consumer economy and the labor market constitute a conjoined system.[47]

Second, the outlook of this book is broadly consistent with work on socio-technical transitions (in this sense consumer society can be viewed as a system) though I do not make an explicit effort to embed the discussion in the specialized terminology, conceptual categories, and analytical tools associated with this area of inquiry.[48] Readers familiar with this research will recognize that I am for the most part concerned here with the landscape conditions of the so-called multi-level perspective that has in recent years received considerable attention from scholars in innovation studies and related fields.[49]

Third, it is useful to say a few words about where this volume seeks to situate itself in a larger milieu of evolving thought about the realignment of consumerist lifestyles. Recent years have seen publication of a number of books on the emergence of new provisioning practices and the current work finds common cause with several of these efforts as it seeks to advance the study of post-consumerist possibilities.[50] As the physicist Nils Bohr famously noted, "Prediction is very difficult, especially if it's about the future." Nonetheless, a key challenge for the social sciences over the next decade will be to assess the evolutionary pathway along which the advanced countries are currently transitioning.

Fourth, it may seem incongruous to some readers to suggest that consumer society is losing its salience when the real and virtual worlds that surround us are suffused with commercial appeals delivered through evermore inventive and provocative strategies. It merits recognizing that the promotionalism that is, in many respects, an inseparable part of consumerist lifestyles is just the outer shell of the prevailing economic model and we need to be careful not to confuse its most readily visible attributes with underlying fundamentals. It is the core preconditions of consumer society that are in flux and it will take time for these circumstances to be acknowledged in the vast industries committed to reproducing customary practices.

Finally, it merits mentioning what this book is not. Interest in the future of consumer society often lapses into appeals encouraging people to embrace the ideals of voluntary simplicity and its related lifestyle movements.[51] Some readers may find important value in this guidance, and indeed there is inevitably overlap between the primary thrust of the current volume and efforts to seek out more parsimonious ways of contentment.[52] Moreover, a genuinely sustainable future will ultimately require significant reductions in energy and material throughput on the part of the world's most affluent consumers, as well as cultural validation of a commitment to sufficiency.[53] However, because most expressions of frugal living rely on individualized processes of discovery they are unlikely to offer a compelling prescription to more than a handful of individuals in otherwise prosperous countries who are predisposed to such practices. Furthermore, appeals for self-imposed downshifting will not be favorably received by the growing ranks of people forced to face increasingly precarious social and economic circumstances due to temporary unemployment or increasing privation because of a complete loss of steady work.[54] The challenge for the future instead will be to identify alternatives for moving beyond consumer society and that simultaneously satisfy all three pillars of sustainability—social, environmental, and economic.

* * *

Chapter 2 introduces a conceptual framework for studying changes currently taking place with respect to the macroscale features of contemporary consumer society. Though it is possible to trace emergent developments back to the 1970s, the 2008 financial crisis accelerated and made more tangible several of the most important trends. The chapter also describes the relevance of household consumption practices to current debates surrounding efforts to anticipate and plan for a more sustainable future. Central to this interpretation are the economic and societal impacts of demographic ageing, wage stagnation, new lifestyle priorities, political paralysis, and constrained resource availability which in combination are impeding the ability of households to reproduce customary consumerist lifestyles.

Chapter 3 turns attention to manifestations of these changes by examining the so-called sharing economy which is premised on establishing ways to redefine the boundaries between product ownership and use and creating opportunities for collaboration between producers and consumers. The most popular "platforms" extend already familiar notions of peer-to-peer provisioning to livery services, overnight accommodations, and clothing exchanges but there is considerable divergence between idealized conceptions of the sharing economy and actual performance. While supporters of the sharing economy continue to describe these developments as evidence of spreading mutuality, detractors regard them as another manifestation of growing reliance on contingent labor and spreading economic insecurity.

Chapter 4 focuses on 3D printing, homecrafting, and other activities comprising the Maker Movement which blurs the traditional dividing lines between production and consumption (sometimes known as "prosumption"). Whether working from a spare room at home or as a tenant of a "makerspace" in a renovated industrial building, recent years have seen a proliferation of interest in all manner of do-it-yourself (DIY) fabrication. Numerous cities in the United States and elsewhere regularly host "Maker Faires" and a growing number of communities have embraced making as way to generate new employment opportunities and to reenergize languishing manufacturing districts.

The third case presented in Chapter 5 investigates what may be the most familiar strategy for forging new provisioning arrangements. Farmers' markets, neighborhood breweries, and downtown shops that sell proximately branded goods are all examples of economic localization. Proponents are motivated by a desire to offer alternatives to the mass-marketed merchandise at big-box retailers, to reduce the need for long-distance transport of products (and their associated carbon emissions) from far-flung factories, and to build more intimate and solidaristic economies less premised on anonymous transactional relationships.

Chapter 6 takes a slightly different perspective and seeks to understand how consumer society is likely to be further transformed by changes in the organization of work. Consumption patterns are strongly shaped by the availability and terms of employment and we seem to be standing on the verge of major upheaval from a new generation of digital technologies that promises to substantially reduce demand for labor. Based on artificial intelligence and robotics, these applications threaten to disrupt entire professions, from accounting to medicine, and to markedly shift the capacity of people to partake in customary provisioning routines. This chapter considers the anticipated scope of these developments and offers a number of recommendations on how we might reduce some of the dislocation caused by their diffusion.

Finally, Chapter 7 returns to themes consistent with a broadly historical perspective of sequential transition from agrarianism to industrialism to consumerism and considers longer-term processes in the United States and other countries. The intention is to regard these developments—both ongoing and prospective—as not merely evanescent trends but rather as early indications that consumer society is receding and nascent alternatives are slowly starting to coalesce into distinguishable forms. This future is not prefigured, though important questions clearly pertain to our capacity to act with wisdom and compassion and to pursue the most efficacious pathway.

2

Fathoming Consumer Society

Introduction

Nearly four decades have elapsed since policymakers in the United States devoted serious attention to the future of consumer society. Wracked by rampant inflation, high unemployment, flagging economic growth, and crippling resource shortages, and gripped by a mood that was described at the time as "malaise," speculation was rife that consumerism as the predominant system of social organization was in jeopardy.[1] As it turned out, this anxiety was unwarranted, or at least premature. During the intervening years, government officials managed to forestall, and then reverse, the envisaged breakdown. Construction of expansive new shopping malls resumed, women went to work in larger numbers, consumers bulked up on credit cards, inexpensive merchandise flowed in from China, and, before long, any unease about the apparent durability of consumer society was successfully dispelled.

During the following decades, at least in places that were able to avoid being upended by the untoward effects of globalization, the prevalent mood became one of blithe confidence. Policymakers encouraged consumers to suppress their transactional inhibitions and to partake in a rash of hedonistic indulgence. Permissive consumerism was, after all, good for business and, perhaps most importantly, contributed positively to the macroeconomic indicators on which politicians measured their success. While this compelling narrative remained more or less intact for three decades, the triumphalism surrounding consumer society was part of a larger syndrome asserting that there was no need for apprehension about the future because we had, at least according to the impulsive appraisal of some commentators, reached "the end of history."[2]

If we turn the clock back to the years following World War II, we discover that the era was marked by widespread popular fascination and expansive scholarly inquiry about the future. Prominent authors wrote magisterial volumes charting the effects of converging and diverging trends and sought to understand the deep processes of social change shaping the evolutionary trajectory of societies.[3] Legions of visitors flocked to futuristic world fairs and, coincident with the diffusion of television, became entranced by the Mercury, Gemini, and Apollo space programs. Ambitious political projects to improve social welfare, housing, and transportation while breaking down barriers of racial and gender inequality promised an age of unprecedented progress.

While it is difficult to pinpoint with precision when policymakers began to lose interest in the future, the early 1980s emerges as a key transitional moment. The neoliberal insurgencies that took control of government in the United States and a number of other countries around the world during these years had little affection for planning and consideration of alternative pathways. The predominant *Weltanschauung* was—and to a large extent continues to be—driven by market imperatives and advocates of this view insisted that there was no need to get involved in trying to make sense of longer-range processes or to develop capacity for anticipation. Anyone who tried to do so was denounced as a fool, an irrepressible romantic, or a socialist. Indeed, the travails of the Soviet Union, and then its eventual dismantlement, only served to reinforce the influence of this perspective across the political spectrum. Social forecasting, technology assessment, and futures road-mapping were replaced by more mundane activities involving the estimation of market potential and the preparation of cost-benefit analysis.[4]

Within academic circles, three additional reasons contributed to the withering of interest in the future. First, the quantitative revolution favored the development and deployment of computerized algorithms to assess vast amounts of historical data, but the underlying methodologies were mostly premised on linear extrapolations. Because studies of the social dynamics of prospective futures do not lend themselves to such techniques, and instead require more artfully constructed methodologies, they fell victim to the rush to embrace the computer and an inability to offer an assured route to remunerative professional opportunities. Colleges and universities steered their most capable students toward different specialties to ensure that they would be able to find gainful employment. The most unfortunate ramification of these developments was that systematic consideration of the future came to be centered on questions involving, for example, when Moore's Law would run its course or what Steve Jobs would conjure up as the next Apple innovation.

Second, decline of concern for the future was abetted by processes of intellectual fragmentation (often called "silo-ization") as each discipline retreated into its own cloistered enclave to pursue matters of limited value beyond its own walls or to the world at large.[5] This pattern of withdrawal was driven by declining regard for the non-economics social sciences in contributing meaningfully to policy processes, but it also stemmed from the fact that expansive theorizing about the future requires appreciation for multiple—and not infrequently conflicting— disciplinary perspectives. Graduate programs in the major universities focused their resources on training technical experts and over a couple of generations this trend has exacted a heavy toll on intellectual creativity and willingness to ask tough questions about big problems.

Finally, the post-1980 neoliberal revolutionaries regarded consideration of longer-range futures as tantamount to communist-era central planning and defunded research programs dedicated to this work. The *Global 2000* report published in 1980 was the last time that the federal government in the United States embarked on a broadly conceived and publicly accessible research project of its type.[6] Commissioned three years earlier by President Carter, the report was widely vetted by scientific councils and received extensive coverage in the popular media.[7] However, because the appraisal offered a decidedly downcast interpretation of prospective developments, particularly in terms of resource availability and ecosystem health, it received a cool political reception.[8]

And then things changed radically. One of the first indications that something new was in the air came during the early autumn of 2007 when nervous depositors started to queue up at branches of the British bank Northern Rock.[9] Soon afterward news stories began to appear about dodgy dealings at an array of Icelandic banks with insouciant names like Icebank. The next shoe to drop involved initial disclosures outlining the monumental scale of the predatory lending practices of a number of major American financial institutions and a whole new vocabulary of once-obscure terms cascaded into the daily lexicon: collateralized debt obligations, credit-default swaps, and mortgage-backed securities. A surprisingly large number of seemingly savvy, but ultimately credulous, investors soon discovered that their life savings had gone down the drain of a gargantuan Ponzi scheme engineered by the criminal

Bernie Madoff. Panicked governments were pressed to the wall, desperately lending vast amounts to effectively insolvent banks to keep the global economy afloat and later printing billions more through a curiously called practice known as quantitative easing. In little more than the blink of an eye, the flush days of unbridled enthusiasm had turned dark and the future of consumer society was no longer so unreservedly assured, and it was not just the usual disaffected chorus grousing from the sidelines.

Stephen Roach, the former chair of Morgan Stanley Asia, was one of the first to clang the bell when he forthrightly proclaimed late in 2008 that "It's game over for the American consumer."[10] A parade of eminent economists followed with their own ominous declarations. Using language that had been dormant since the 1970s, Nobel laureate Joseph Stiglitz observed that the United States economy was in a "long malaise" and that "the American dream, a good life in exchange for hard work . . . is slowly dying."[11] Northwestern University economist Robert Gordon, issued a report under the august banner of the National Bureau of Economic Research with the unnerving title, "Is U.S. Economic Growth Over?"[12] Steven King, the chief economist for HSBC, postulated in the title of his widely read book that we had reached "the end of Western affluence."[13] And this was just the beginning, nor was consternation confined to academic seminars and Wall Street boardrooms. Even in sundrenched southern California, in many respects the birthplace of contemporary consumer society, Los Angelenos awoke one morning in 2009 to a litany of disturbing questions from one of the city's most popular media outlets:

Is this the end of the consumer society? The evidence is growing that America is undergoing a fundamental economic restructuring . . . [and there is] the possibility that some radical cultural shift is taking place . . . How does America adjust to a zero growth society? Can we live without all the toys of a hyperconsumer society?[14]

These concerns about the shaky prospects of consumer society had a certain catalytic effect and unleashed a form of cultural criticism that in the United States had long been suppressed, or at least marginalized, for the better part of thirty years. Jeremiads against consumerist lifestyles are, of course, as old as the system itself and its most excessive practices have not been difficult to disparage.[15] Nonetheless, rabid denunciations seemed by the early 1980s to have fallen out of favor, but that is the case no longer.[16] The financial crisis released a reservoir of pent-up frustration and the last few years have given rise to a veritable flood of condemnation of the presupposed banality of consumer society and, in some cases, hopeful enthusiasm for what is anticipated will be its pending denouement.[17] New channels have also opened up to authors interested in communicating the results of lifestyle experiments premised on rejection of the world of goods and to advocates of self-help therapies intended to cure what are described as "shopping addictions."[18]

Claims that consumerist lifestyles are attenuating have also fueled wide-ranging debates on the future of capitalism, the viability of the American Dream, and the ability of the United States to maintain its commanding position in international affairs.[19] A recent characterization by journalists Robert Borosage and Katrina vanden Heuvel is emblematic of this dire perspective:

Every element of the dream is imperiled. Wages for the 70% of Americans without a college education have declined dramatically over the past forty years, although CEO salaries and corporate profits soared. Corporations continue to ship good jobs aboard, while the few jobs created at home are disproportionately in the low-wage service sector. One in four homes is underwater, devastating what has been the largest single asset for most middle-class families. Healthcare costs are soaring, with nearly 50 million uninsured. Half of all Americans have no retirement plan at work, pensions are disappearing and even Social Security and Medicare are targeted for cuts. College debt now exceeds credit card debt with defaults rising and more and more students priced out of higher education.[20]

A related phenomenon is how the fine print of economic analyses—for instance, monthly employment estimates and projections of new-home construction—have seeped out of government bureaus and policy think tanks to become part of the daily news cycle. Moreover, if the regular release of these data was not sufficient, even the revisions that are subsequently issued to adjust key figures on the basis of more robust aggregations have become fodder for raucous debate in bars and online forums. For instance, it is not uncommon to encounter exchanges about whether the downward adjustment in the latest jobs report was due to a severe snowstorm that kept shoppers stuck at home or an unexpected spike in gasoline prices.

A still further trend of perhaps even greater wonderment is how dour-faced central bankers have become celebrities with television commentators opining on the brand of their latest suit and the style of their recent haircut.[21] Every carefully articulated syllable is parsed and disambiguated with Talmudic precision in the hope of discerning a clue about the future direction of interest rates or adjustment of the money supply. Part of this strange turn of events stems from the fact that media venues have a lot of space to fill and need to manufacture conversation to occupy the long hours. We should, though, not underestimate the extent to which all of this scrutiny reflects preoccupation with the fragility of the economy and widespread recognition that current conditions are deeply unsettled.

Contemplating this situation, futures thinker Paul Raskin writes, "We live in an extraordinary time, a turbulent interregnum between the familiar world of the past and a very different one in the making" and many observers of the current historical moment would likely not disagree.[22] This chapter takes this contention as its point of departure and explores its implications from the standpoint of contemporary provisioning practices. The next section, "Defining Consumer Society," advances the concept of the consumer society as a focus for serious scholarship. The third section, "The Precariousness of Consumer Society," outlines the reasons for the current instability of consumerist lifestyles and the fourth section, "A Transition beyond Consumer Society?" surveys evidence of a putative transition. The contours of a successor system of social organization have not to date received a great deal of attention and the penultimate section, "Envisioning Post-Consumer Society," takes up the challenge of discerning its broad outlines. The conclusion to this chapter offers a roadmap of the remaining chapters of the book which are intended to provide more grounded insights on the future of consumer society.

Defining Consumer Society

A reasonable question to ask is whether the compilation of indictments issued against consumer society in recent years constitutes an ultimately disabling assessment of its future durability. Guardians of the status quo often contend that all countries use resources to a greater or lesser extent and that this appropriation is hardly a remarkable attribute of lifestyles in the United States or anywhere else. Moreover, this customary rejoinder often further observes that avid pursuit of material goods is not a new fascination—consumption has been a quotidian feature of life throughout history.[23] It is notable that this understanding, prevalent though it may be, fails to recognize just how deeply consumerism has penetrated the fiber of daily existence and how truly pervasive its logic has become in reproducing large parts of the contemporary world.

According to the World Bank, 68.6 percent of the gross domestic product (GDP) in the United States in 2013 was attributable to consumption (the remainder comprises investment and government spending).[24] The comparable figure for France was 55.3 percent and 64.6 percent for the United Kingdom.[25] An important tenet of this book is that these amounts are not just aggregate measures of the monetary value of physical quantities. In a consumer society, it is through the use of goods (and services) that we forge our identities and develop an understanding of our place in the world.[26] It is through consumer purchases—and the way that we display them—that we communicate with our friends, co-workers, family members, and others about what we regard as important and what we want to signal about ourselves.[27] While the term is often used in jest or as a form of self-deprecation, the point here is that we *really* do live in consumer society.

The *Oxford English Dictionary* defines consumer society as "a society in which the buying and selling of consumer goods and services is the predominant social and economic activity" and traces the first usage of the term to 1920.[28] We can attribute development of this mode of social organization to four interlocking processes that have unfolded over the past two centuries: disembedding, social atomization, pseudo-individualization, and commodification. Each of these factors has been constitutive of the seemingly ineluctable march of modernization but as a practical matter has also been harnessed by both government and business to intensify and deepen the development of consumer society.

First, human relations have come to be increasingly disembedded from local contexts where tradition and established standards previously provided the basis for determining socially sanctioned conduct.[29] Interactions, especially for economic purposes, are now carried out over longer distances (sometimes referred to as distanciation) and with respect to consumption have been grounded in abstract systems like money rather than in more proximately negotiated arrangements centered on reciprocity and solidarity. As a commercial strategy, disembedding has been extremely effective in moving activities that were once performed individually or within kinship networks into the realm of the market where they have become subject to transactional logic and susceptible to manipulation for strategic purposes.

Second, social atomization refers to the fragmentation of a preexisting collectivity or community into smaller and more distinct units, a process that weakens interpersonal cohesion and the connections that people have to larger aggregations. Adam Smith famously asserted that "social atomization was a prerequisite to perfect competition" because it frees people from established modes of thinking, positions them in oppositional relationships, and encourages a greater sense of personal responsibility.[30] It can, however, be extremely challenging for people to construct an individualized biography without reference to larger social constructs and to navigate in the world without the surety offered by fixed points of orientation. Under such circumstances, assistance in building larger conceptual frameworks—whether from demagogic leaders or clever marketing managers—can provide comfortable assurance and offset fears that we need to cope entirely on the basis of our own capabilities.

Third, the notion of pseudo-individualization is generally attributed to the German sociologist and philosopher Theodor Adorno who in his critique of the "culture industry" highlighted how consumers are induced to purchase goods that confer a superficial measure of individuality while at the same time retaining commitment to mass production and the efficiencies inherent in standardization.[31] In such a way, consumer society is able to perpetuate a narrative of freedom and personal self-expression without having to incur the expenses that actual individual customization would entail. This business model allows for the sale of an ever-expanding array of goods with superficial differences but that can nonetheless offer consumers a sense of uniqueness. We thus have an array of automobiles that diverge from one another only with respect to their minor stylistic or operational variations but are nonetheless amenable to the infusion of a distinctive marketing story.[32]

Finally, commodification is the modernization process that captures the Marxist idea of transforming previously noncommercial goods and services into saleable products.[33] Because the capitalist system faces an insatiable need to expand, there is a powerful imperative to continually seek out new markets to exploit. One way to accomplish this objective is to draw goods into the system that are otherwise outside of the realm of transactional relations (and hence freely available) and to induce consumers to pay for them. The discovery that people could be convinced to pay for bottled water—instead of getting it essentially for free from the tap—and converting water into a marketable good is a prime example of successful commodification.[34] More ambitious initiatives have involved the reconfiguration of urban space so that a reliable car becomes, for all intents and purposes, the only way to accomplish daily tasks.[35]

While consumer society has categorically contributed to significant improvements in material standards of living in the United States and elsewhere, its associated lifestyles have a voracious appetite for energy and other resources.[36] To be sure, certain efficiency improvements have helped to contain some of these impacts, but in aggregate the demands that consumer society imposes on a world of constrained biophysical capacity have been immense and continue to increase.[37] This situation is largely a result of the limitlessness of consumption desires which are compelled to continuously increase due to the dual, but reinforcing, processes of consumers pursuing novelty and producers cultivating new markets.[38] The subsequent dynamic unleashes a number of perverse incentives including the operationalization of business strategies that rely on premature product obsolescence, overly rapid fashion cycles, sale of products of dubious social value, questionable promotional techniques, and recruitment of children and other vulnerable populations.[39] The social practices embodied by consumer society also lead to familiar maladaptive outcomes including climate change, obesity, and various unhealthy compulsions as well as sub-optimal results with respect to both collective and individual well-being.[40]

In the current neoliberal age there is a pervasive tendency to reflexively acclaim the sacrosanctity of entrepreneurial heroism and to denigrate government intervention.[41] Accordingly, often overlooked, even by its most ardent champions, is the paradox that in the United States the foundation stones of consumer society were set by robust public programs originally conceived to boost demand for the country's prodigious industrial output.[42] Starting with the implementation of a progressive income tax and the provision of guaranteed pensions, the federal government enacted an expanding array of measures to enable consumerist lifestyles. Other initiatives over the years have included the tax deductibility of mortgage interest, the provision of grants and low-cost loans to local jurisdictions for infrastructure development, and the construction of transportation systems to inexpensively haul raw materials and finished products.

This book approaches the future of consumer society largely from the vantage point of sustainable consumption which provides a useful critical lens for appreciating the material dimensions of consumerist lifestyles and assessing the efficacy of alternative systems of social organization. A policy agenda around the sustainability dimensions of contemporary consumption practices first gained prominence during the preparatory stages for the United Nations Conference on Environment and Development (dubbed the Earth Summit) in Rio de Janeiro in 1992.[43] The cornerstone document of the event was Agenda 21 (Agenda for the 21st Century) and one of its chapters was entitled "Changing Consumption Patterns." This chapter proved to be massively contentious, in part because it characterized prevailing consumption practices in the affluent countries of the world as "unsustainable" and among other objectives encouraged the adoption of policies to "reduce environmental stress" and to "meet the basic needs of humanity."[44]

The years following the Rio conference were a time of energetic activity by several multilateral organizations to further elaborate the concept of sustainable consumption and to generate political support. One of the more notable conclaves was held in Oslo in 1994 where conferees defined sustainable consumption as "the use of services and related products which respond to basic needs and bring a better quality of life while minimizing the use of natural resources and toxic materials as well as emissions of waste and pollutants over the life cycle of the service or product so as not to jeopardize the needs of future generations."[45] During the subsequent decade, sustainable consumption came to be integrated into global environmental politics and attracted interest from a widening array of nongovernmental organizations (NGOs) as well as from national governments and transnational governance bodies, especially in Europe.[46]

This activity prompted establishment of programs funded by scientific councils and development of a research community, though at the time work pertaining to sustainable consumption was largely centered on individual consumer decision-making, dissemination of nominally "green" products, waste minimization, information provision (through ecological labels), consumer education, and institutional procurement. To facilitate more environmentally responsible manufacturing processes, initiatives were pursued under the conceptual umbrella of "sustainable consumption and production" which has involved related attention on energy and materials efficiency and clean manufacturing. In more recent years, the field has begun to move beyond this earlier focus on individual behavior change and technology-led improvements. Inquiry has shifted instead toward more macroscopic perspectives related to the political economy of consumerism, the ecological economics of consumption, the design of strategies for socio-technical systems innovation, and the development of practice theoretical approaches to consumer action.[47] Part of the impetus for this new emphasis has been the realization that policies premised on rational actor prescriptions are unlikely to contribute to unambiguous improvements and efficiency-focused strategies are destined to generate unintentional rebound effects and other adverse outcomes.[48]

To suggest that consumer society is giving way is obviously an ambitious claim, but we can start to grasp the possibilities that it opens up if we are attentive to how predominant systems of social organization evolve over time. In the first instance, it bears keeping in mind that though the term "Industrial Revolution" was coined as early as 1799 it only began to enter into popular usage after the posthumous publication in 1884 of the lectures delivered by economic historian Arnold Toynbee.[49] This is important to note because the era that we commonly regard today as constitutive of a period of world-shattering importance only came to be generally acknowledged for its exceptionality after the passage of considerable time. The point here is that for nearly a century it was only among the most prescient observers of the day—people like Wordsworth, Blake, Marx, and Engels—that the turmoil that we now perfunctorily refer to as the Industrial Revolution held much significance.

Complicating matters is that while it might have been at an earlier moment appropriate to conceive of national economies as relatively self-contained systems impelled by their own internally determined paces of change, it has become increasingly difficult to substantiate such an assertion.[50] Despite evident regional variations, most relatively affluent countries have been absorbed into a thoroughly globalized world and we need to exercise care when considering the extent to which its constituent parts have capacity for independent change.[51] Concomitantly, we should recognize that nations are not fatalistically locked into an all-encompassing juggernaut and they do retain some evolutionary autonomy. However, determining the limits of this capacity will always be tenuous due to inherent uncertainties in the nested system and the fact that relationships across scales are dynamic and continually shifting.

This book seeks to expose some of the gathering trends that are beginning to prompt questions about the future of consumer society and its ability to endure as a predominant system of social organization in the United States and elsewhere. It is very conceivable that over the coming decade the customary consumption landscape will change in striking and irreversible ways. Indeed, substantiating evidence of breakdown is already apparent and more widespread recognition of the underlying processes might help to prepare our minds for future developments, some of which are likely to have an unsettling effect on prevailing aspirations.

Given these circumstances, it is striking that social scientists have to date been so confident about the apparent indomitability of consumer society and have evinced little interest in anticipating what might follow. This is even the case among critical social theorists who have presumably been more thoroughly exposed to the sharp criticism of past decades and might have an inclination to reflect on alternative visions of the future.[52] With the exception of some consideration of the idea of "post-consumerism," the repositories of knowledge are lamentably empty on questions pertaining to how a transition beyond consumer society might transpire and what the key features of a new system of social organization might be.[53]

The Precariousness of Consumer Society

As briefly described earlier, all societies are characterized by an under-lying organizational logic that shapes their arrangements for economic exchange, social interaction, and political decision-making. According to prevalent historical understanding, the past few hundred years have been marked by three generic models that have tended to transpire in stepwise succession: agrarianism, industrialism, and consumerism. Each of these archetypes rests on a set of determinants that the following discussion refers to figuratively as "pillars." These pillars are not everlasting and require periodic reinforcement to ensure continued viability. In the absence of persistent maintenance, they will gradually deteriorate or, in certain more pronounced cases, fall into precipitous decline.[54]

During the middle third of the twentieth century (roughly 1930–1980), the solidification and extension of consumer society in the United States was premised on three essential pillars: propitious demographics, com-paratively equitable income distribution, and mutable cultural values.[55] To further build on this metaphor, connecting these props were reliable joists, most notably in the form of facilitative government policies that put consumers at the center of an imperative for economic growth and sought to ensure relatively unencumbered access to natural resources. These determinants gave a specific shape to life during the middle decades of the twentieth century and their fortuitous convergence lifted a broad segment of the population to steadily improving material standards of living and helped to imbricate consumerist sensibilities into a wide array of routine practices.[56]

During the 1980s, governments were compelled to champion a combination of initiatives—economic deregulation, trade liberalization, technological invigoration, and militarization—to recharge a then-flagging consumer society. Especially important in the United States was the relaxation of controls on financial institutions that led to massive expansion of consumer credit that more than compensated for the slowing of wage growth.[57] Despite these interventions to keep consumer society in smooth-running condition, several cross-cutting currents continued to undermine its most important pillars. First, the American population has been growing older and this process of demographic ageing has now begun to prompt sweeping changes in consumer behavior. Second, middle- and lower-earning households have been experiencing several decades of wage stagnation and these circumstances have taken a toll on their capacity to consume. Third, the so-called millennial generation has come of age during a difficult economic period and are more circumspect about embracing lifestyle priorities founded on material accumulation. Fourth, state and federal governments have elevated austerity to a political priority and have curtailed public investments to stimulate and enable private consumption. Finally, the combined effects of declining resource availability and increasing international competition for extant supplies have put pressure on critical natural resources and raised questions about the long-term abundance of several raw material inputs critical to consumer society. The following discussion takes up each of these factors.

Demographic Ageing

The median age of the American population reached its post-World War II nadir of 28.3 years in 1970 (Figure 2.1). It is currently 38.0 years and projected to be 41.7 years in 2050 and 44.7 years by 2100. Driving this process to date has been the ageing of the "baby boomers" born between 1956 and 1964. The birth of this generation reversed the prior maturating trend, injected an unprecedented youthfulness into the country's

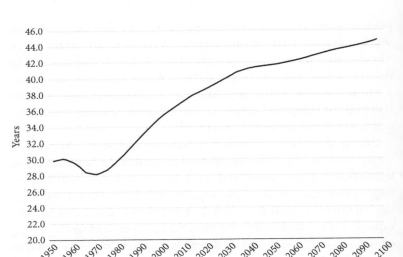

Figure 2.1 Median age of the population, United States, 1950–2100

Note: Projections for 2020–2100 are based on the medium fertility scenario.

Source: Probabilistic Population Projections Based on the World Population Prospects: The 2015 Revision, Population Division, United Nations Department of Economic and Social Affairs (available at http://esa.un.org/unpd/ppp).

demographic profile, and triggered unprecedented demand for material goods. Also notable from the perspective of this book is that baby-boomer households in the United States launched the first mass wave of suburbanization and enlivened and transformed middle-class consumer culture in entirely novel ways.[58] The tremendous burst of economic activity associated with this internal migration and its subsequent infrastructural reverberations—residential subdivisions, shopping malls, business parks, and highways—is extremely difficult to replicate.[59]

These developments continue to be consequential because the baby boomers are still the largest demographic cohort in the country (the other outsized cohort is the children of baby boomers—the so-called echo boomers—discussed separately later).[60] As boomers reach retirement age, their consumption preferences are shifting toward smaller homes and more healthcare services. Accordingly, we are now witnessing a contraction in demand for customary consumer goods and a downscaling in the overall material dimensions of everyday life.[61]

This retrenchment is contributing to changes in the merchandising landscape across the United States. Retail sales (annually now approximately $4 trillion) have been flatlining over the last few years and even normally ebullient industry spokespeople are ambivalent about opportunities for future improvement. In particular, establishments that cater to a predominantly middle-class clientele are under increasing pressure. Announcements of the downsizing or liquidation of familiar firms is becoming a regular and relatively unremarkable occurrence. Explanations attributing the downturn to lingering effects of the post-2008 financial crisis are starting to wear thin as demographic change continues to disrupt established consumer expenditure patterns.[62]

Wage Stagnation

During the years following World War II, robust industrial employment, relatively progressive tax policies, and vigorous trade unionism in the United States combined to steadily lift wages over the ensuing decades.[63] Median household income reached a high of $57,843 in 1999 (2014 dollars), but then began to reverse course. By 2012, just a little more than one decade later, this income measure had declined by nearly 10 percent to $52,605 (Figure 2.2). Disaggregating the data by income

Figure 2.2 Real median household income, United States, 1984–2014

Source: United States Bureau of the Census, "Real Median Household Income in the United States" [MEHOINUSA672N], retrieved from FRED, Federal Reserve Bank of St. Louis, https://research.stlouisfed.org/fred2/series/MEHOINUSA672N (accessed May 8, 2016).

group (termed "strivers," "middle class," and "strugglers") provides a more variegated—and disconcerting—view with increases over most of this period concentrated disproportionately among the "strivers" and stagnation (and even decline) among "middle class" and "strugglers" (Figure 2.3). Income inequality, as measured by the Gini coefficient fell to a historic low in the late 1960s and then changed direction (Figure 2.4).[64] While easy access to consumer credit cushioned some of the trends, it also contributed to rising levels of household indebtedness, bankruptcy, and foreclosure, especially among the poor.[65]

These developments raise a critical question: Can consumer society persist in the face of continued wage stagnation and related contraction of the middle class? It seems unlikely, because increasing income inequality deepens the divide between well-heeled buyers of positional goods and cash-strapped shoppers of everyday commodities.[66] Reversal of this trend is a political task, but at least for the foreseeable future there seems to be little motivation to marshal the necessary will to do so. Modernization theorist Ronald Inglehart is notably pessimistic about prospects for action on this front. He has recently asked, "Will enough

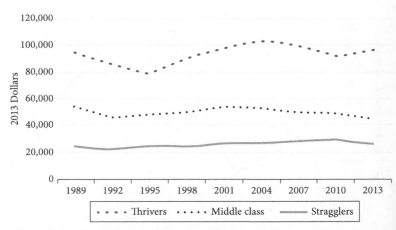

Figure 2.3 Median income of "thrivers," "middle class," and "stragglers," United States, 1988–2014

Source: https://www.stlouisfed.org/publications/in-the-balance/issue11-2015/the-middle-class-may-be-under-more-pressure-than-you-think. © Federal Reserve Bank of St. Louis, 2015. All rights reserved. Reproduced with permission of Federal Reserve Bank of St. Louis (https://www.stlouisfed.org, accessed May 8, 2016).

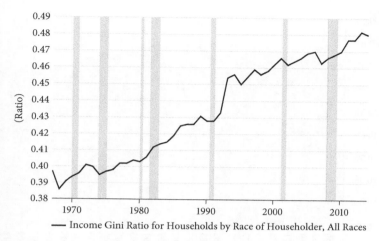

Figure 2.4 Gini coefficient for households, United States, 1965–2015

Source: United States Bureau of the Census, "Income Gini Ratio for Households by Race of Householder, All Races [GINIALLRH]," retrieved from FRED, Federal Reserve Bank of St. Louis, https://research.stlouisfed.org/fred2/series/GINIALLRH (accessed May 8, 2016).

of today's dispossessed develop what Marx might have called 'class consciousness' to become a decisive political force"? He responds by observing: "In the short run, probably not, because of the presence of various hot-button cultural issues cutting across economic lines."[67] When taking a longer view, Inglehart is more sanguine, suggesting that resentment will mount and growing dissatisfaction will translate into political action. In the meantime, new business strategies grounded in the concept of an "hourglass society" are gaining ground as firms realign products away from the middle-income mass market and toward the upper or lower ends of an increasingly bifurcated income distribution.[68]

Lifestyle Priorities

Market research suggests that the current youth generation, comprising people born during the 1980s and 1990s and often referred to as the "millennial generation" (or "Generation Y") has decidedly different consumption preferences than its predecessors.[69] In particular, this cohort seems to evince diminished interest in material possessions, subscribes to less regularized employment practices (in part owning to changing labor-market conditions), and relies heavily on social media to flexibly and fluidly manage relationships and daily activities.[70] Novel

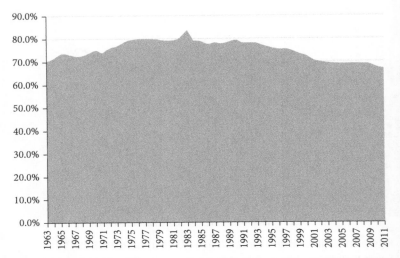

Figure 2.5 Percentage of 16–24-year-olds with driver's licenses, United States, 1963–2011

Source: Dytzik, Tony and Phineas Baxandall. 2013. *A New Direction: Our Changing Relationship with Driving and the Implications for America's Future.* Washington, DC: U.S. PIRG Education Fund and Frontier Group, p. 21 (available at http://www.uspirg.org/reports/usp/new-direction, accessed May 8, 2016). Reprinted with permission.

routines pioneered by Generation Y-ers are beginning to induce broader changes in consumer society, and an especially salient example pertains to the hitherto most celebrated good: the personal automobile. In the United States and similar countries, a growing proportion of the current youth generation is not even bothering to acquire a driver's license, let alone purchase a vehicle (Figure 2.5).[71] Transportation planners have dubbed the phenomenon "peak car" and the shift also points to declines in the number of vehicle miles traveled per year (Figure 2.6).[72] Not surprisingly, automobile manufacturers have become increasingly disconcerted by their inability to cultivate among members of this age group the kind of passionate enthusiasm for cars that has long been an undisputed tenet of youth culture and consumerism more generally.[73]

It is not difficult to intuit the reasons for this new mindset.[74] After all, for a typical teenager a car is, first and foremost, a means of maintaining connectivity with a social network, and motorized transportation is less essential in an era of ubiquitous mobile communications. The

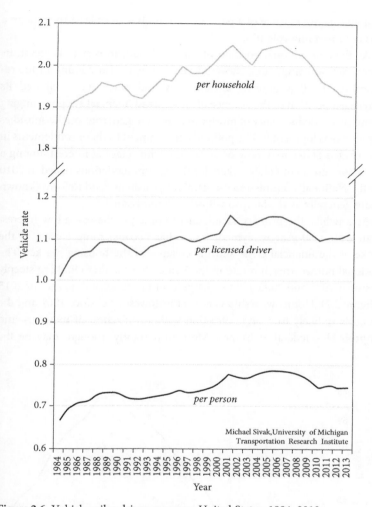

Figure 2.6 Vehicle miles driven per year, United States, 1984–2013

Source: Michael Sivak, "Has motorization in the U.S. Peaked? Part 7: Update through 2013 (UMTRI-2015-10)." Ann Arbor, MI Transportation Research Institute, University of Michigan, March 2015 (available at http://deepblue.lib.umich.edu/bitstream/handle/2027. 42/110979/103186.pdf, accessed May 8, 2016). Reprinted with permission.

commodity fetishism previously associated with cars has been trans-
ferred to smartphones and other hand-held electronic devices. In addition, Generation Y-ers in the United States and elsewhere are expressing
preference for urban lifestyles, making it possible to dispense with the

cost and inconvenience of a personal automobile or at least to reassign a less commanding role to it.

As the conventional position of cars in American society is recast, its consumption companion, the suburban home, is also coming in for re-examination. This housing alternative would never have achieved its privileged position in the absence of widespread financial support ranging from the tax deductibility of mortgage interest to generous public subsidies for land development.[75] The political commitment to these entitlements in the United States may now be softening, with ongoing interest among a bipartisan group of policymakers for the recommendations issued in 2010 by the National Commission on Fiscal Responsibility and Reform (known more generally as the Simpson-Bowles Commission).[76]

Meanwhile, the primary facilitator of home purchases—a low-interest loan with a 30-year repayment term—has become more elusive in the wake of the financial crisis and the collapse of the housing market. The national homeownership rate in the United States, after climbing steeply between 1995 and 2005, fell to 63.4 percent in the second quarter of 2015 (Figure 2.7). Homeownership is now at its lowest level since 1967 and the trend is unlikely to change direction without injection of massive—and improbable—federal assistance. More importantly, though, may be the

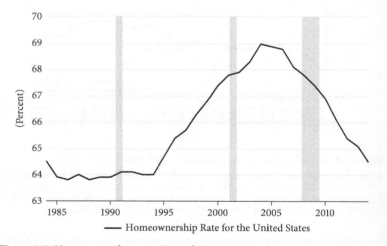

Figure 2.7 Homeownership rate, United States, 1980–2015

Source: United States Bureau of the Census [USHOWN], retrieved from FRED, Federal Reserve Bank of St. Louis, https://research.stlouisfed.org/fred2/series/USHOWN (accessed May 8, 2016).

shift that the real-estate debacle has prompted in terms of the sacrifice that borrowers are prepared to make to retain a home in the face of financial adversity.[77] Strategic default now carries less social stigma and without the ability to rely on moral suasion to ensure repayment, long-term home financing at fixed rates becomes a much more uncertain prospect. Additionally, a sizeable fraction of the country's distressed suburban housing stock has been acquired in recent years by hedge funds and private equity firms and offered to occupants on a rental basis.[78] While resale at some point in the future is probable, the vast size of these investment portfolios may make it difficult to do so at scale without depressing the market. In some parts of the country, neighborhoods that were once comprised exclusively of owner-occupied homes are now inhabited by an increasing number of renters.[79] This development suggests the possibility of an enduring structural shift in how housing in the United States will be provided in the future. The growing popularity of home rental is also likely to have implications on public policies ranging from the provision of municipal services to the design of household energy-efficiency programs.

Political Paralysis

Most of the post-World-War-II era in the United States has been marked by an undisputed political consensus on the desirability—and indeed the non-negotiable necessity—of economic growth.[80] There has been in the country, regardless of party affiliation, a resolute commitment to expansionary policies and to reliance, during periods of slack demand, on deficit spending by government. Concurrently, economic growth, by increasing public revenues, has ameliorated numerous governance problems, particularly conflicts surrounding equitable distribution. In short, "growthism" has served as grease on the wheels of political decision-making.[81]

During the immediate aftermath of the 2008 financial crisis there were indications in several affluent countries of a turn toward neo-"New Deal" economic policies (sometimes even expressed as a "Green New Deal").[82] However, the prospect for such action quickly faded in the face of implacable political divisions. Plentiful rhetoric, to be sure, continues to be devoted to the inviolability of economic growth, but there is little common ground between adherents of "free-market" neoliberalism and proponents of a return to Keynesian fiscal policy. The present stalemate in the United States, in all likelihood, will continue for some time at the federal level.[83] Many sub-national jurisdictions have gotten caught up in their own ideological traps and implemented policies that perversely sap the potential for meaningful rejuvenation.[84]

Dissolution of the political consensus on economic growth is taking a toll on several fronts relevant to maintaining consumer society in the United States. Education is just one area where the ramifications are particularly evident. Current political dysfunction is closely bound up with faltering commitment to quality public education and this situation raises concerns about the country's ability to compete in a globalized economy in coming decades. Despite a seemingly endless stream of reports from august commissions over the last couple of decades, there has been little systemic effort to stem the attrition, let alone move the country onto a different trajectory with respect to educational perform-ance.[85] The United States seems to be reaching a critical tipping point where a positive and debilitating feedback loop has been created with further consequences for economic growth. A cycle of decline is becom-ing manifest where falling levels of educational achievement reinforce a parochial understanding of civic affairs, diminish public capacity to appreciate complexity, stimulate a tendency to embrace superficial policy interventions, and narrow worldviews.[86] These circumstances can make it extremely difficult for more informed perspectives to break through the din of strident appeals designed to appeal to populist sensibilities.

Resource Availability

The global system faces several types of resource scarcity, ranging from shortages of precious metals to insufficient fresh water in densely popu-lated regions. However, it is the remaining supply of oil that has captured notice because of the pivotal role that relatively inexpensive fossil fuels has played for the past century powering industrial production and existing modes of transportation.[87] Cheap petroleum and coal have also been indispensable in propelling consumption-driven economic growth during this period and it is extremely challenging to envisage how we might maintain even modest expansion in the face of steadily increasing prices and dwindling supplies.[88]

Most recent attention on the future of energy has centered on "peak oil," the point at which global production reaches its zenith and then begins to inexorably decline. Though extant conditions of plentiful supply suggest otherwise, we may nonetheless still be nearing this his-toric juncture.[89] The rate of discovery has slackened considerably in recent decades and we are presently consuming four barrels of oil for every newly identified one.[90] In addition, the growth of deep-water drilling and the aggressive effort to exploit tar sands and other noncon-ventional sources suggest that the era of readily exploitable supplies is coming to an end and in future years it will be necessary to pursue evermore inaccessible—as well as expensive and environmentally problematic—sources in geographically remote regions.[91]

It is, though, unnecessary for current purposes to scrupulously parse the debates on each of these points. Instead, we need only focus on the extreme price volatility that exists in oil markets today due to erratic demand in China, India, and other developing countries.[92] One would need to search for quite some time to find a reputable analyst who envisions a scenario of reliably low prices over the medium to long term. The return of upward-trending prices will pose pronounced diffi-culties for the United States because the country has not done an especially effective job of improving its fuel efficiency. In particular, Americans have been slow to reduce oil dependency of the surface transportation fleet and to encourage large-scale uptake of alternative fuel vehicles. Arguably more than other nations, the United States has, over the course of the past two centuries, benefited from low-cost sources of energy and this situation has facilitated the development of an entrenched and extremely fuel-inefficient consumer society.[93]

A Transition beyond Consumer Society?

Does this assemblage of factors point to impending evolution away from consumer society as the predominant system of social organization in the United States? The social commentator Ziauddin Sardar observes that we live in "postnormal times" which is a historical moment:

When little out there can be trusted or gives us confidence. The *espiritu del tiempo*, the spirit of our age, is characterized by uncertainty, rapid change, realignment of power, upheaval and chaotic behaviour. We live in an in-between period where old orthodoxies are dying, new ones have yet to be born, and very few things seem to make sense. Ours is a transitional age, a time without the confidence that we can return to any past we have known and with no confidence in any path to a desirable, attainable or sustainable future. It is a time when all choices seem perilous, likely to lead to ruin, if not entirely over the edge of the abyss. In our time it is possible to dream all dreams of visionary futures but almost impossible to believe we have the capability or commitment to make any of them a reality. We live in state of flux beset by indecision: what is for the best, which is worse? We are disempowered by the risks, cowed into timidity by fear of the choices we might be inclined or persuaded to contemplate.[94]

While this characterization may be overly dark and dramatic, there is little question that any mention of prospective attenuation of consumer-ist lifestyles evokes for many people unsettling images of indolence, of lives diminished and without much dynamism. This is the disquieting vision that many observers of the current scene hold for the United States, with the country sliding down much the same slippery slope that Japan has travelled over its past two "lost" decades.[95] But while prevalent, is such an inauspicious future necessarily justified? We are seeing today in certain locales a notable upsurge in social innovation to reinvent food-and energy-provisioning systems on the basis of grassroots strategies.[96] In some places, utility companies, regulatory agencies, and other incumbent institutions are involved in efforts to adapt large-scale systems using more customary strategies.[97]

Whether these initiatives can scale up, diffuse, and eventually supplant presently dominant modes of household provisioning remains a critical question. In addition, there is uncertainty about whether these reinventions have the capacity to not only displace existing production technologies but also to transform widespread social practices. Some proponents working from the perspective of systems theory contend that prevailing conditions are emblematic of emergent change in a complex adaptive system and that opportunities exist to transcend current consumerist lifestyles.[98] They argue that our inability to foretell at this point how these processes will in due course unfold should not detract us from acknowledging the consequence of the present moment. Such speculation raises a range of interesting issues about social change and how new arrangements become instantiated over time. If the past is any guide, a societal transformation of this order of magnitude will proceed in fits and starts, with variance across regions. Almost inevitably, some people will benefit and others will come up short, perhaps severely so. When considering such developments it merits keeping in mind that prior transitions required extensive micro- and macro-scale adjustment over time and catalyzed significant disruptions in political power, economic institutions, and rhythms of everyday life. There is no reason to think that evolution away from consumer society will be any less traumatic.

By contrast, defenders of the status quo correctly observe that the prevailing system of social organization has overcome various challenges in the past and, in all likelihood, will reassert itself and thwart the intentions of insurgent alternatives. Accordingly, declarations of decline and fall are unjustified, and talk of an impending transition is not only extremely premature, but also reckless. Some champions go so far as to maintain that consumerist lifestyles are essential to human flourishing and we would be extremely foolhardy to allow current arrangements to slip away.[99]

Let us though provisionally assume that historic change in the structural underpinnings of consumer society is indeed afoot. If this is the case, where might one go to glimpse it in fledgling form? Such a question is not unprecedented. Someone in the late eighteenth century interested in the nascent industrial age would have been wise to head to Lancashire or Manchester. Los Angeles would have been an excellent place to witness firsthand the incipience of post-World-War-II consumer society. In the United States today, the comparable nexus might be the hipster neighborhoods of Brooklyn, which because of their social diversity and cultural creativity may have vanguard status in a putative transition beyond consumerism.[100] Other notable locales could conceivably include Portland (Oregon), Berkeley (California), and Burlington (Vermont), though the nomination of these particular candidates is unlikely to be surprising to anyone with an interest in progressive change.

The showcasing of these examples is not intended to suggest that inchoate efforts to transcend consumer society are geographically circumscribed as indications of alternative provisioning practices are by no means limited to these places. The point here is that new routines can be nurtured in these communities, in part because they have become destinations of "idio-cultural migration."[101] In other words, the development of these niches of innovative lifestyles has become sufficient to induce the relocation of like-minded people, and this movement continues to expand as a kind of social-agglomeration effect gathers momentum.[102] Paradoxically, several of these forerunner locales probably owe some of their comparative advantage to geographic proximity to city-regions that are vital centers in the incumbent system. They are able to draw on the financial and social capital of the mainstream economy and to redirect resources to jumpstarting insurgent alternative provisioning systems. A stylized example might be a household where one member is a partner in a Wall Street investment bank and her spouse engages in community gardening, clothing swaps, and time banking in the couple's residential neighborhood in Brooklyn.

Such cases point to a close entwining—perhaps even an inextricable linkage and unavoidable dependency—between the old and the new. The core institutions—shopping malls, consumer-finance companies, distribution infrastructure, and so forth—that uphold consumer society are not apt to disappear completely any time soon. Incipient routines tend to emerge in a halting and partial manner and do not quickly or thoroughly displace preceding practices. After all, industrialism only gradually supplanted agrarianism, developing a codependent relationship with it (industrial workers had to eat and farmers increasingly needed tractors). Rather than leaving consumerist lifestyles completely behind, ongoing changes will progressively destabilize the prevailing system of social organization as it continues to lose its capacity to deliver satisfactory livelihoods. These changes demonstrate that even if we do transcend consumer society, its vestiges are likely to remain with us for some time to come.

Envisioning Post-Consumer Society

History suggests that we first create rough mental constructions of the future and these renderings gestate in our minds before they begin to assume tangible form. The capacity to effectively conjure shared nascent visions is a matter of collective temperament and disposition. In other words, a critical mass of people needs to think in different ways before an alternative system of social organization begins to acquire a physical existence. The Industrial Revolution is a useful case in point. This period of rapid and expansive social change did not commence, as standard treatments allege, with Thomas Newcomen's steam engine in 1712 or James Hargreaves spinning Jenny in 1764, but rather some centuries before when ingenious souls first began to anticipate—often in quite far-fetched ways—the possibilities afforded by mechanization. Leonardo Da Vinci's fifteenth-century drawings of flying machines are legendary, but the pre-industrial age engaged the imaginations of thousands of other less-renowned figures whose observations, surveys, and prototypes prepared the cognitive landscape for the eventual industrial era.[103] In England and Scotland, the most important institutional manifestation of this preparatory activity was the eighteenth-century network of literary and philosophical societies that evolved into the first Mechanics Institutes which played an important role moving people from a receding agrarian past into an emerging industrial future.[104]

A similar process was emblematic of the transition from industrialism to consumerism and the work of sociologist Colin Campbell is especially illuminating in this regard.[105] He persuasively asserts that the origins of contemporary consumer society—as opposed to medieval forms of material acquisition—are rooted in Romantic literature of the eighteenth century and especially the novels targeted to a largely female readership. These books taught women, Campbell argues, to imagine new forms of hedonistic pleasure and they satisfied these impulses by partaking in the splendor of an expanding marketplace. The grandeur of shopping reached new heights with establishment of the first department stores during the middle of the nineteenth century and in the ensuing decades the sponsors of these ventures became increasingly adept at using architecture and elaborate displays of goods to create experiences that pushed the boundaries of otherworldliness and escapism.[106]

However, we should not allow ourselves to fall into a nostalgic trap, one that treats societal transformation in unambiguously positive and ineluctable terms. For example, the frequently referenced notion of "creative destruction" suggests that periodic reinvention ultimately contributes to human betterment by sweeping away outmoded institutions and practices.[107] This idea is anchored in an Enlightenment understanding of continual improvement and the prevalent view that change is tantamount to progress. There is no skirting the fact that sequential transitions, first from agrarianism to industrialism and then to consumerism, were wrenching and often bewildering for people caught up in the throes of reorganization. Laws were rewritten, new infrastructure was built, and familiar routines were torn asunder. One need only read the work of nineteenth-century political economists to appreciate the havoc caused by the wholesale shift from a primarily agricultural system of production to arrangements based on industrial manufacturing.[108] The more recent process of deindustrialization—a parallel development in the shift to consumerism—that began in the second half of the twentieth century was, and continues to be, similarly disruptive.

The stranded remains that occupy many once-vibrant industrial cities, and the broken souls that congregate in their shadows, are evidence of both the disarray that accompanies new modes of social organization and the inevitable incompleteness of any transition.[109]

Let us therefore presume that we are today at a similar preparatory moment, but in this case evolution is away from consumerist lifestyles toward a new system of provisioning, one that we can at the moment only fathom in vague terms. There has been in recent years a notable upsurge of interest in collaborative consumption, peer-to-peer provisioning, self and communal fabrication, and local-living economies that suggests purposeful initiative to reconfigure certain social practices. We are also seeing efforts to deploy new business models predicated on distributed networks, novel allocation of surplus capacity, and leasing schemes that unbundle the use of goods from actual ownership of them. Within the sphere of marketing, there appears to be growing interest in "value co-creation" and, under certain conditions, a desire to nurture what some analysts refer to as "mindful consumption."[110]

While little more than experiments at this stage, these initiatives are challenging familiar arrangements for delivering goods and services to households and demonstrating some potential for replication. For instance, the trading of second-hand goods has become valorized, swap meets are increasingly popular social activities, and craft-reskilling is now a trendy pastime. It might be tempting to surmise that these developments are confined to marginal subcultures, but such a conclusion would fail to recognize that, for better or worse, mainstream commerce is getting actively engaged. We also need to acknowledge that at present it is impossible to know whether these insurgent routines should be dismissed as transient phenomena or heralded as harbingers of a more deeply seated transition. There is moreover still much to learn about the extent to which ostensible relinquishment of the appurtenances of consumer society is attributable to volition or desperation.

Conclusion

This chapter outlines the challenges confronting consumer society as we approach the end of the second decade of the twenty-first century. The intention of this book is not to posit the ignoble end of consumerist lifestyles, but to discount completely the prospect of a transition away from this system of social organization would seem to misinterpret—or ignore altogether—a mounting accumulation of evidence. While there is currently in some circles a great deal of excited talk about the scalability of inchoate alternatives, we need to be realistic about their potential to endure and diffuse. It is also imperative to acknowledge that the primary beneficiaries of consumer society will continue to fight mightily to keep the incumbent system propped up regardless of its degree of dysfunctionality.

Nonetheless, unease continues to expand, in part because existing provisioning arrangements are falling seriously short of expectations for a growing number of households.[111] Disaffection has not yet coalesced into a social movement, but rather is being vented through random expressions of anger as downward mobility becomes more obdurately entrenched in societal structures. We may be reaching a cross-roads. The dilemma is that at present post-consumerist alternatives are haphazardly organized, difficult to recognize as coherent assemblages, insufficiently reliable, and, in some cases, informed by a politically unpalatable countercultural agenda. People, at the same time, are justi-fiably unsure whether the incipient and partially constructed options will be durable and efficacious, so for the time being they hold fast to familiar routines despite their patent inadequacy.[112]

Each of the following three chapters (Chapters 3–5) explores an extant strategy that has generally come to be regarded as offering the prospect for more sustainable consumption while concomitantly conferring greater economic security. The main question is whether the emergent manifestations of putative sharing, do-it-yourself making, and economic localizing are harbingers of a transition beyond consumer society. At the same time, work is being reorganized by a new wave of digital technolo-gies that is sweeping through sectors of the economy once thought to be impervious to such disruption. The unsettling question is whether these developments will undermine incumbent provisioning systems to a point where a new system of social organization becomes palpably apparent.

3

The (Mostly) Empty Promise of the Sharing Economy

Introduction

As the middle class in the United States has ruptured due to stagnating incomes, overburdening household debt, employment insecurity, and general economic angst, a growing number of observers has started to doubt the continued viability of consumer society as the country's dominant system of social organization.[1] This skepticism is prompted in part by evidence of the emergence of alternative provisioning practices, an especially notable example of which is the so-called "sharing economy."[2] Over the span of just a few years, startups like Airbnb, Uber, Lyft, and Poshmark have become increasingly recognizable fixtures of a new commercial landscape.[3] And these online companies represent just the tip of an ever-expanding iceberg. There are today scores of digital marketplaces that allow consumers with little more than a smartphone and a credit card to conveniently acquire just about anything—from a car to an electric drill to a wedding dress—for a short period of time. Other websites emblematic of this putative sharing economy enable users to recruit a babysitter, borrow money, or order a pizza. Some trend-watchers have even suggested that the remarkable success of these "platforms" marks a break from the familiar era of ownership-based consumption to a new age predicated on shared access.[4]

Proponents of this idea assert that our experiences downloading music files and interacting through social media have re-enlivened latent sensibilities that transcend long-standing affinity for proprietary acquisition.[5] They contend that consumers are coming to embrace lifestyles that curb material accumulation and forsake the responsibilities of ownership. It is alleged that we are rediscovering the simple pleasures and financial attractiveness of exchanging second-hand consumer goods.[6]

Some commentators anticipate that spreading acceptance and normal-ization of shared access provides a promising path to a more sustainable future.[7] They maintain the sharing economy simultaneously ameliorates consumerist excess and satisfies the three dimensions of sustainability (social, environmental, and economic).[8] First, from the standpoint of social sustainability, decades of competitive striving, coupled with contraction of the public sphere, have stripped large parts of the United States of the communal connections indispensable to both individual and collective well-being.[9] Despite the severity and geographic extent of these deteriorated social conditions, the image of neighbors trading freshly baked goods across the backyard fence retains important nostalgic power and kindles a yearning for association.[10]

Second, from an environmental vantage point, swelling anxiety sur-rounding a range of ecological dilemmas—from traffic congestion to waste disposal to climate change—has begun to provoke a reassessment of contemporary consumption practices.[11] However, there still remains a chasm between civic consciousness and individual resolve to take con-crete, and ultimately meaningful, action. As author David Owen sardon-ically observes, for most people sustainability means living "pretty much the way I live right now, but maybe with a different car."[12] Expressed slightly differently, despite growing unease, consumers are extremely disinclined to voluntarily alter their current lifestyles and continue to hold out for technological breakthroughs as the answer to outsized utilization of energy and other resources.[13]

Finally, from an economic angle, shared access strikes many con-sumers as eminently sensible during a time when a sizeable number of households need to pinch pennies to make ends meet. Attention to this dimension of sustainability calls for rethinking prevalent cultural dis-positions that equate sharing with privation and there are indications that a change of mindset is taking place. If the household budget no longer supports the purchase of a new Gucci clutch, the rental of one from Bag Borrow or Steal may not be an unappealing option. And better still, who will even know that the handbag has been acquired on loan. In a similar vein, *The New York Times* columnist David Brooks attributes the willingness of homeowners to serve as Airbnb hosts to revived interest in the "boardinghouse model of yesteryear" when renting out the backroom provided a ready way to generate extra income.[14] The sharing economy has also attracted attention as a way to shake up a number of slow-to-change industries—from taxis to hotels—and stirred hopefulness that a rash of insurgent startups will propel local economic growth.[15]

Pulling this all together, of course, is the diffusion of Web 2.0 platforms that are precursors of the "Internet of Things."[16] Laptop computers and handheld electronic devices are no longer just tools for transmitting ethereal bits to corporeal human beings at lightning speed but are rapidly becoming the means to communicate with otherwise inanimate objects and to control the operation of consumer goods from a distance by touching a few buttons. The frontrunners of this trend are focused on the use of automobiles, the renting of short-term tourist accommodations, and the exchange of apparel but the most ardent champions of shared access insist that this is just the beginning and the media have by and large obediently helped to propagate this view. Writer Susie Cagle ironically observes:

For the past few years, the "sharing economy" has characterized itself as a revolution: Renting a room on Airbnb or catching an Uber is an act of civil disobedience in the service of a righteous return to human society's true nature of trust and village-building that will save the planet and our souls. A higher form of enlightened capitalism.[17]

The next section, "A Brief History of the Sharing Economy," offers a succinct historical account of how the sharing economy has achieved such rapid and impressive diffusion in a relatively short period of time. The third part, "What Do We Really Mean by 'Sharing'?" imposes necessary checks on the permissive, and unfortunately disingenuous, way in which the notion of shared access has come to be applied. Once these issues have been ironed out, the chapter assesses the sharing economy in terms of the three dimensions of sustainability. The emphasis is largely on what has come to be termed "Big Sharing," the vanguard of successful startups in the urban mobility and tourism sectors that have experienced exponential growth and already have market capitalizations in the tens of billions of dollars.[18] Some limited consideration is also devoted to the diverse array of platforms involved in the sharing of clothing and fashion accessories. The conclusion identifies reasons for the headlong rush to situate these firms under the enticing rubric of sharing and the need for more circumspect understanding of its potential as a pathway toward a more sustainable future.

A Brief History of the Sharing Economy

Sharing is an age-old practice for managing the distribution and utilization of resources and contemporary expressions are not, at least in principle, notably different from what has gone on in one form or another for millennia. It is, though, not necessary to turn the clock back to the beginning of recorded time to appreciate the venerability of sharing and the following discussion instead adopts a more historically modest approach that simply aims to call attention to a few appropriate antecedents. During the nineteenth century, fraternal organizations, friendly societies, and mutual aid groups frequently promoted the sharing of durable products as a form of social welfare.[19] Perhaps less obvious, but nonetheless regularized, forms of sharing of the time also included municipally licensed horse-drawn carriages and trams (which were apportioned both concurrently and sequentially and hence "shared" conveyances) and were followed in due course by the advent of motorized taxis and other public services that were built on the same general model.[20]

Also during this period, the rough taverns and inns of the earlier era gave way in the United States and other countries to grand hotels that served as homes away from home for wealthy travelers. These facilities—significant for current purposes because they entailed the short-term "rental" of rooms—co-evolved with the railroads and, as journeys became less onerous and more accessible to people of diverse means, came to be distinguished by different service standards.[21] Automobile tourism first started to gain popularity during the 1920s and it was initially common for farmers to accommodate travelers in their barns but these rudimentary arrangements soon gave way to purpose-built auto-camps, cabin courts, tourist homes, and motels.[22] The 1950s saw establishment of national hotel chains like Howard Johnson's (that started out as a restaurant company) and Holiday Inn which assembled hundreds of properties under a single identifiable brand.[23] By the 1970s, vacation residences—first in Florida and then on a nationwide scale—became widely available on a timeshare basis where a family or group purchased a fractional number of weeks of occupancy at a particular resort.[24]

The sharing—or more precisely the rental—of cars is nearly as old as the automobile itself. Historians credit a 1904 advertisement by a bicycle shop in Minneapolis as the first instance of vehicles being made available for short-term use in the United States. One of the earliest recognizable car-rental ventures, though, was launched in 1915 by a realtor in Omaha who conjured the idea when he found himself in need of a replacement vehicle after his own car became temporarily inoperable. Meanwhile, a Chicago businessman named Walter Jacobs acquired in 1918 a dozen Ford Model T's and called his fleet the Yellow Driv-Ur-Self System. By the 1920s, the letting of cars was commonly available in most cities with vehicles prepositioned for pick up at curbside locations. In 1923, Jacobs sold his business to John Hertz, President of the Yellow Cab and Yellow Truck and Coach Manufacturing Company. Three years later, the firm was acquired by General Motors which retained ownership until 1953. Before long, the new owner, the Omnibus Corporation, renamed it Hertz Rent-a-Car and the company became a leader of an industry now populated by a handful of international firms and thousands of local competitors.[25]

The rental of clothing and the logistical organization of second-hand apparel (a broad range of activities that encompasses borrowing, bartering, cooperative purchasing, swapping, donating, consigning, pawning, repurposing, and gifting) have recently come to be recast as "sharing" but are nonetheless practices of long-standing duration. In the nineteenth century and earlier it was accepted practice for gentlemen to exchange dress uniforms and tailcoats and for ladies to trade court dresses. It was furthermore not unusual for wardrobes to be bequeathed across the generations due to their high monetary value and sentimental significance.[26] Such treatment of formal apparel became less common with the appearance of ready-to-wear fashion, though the commercial rental of tuxedos, party costumes, and uniforms for certain types of manual work remained notable exceptions. With respect to the far more prevalent supply of casual garments, reassignment to subsequent users remained a widespread practice until the early decades of the twentieth century.[27]

As the volume of industrially manufactured household products steadily increased and suburbanization was interwoven into ongoing development of consumer society, it became financially and logistically inadvisable to encourage—or indeed to tolerate—the sharing of consumer goods.[28] Common use and the extension of product lifetimes through second-hand trading were not consistent with the need to move the vast supplies of inventory building up in the country's warehouses and freight yards. The challenge was perceptively apprehended in 1955 by retail analyst Victor Lebow who wrote in a frequently quoted passage that:

Our enormously productive economy demands that we make consumption our way of life, that we convert the buying and use of goods into rituals, that we seek our spiritual satisfactions, our ego satisfactions, in consumption. The measure of social status, of social acceptance, of prestige, is now to be found in our consumptive patterns. The very meaning and significance of our lives is today expressed in consumptive terms. The greater the pressures upon the individual to conform to safe and accepted social standards, the more does he tend to express his aspirations and his individuality in terms of what he wears, drives, eats—his home, his car, his pattern of food serving, his hobbies. These commodities and services must be offered to the consumer with a special urgency. We require not only "forced draft" consumption, but "expensive" consumption as well. We need things consumed, burned up, worn out, replaced, and discarded at an ever increasing pace. We need to have people eat, drink, dress, ride, live, with ever more complicated and, therefore, constantly more expensive consumption.[29]

Despite Lebow's entreaties, premature obsolescence, shortened fashion cycles, and related design and marketing techniques did not completely extinguish culturally embedded forms of collaborative consumption. For example, the exchange of garden tools between neighbors and the passing down of children's clothing remained commonplace, even as the practice of, say, parceling out cars beyond the members of a household became more exceptional. Shared use and second-hand trading were in many communities a largely unremarkable part of daily routines that attracted little attention from social scientists, data-gathering organizations, or policymakers entranced by new acquisition. In the face of refortified promotional efforts touting the advantages of newly minted consumer goods during the 1950s, communal use acquired a distinct social odor and came to be regarded as suitable for only the least affluent consumers. The notion of owning a home, along with a full complement of appliances and other equipment, became a widely celebrated feature of the ascendant American Dream.[30]

Contemporary interest in more purposeful forms of consumer cooperation traces back to the car-sharing clubs that began to form in Switzerland, Germany, and elsewhere in Europe following World War II.[31] Inspired by a combination of frugality and environmental awareness, the practice typically entailed the formation of a communal association that would jointly acquire a small fleet of vehicles and negotiate a formula for allocating them to members. These arrangements proved workable while the number of participants in the scheme was relatively small, but scheduling and management often became unwieldy as the group increased in size. In addition, evolving social norms privileging personal ownership—combined with pronounced stigmatization of collectivization—ensured that car-sharing remained a distinctly countercultural activity.

The 1990s brought forth the Internet, the rise of open source as a development model for innovation, the arrival of online exchanges for music and other intellectual property, and the partial relaxation of social strictures concerning alternative modes of access to consumer goods. By the new millennium, the founders of Zipcar, Antje Danielson and Robin Chase, were assembling these pieces into a workable business model and adapting the earlier social experiments around car-sharing into a viable commercial undertaking.[32]

Then came the 2008 financial collapse, undermining customary career paths and prompting a new generation of savvy entrepreneurs to cast their gaze across the broad expanse of the consumer economy, scouring opportunities to bring buyers and sellers together, to exploit the potential of "slack" capacity, and to fulfill inchoate cravings for sustainability.[33] The original, but less trendy, forums for online sharing like eBay, Craig's List, and Freecycle were largely swept to the side. A small cadre of crusading authors construed these developments as the initial phase of a radically new form of commerce, one suffused with nearly limitless potential for visionary startups.[34] The concept of partitioning durable products into smaller consumable units went viral with a loosely conceived conception of "sharing" getting applied to a panoply of activities.

We are now at the point where clever millennials are unearthing possibilities for shared access in all manner of places and several of the more successful initiatives have attracted very substantial investment from venture capitalists. This financial model has imposed tremendous pressure on these entrepreneurs to rapidly scale up operations and there has been no shortage of breathless commentary heralding Uber, Lyft, and Airbnb as the front edge of a tidal wave of disruption sweeping through consumer markets. The following sections scrutinize the sharing economy in detail and assess its current status and prospects as a sustainability strategy.

What Do We Really Mean by "Sharing"?

Before seeking to assess the sharing economy it is instructive to first sharpen appreciation for what this phenomenon actually entails and a useful place to begin is the etymology of the term. The word "sharing" derives from the Old English term *scear* meaning to cut and the *Oxford English Dictionary* defines its contemporary use as "a part or portion of a larger amount that is divided among a number of people, or to which a number of people contribute." We typically encounter the concept colloquially at an early age and learn that it is about splitting a stock of divisible items into more or less equitable portions. If pressed to do so, most people would likely be able to identify authentic instances of sharing without too much trouble. However, closer examination reveals the existence of substantial ambiguity in how consumer goods are practically deployed. More to the point, many common products evince hybridity and do not fit cleanly into binary categories of sharing and non-sharing.

The case of residential accommodation appears, at least at first, to be relatively unproblematic. We typically regard an occupied home to be an owned possession (even if there is a mortgage) but when several related people dwell under the same roof is it not a "shared residence"? How should we treat a rental house or apartment, particularly one that turns over on a frequent basis and is tenanted by a serial rotation of occupants? Moreover, into which category does a condominium fall? This legal structure provides for private title to one's residential space but joint ownership of common areas. This, though, is just the beginning of a very slippery taxonomic slope.

Public services of various kinds, ranging from trains and buses to schools and swimming pools, are regularly used on a collective basis though we do not normally think of them as entailing sharing. Access in these facilities is typically non-exclusive (a single person or party does not have sole use at a particular point in time) or temporally serial (usage by a sequence of persons or parties over time). Once we start looking, we realize that commercial air travel is a form of sharing and even affluent travelers that fly on private aircraft are invariably tethered to shared systems of air-traffic control and ground facilities.[35] In a noteworthy recent book, sociologists Harvey Molotch and Laura Noren remind us that even the humble public restroom is a shared amenity.[36] To this we could add any number of other examples including washing machines in laundromats, exercise equipment in health clubs, and tables in coffee shops. All of these places feature assets that are utilized for a period of time by a single person or party, surrendered, and appropriated by a successor—in other words, they are shared.

The intent here is not to play semantic games, but rather to suggest that a rigorous discussion of sharing is headed for some dangerous conceptual shoals. Consumer goods do not neatly categorize themselves. Moreover, even products that are used on a collective basis are owned by some entity, normally a public authority, shareholder-owned corporation, or nonprofit organization. The upshot here is that the task of distinguishing sharing from other modes of possession can, in practical terms, be a tricky undertaking.

To make some constructive headway, it first helps to carefully differentiate between the *ownership* and the *usership* of a product. Prevalent social practices tend to vest both ownership and usership of particular items in a single individual or group. The ubiquity of this organizational mode derives from public policies that have actively instilled the conflation of ownership and usership due to recognition that it is the most effective way to encourage material consumption and to facilitate conventional notions of economic growth.[37] Contemporary interest in sharing derives from a desire to separate ownership and usership and the workability of this division rests on an understanding that an owner cannot dispossess a user prior to a previously negotiated deadline. It also requires the cooperation of the user in the sense that she will not damage or unduly devalue the product during the period it is in her custody. It further merits noting, as outlined earlier, that proponents of shared access frequently impose an all-purpose conception of sharing on distinct modes of common use including borrowing, bartering, and swapping that may, depending on the social context, create different reciprocal obligations between providers and receivers.

Social Sustainability of the Sharing Economy

When considering the social sustainability of the sharing economy it is instructive—counterintuitive though it may seem—to initially forget about sharing altogether and to regard the leading Web 2.0 platforms as digital marketplaces. If we take this as our point of departure, the

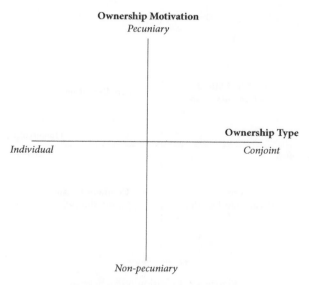

Figure 3.1 Provisioning typology

ownership of consumer goods can take two basic forms: they can be owned either *individually* or *conjointly*. This distinction is depicted along the horizontal axis of Figure 3.1. The mode of ownership matters because we continue to live in a world of physical products that are ultimately embedded in proprietary systems. Despite the efforts of some designers to "ephemeralize" certain material goods, actual progress on this front has to date been nominal.[38] Aside from the technical challenges of dematerializing individual items, it is useful to recognize that virtualization does not typically exist *sua sponte* and the utility of incorporeal services are generally closely coupled with tangible products. For instance, the service of housecleaning presupposes the existence of a residence and electronic music files have little value without access to a compatible device on which to play them.

It is also necessary to differentiate the motivations for owning specific consumer goods, which in practical terms means inquiring whether a product is held for profit-making purposes or for more intrinsic or ancillary (or at least less financially instrumental) purposes. This dimension extends from *pecuniary* to *non-pecuniary* and is depicted by the vertical axis in Figure 3.1.

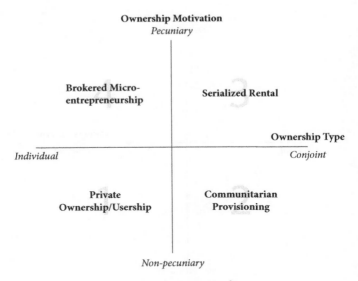

Figure 3.2 Provisioning archetypes

The juxtaposition of these two ownership features—type and motivation—generates a taxonomy of the contemporary sharing economy comprising four archetypes. Before offering a more detailed explanation, it is instructive to note that the two modes on the left-hand side of the figure are based on personal ownership and the two options on the right-hand side are predicated on ownership by an organization or group. Correspondingly, in the lower half of the diagram ownership is not impelled by profit-seeking intentions while commercial exchange is the primary impetus for the archetypes in the upper half.

We can now consider the qualities of each of the quadrants with the assistance of Figure 3.2. Quadrant 1 is straightforward as it represents consumer goods that are routinely held for non-pecuniary purposes in *private ownership/usership* (and is hence not in fact directly germane to the sharing economy and is set aside for current purposes). Moving in a counterclockwise direction, Quadrant 2 is the domain of *communitarian provisioning* where consumer goods are deployed for non-pecuniary purposes by a public agency or cooperative organization. Quadrant 3 represents the sphere of the sharing economy where objects are conjointly owned with pecuniary intent and made commercially available on the basis of *serialized rental*. The variant of the sharing economy in

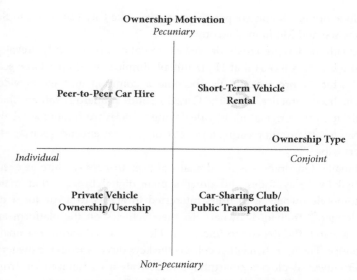

Figure 3.3 Social organization of urban mobility options

Quadrant 4 combines individual ownership with pecuniary motivations and is termed *brokered micro-entrepreneurship*.

The taxonomy and constituent archetypes become more useful if we apply this model to a few concrete examples as displayed in Figure 3.3. The following discussion highlights the various ways in which ownership/usership of urban mobility options is socially organized.[39] Again, starting in the lower left-hand corner, Quadrant 1 is the unexceptional case of private vehicle ownership/usership in which a car is individually held and serves generally non-pecuniary purposes such as driving children to school or taking weekend excursions. It is important to note that a vehicle in the sense described here can also be used to commute to work, but it is not instrumentally used as a direct source of income.

In Quadrant 2 we have the case of traditional car-sharing as facilitated by a club or cooperative organization, but this category also includes, due to the emphasis on joint ownership/usership, most familiar forms of public transportation. The general model involves a group of people jointly owning—oftentimes through the intermediation of a local mutual association or public-purpose agency—a fleet of vehicles and using them in accordance with a set of stipulated operational rules. Notable examples include nonprofit and cooperative providers like City Car Share in San Francisco and Modo in Vancouver.

Quadrant 3, represents serialized car rental and is especially prevalent as the business model that Hertz initially implemented on a large scale and which more recently has become a common and more widely normalized practice. Zipcar, Car2Go, and numerous others have built upon the original idea by deploying vehicles from more accessible urban locations and creating a price structure that encourages usage for short trips.

Finally, Quadrant 4 is the domain of peer-to-peer car hire as exemplified by Relay Rides and other similar digital brokers that match automobile owners with users interested in access to a car for a day or longer.[40] Individual owners list their vehicles on the platform and users search the website to find a suitable car parked within reasonable distance. The user then either collects the keys directly from the owner or alternatively deploys a smartphone to activate a customized electronic device that unlocks and starts the vehicle. Payment is made via pre-registered credit card with the platform receiving a commission of approximately 25 percent.

As the sharing economy has expanded—both in general and with respect to urban mobility in particular—it has begun to evolve in different ways with some notable variation evident, for instance, between the United States and Europe. Serialized car rental is now available in many cities on both sides of the Atlantic but explicit public policy measures, higher population densities, lower rates of automobile ownership, and complementary public transportation systems have encouraged greater uptake in Europe. By contrast, ride-sharing in the United States has advanced primarily on the basis of brokered micro-entrepreneurship with the digital marketplaces established by Uber and Lyft achieving rapid user acceptance. There has arguably been in Europe less emphasis on exploitation of the commercial potential afforded by the sharing economy and more on its solidaristic possibilities, but the trans-Atlantic comparison requires more detailed research than has been carried out to date.[41] An illustrative, but admittedly anecdotal, example of the different ways in which these new forms of collaboration are being shaped by economic culture is the French startup BlaBlaCar which creatively fuses elements of brokered micro-entrepreneurship and communitarian provisioning. A participating car owner uses the website to recruit one or more passengers to travel between, say, Paris and Lyon but rather than charging a profit-seeking rate, the fare is set at a level that covers just the direct and indirect costs of the trip. Because expenses are pooled, a journey booked through the platform is typically competitive on a per-person basis (even accounting for a 12 percent commission) with trains and other modes of public transportation.[42]

Turning our attention back to the United States and the sharing economy typology in Figure 3.2, it becomes difficult to substantiate key claims advanced by proponents of shared access. First, aside from the technological interface, there is nothing particularly novel about the underlying business models. Despite all of the assertions about disruptive innovation, the vanguard firms are applying standardized strategies based either on the serialized rental of consumer goods or the matching of underutilized physical or human resources with transitory opportunities. Second, there is a troubling contradiction at the core of the sharing economy that arises from the fact that little actual sharing seems to be taking place, at least in terms of how the term is conventionally understood.[43] Communitarian provisioning as expressed by, for example, clothing swaps, community kitchens, and public libraries are interesting exceptions because the emphasis is not on transactional commerce but rather on fostering genuine forms of mutual exchange. However, this dimension of the sharing economy is, at least in the United States at present, vastly overshadowed by the commercial alternatives. Serialized rental and brokered micro-entrepreneurship convey a semblance of social sustainability, but it is largely a pretense and often does not extend beyond the posting of (often anonymous) performance rankings. In sum, most of what has come to be regarded as the sharing economy is premised on a kind of ersatz sharing.

Environmental Sustainability of the Sharing Economy

In addition to claims pertaining to social sustainability, shared-access enthusiasts advance certain environmental intentions, most notably a commitment to more efficient utilization of consumer goods. It is accurately observed that after decades of emphasis on material acquisition, we are overburdened with surplus stock and, furthermore, many products are used only sporadically.[44] For instance, our cars sit idle for most of the day. Our closets are packed with infrequently worn clothing and our tools are stowed away for long periods of time until called into service by the occasional task. In short, from a materials-management standpoint, the consumer society is shot through with vast amounts of waste.

The idea that efficiency is virtuous has, of course, a long history on the production side of the economy where upgrading the productivity of equipment and labor has been a preoccupation of industrial managers at least since Frederick Winslow Taylor and the team of Frank and Lillian Gilbreth conducted their groundbreaking time and motion studies more than a century ago.[45] This work launched the so-called Efficiency Movement during the late nineteenth century though attention was confined only to manufacturing operations. It was not long before home economists and others began to apply the efficiency-enhancing techniques developed on the factory floor to domestic provisioning.[46] A prominent approach emphasized collaborative housing arrangements with shared kitchens and cooperative housekeeping.[47] However, such ideas rapidly disappeared after World War II as new domestic policies that, in combination with modern marketing, emphasized a different set of priorities.[48] The household came to be regarded as having a seemingly limitless appetite for consumer goods and fulfilling its requirements was a way to ensure economic growth and to drive national prosperity. The joint use of appliances, automobiles, and other consumer goods fell out of favor as collaboration was dismissed as superfluous and, ultimately, a sign of financial, or even moral, inferiority. Sharing persisted in significant measure only among the poorest households in the country.

An appropriate way to understand shared access from the perspective of environmental sustainability is to regard the general business model as a way to exploit what Zipcar co-founder Robin Chase has described as "excess capacity."[49] If we strip the sharing economy down to its bare essentials, by setting aside for the moment the smartphone interfaces, the global positioning systems, and the rapid response options, what we have left is a useful way to improve the efficiency with which consumer goods are deployed. For instance, vehicles that are part of Car2Go or Relay Rides spend less time in parking lots or garages. The same holds true for apparel-sharing platforms like ThreadUp or Rent the Runway. Airbnb is essentially a way for hosts to put a spare room (or an entire residential unit) to work. Especially during periods of economic stress, this is a concept that should—and to a growing extent does—have widespread appeal. On one hand, who would not want to earn a few extra dollars renting out underutilized stuff or space—provided there was assurance that it would not be damaged? And, on the other hand, opportunities to share allow users to avoid the expense of sinking large sums of money into consumer goods for which they only have an intermittent need.

Because of its apparently unproblematic allure, efficiency has been assiduously promoted for the past several decades by government agencies and others as a painless way to "save" the environment.[50] For example, energy expert Amory Lovins famously describes efficiency as "not a free lunch, but a lunch you're paid to eat."[51] The Achilles' heel of this approach—and the dilemma is replete in enterprises that populate the sharing economy—is that we have known for at least 150 years that efficiency enhancements have a built-in tendency to backfire. Attribution for initially recognizing this phenomenon is normally assigned to the nineteenth-century British economist William Stanley Jevons who at the height of the Industrial Revolution recognized that consistent improvements in the operating efficiency of steam engines increased rather than decreased domestic coal consumption because innovation drove down the price of fuel.[52] Jevons reasoned that the falling cost prompted people to find more and more uses for the energy source and, in the end, more of it was consumed.

The so-called Jevons Paradox is not a fleeting or idiosyncratic problem and there are numerous cases where it has become perversely manifest.[53] A prominent example is the Corporate Average Fuel Economy (CAFE) standards originally implemented in the United States at the height of the first energy crisis of the 1970s to increase automobile efficiency. Instead of cutting fuel use, the program had the reverse effect of driving up aggregate gasoline consumption (in part because greater efficiency induced drivers over time to travel further and to purchase larger vehicles).[54] Similarly, household refrigeration has become much more energy efficient over the last few decades, but most of the benefits of this achievement have been squandered. As the energy cost per cubic meter of cooling space has declined, overall unit size has increased.[55]

The Toyota Prius, widely celebrated as a "green" car, further illustrates the hazards of Jevon's Paradox. Because the Prius (and other similar models) runs alternately on its gas engine and electric motor, owners of this vehicle enjoy lower per-mile driving costs. This means that they can drive further on a tank of fuel or, if they stick to their customary traveling practices, over the course of a year save a few hundred dollars that would otherwise be spent at the pump. This latter outcome raises a perplexing series of questions: How likely is our Prius owner to retain her savings? Does she spend her windfall on some other form of consumption, say, a winter airplane trip to a warm-weather paradise? The point is that she would need to be an extremely scrupulous household accountant to avoid frittering away her efficiency dividend.[56] The insight to take on board is that innovative technology is rarely a silver bullet and its ultimate effectiveness must be reconciled with the subsequent social counteractions that implementation inevitably triggers.

As awkward as this problem is, it raises another, even more troubling, dilemma, one that rarely factors into contemporary discussions about shared access or, for that matter, sustainability policymaking. As its proponents are not hesitant to suggest, becoming a service user or goods recipient in the sharing economy can be an effective way to reduce out-of-pocket expenses. Occasional reliance on Uber or Lyft instead of a personal vehicle for local trips is apt to cut one's annual urban mobility expenses.[57] The same holds true for fashion-conscious consumers who rent or swap clothing. The affordable pricing that one is often able to access through Airbnb is typically cheaper than conventional forms of accommodation.[58]

For most of us, saving money is a welcome achievement. This is due in part to an inherent consumer-centric bias that selfishly diminishes our capacity to identify with the interests of service providers and product producers who consequently receive less remuneration when prices drop (they may make up this difference through an increase in aggregate demand but this will depend on price elasticity). The aim is not to deny people trips across town, fashionable accessories, or vacations but to acknowledge an incontrovertible truth. Reducing the out-of-pocket expenditures of consumers does not in and of itself offer a more sustainable outcome. *Efficiency* is unquestionably necessary, but it must be coupled with a stringent notion of *sufficiency* to prevent our noble intentions from rebounding in untoward ways. The central challenge that we face in affluent countries is quite simple and straightforward: there are just too many people striving to do too much stuff.[59] Trends favoring shared access over ownership are unlikely to have much beneficial effect unless this transition is accompanied by simultaneous efforts to achieve absolute reductions in resource throughput.[60] There is surely a role here for technological improvements, but engineered solutionism will be inadequate in the absence of fundamental changes in consumer aspirations and practices.[61] The science of sustainability is unambiguous on this point. We live in a world of biophysical constraints and sooner or later we will need to come to terms with the harsh implications of this situation.[62]

We will further pursue this important point later in this book. In the meantime, let us pause to note that it is consumer demand—cultivated by marketing and expressed through expenditures—that drives energy and materials through the global economy. By ignoring this inconvenient fact, proponents of shared access fail to formulate a comprehensive understanding of the system-scale impacts of collaborative use. For instance, they do not differentiate between sharing that substitutes for existing consumption and that which is augmentative or stimulative. To take an example, some car-sharing advocates contend that "every shared car replaces 13 owned cars. 50% of new car-sharing members join to get access to a car who didn't already have access to a car."[63] A sympathetic interpretation is that the sharing of vehicles is beneficially replacing car ownership, but equally plausible is that it is enabling automobile trips that would not have previously taken place (either because the traveler would have otherwise opted to take public transportation or would have deemed the journey too troublesome to embark on at all). Moreover, by giving carless individuals an opportunity to affordably experiment with automobile use, car-sharing has a propensity to play a transitional role toward eventual vehicle ownership.

It is not that proponents of shared access are feckless (quite the contrary, many of them tirelessly work to transcend currently unsustainable practices), but they do demonstrate a tendency to misconstrue the dynamics of complex systems.[64] Under such circumstances, unanticipated and unintentional "side-effects" proliferate because the original problem was defined in overly delimited terms. Sharing advocates are not alone in their incomplete appreciation of the often peculiar and illogical workings of complex systems. Indeed, this shortcoming is more generally apparent, but it raises unique challenges when exhibited by people devoted to championing change. Systems theorist John Sterman writes, "The problem is not the few who are truly uncaring. It is the failure of even those who sincerely care to understand the urgent need for action created by the long time delays, feedbacks, nonlinearities, and other characteristics of complex systems."[65] Unambiguous environmental improvement requires more than inadvertently moving problems from one domain to another—it demands a systems-scale perspective and recognition of the ultimate inadequacy of individualized efforts to enhance the sustainability of contemporary provisioning systems. Most notably, it is impossible to grapple with such matters without considering the crucial role of economic growth and the equity implications of its distribution on resource throughput.[66]

Problems arise even if we apply a more modest test of environmental sustainability to the vanguard firms in the sharing economy and, revealingly, the platforms themselves seem to be aware of the limitations and inconsistencies of their promotional rhetoric. Lyft, acknowledges that its ride-sharing service is not contributing to contraction in the overall size of automobile fleets or to reductions in vehicle miles traveled because the platform is competing primarily with taxis rather than with private automobile ownership.[67] Uber is characteristically cagier on this point, but there is no reason to anticipate a different outcome because it is employing essentially the same business model. The claims of Zipcar and the other car-sharing firms are more interesting because they are ambivalent about the degree to which they are even part of the putative sharing economy.[68] There is also, as noted earlier, the complicated methodological issue of whether sharing rides and cars induces automobile journeys that would not otherwise be undertaken.

Further notable is the fact that several of the serialized clothing-rental services initially made claims touting their environmental sustainability, but no longer do so and instead invoke standard consumerist appeals predominantly based on saving money while expanding the appearance of choice. More communitarian swapping and donating of apparel has a much more realistic potential to constrain the number of garments in circulation and to limit premature discarding.[69]

Finally, Airbnb situates itself in a discourse on sustainable tourism by emphasizing the authenticity of the travel experience that its hosts strive to confer in comparison to conventional hotels.[70] As an alternative to commodified tourism, one that limits demand for new construction and provides opportunities for local businesses to capture tourist expenditures (see Chapter 5), Airbnb constitutes a promising strategy, but is ultimately a double-edged sword.[71] An irreconcilable contradiction of sustainability in the comprehensive sense is that it requires tolerance of cultural differences (and self-directed tourism is an important way to build this empathy), yet making the cost of long-distance vacations more affordable increases demand for both travel and the resources that this form of consumption entails. Strict adherence to sustainability guidelines may in the future require us to forsake energy-intensive modes of travel for alternatives premised on immersive imaging technologies and other means of facilitating virtual tourism.[72]

Economic Sustainability of the Sharing Economy

Economic sustainability of the sharing economy spans a wide scope, but this dimension can be reduced to four overlapping issues: the evasion of established regulations, the avoidance of taxes, the creation of economically competitive cities, and the financial circumstances of a largely itinerant labor force. First, the vanguard firms are disrupting several economic sectors that have a high degree of visibility and have long been managed by expansive regulatory arrangements. Initially implemented to protect consumers from unscrupulous practices and to uphold public health and safety, these regimes have concomitantly shielded incumbents—especially in the accommodation and taxi industries—from competition through the creation of elaborate systems of licensure, performance standards, inspections, and, in some cases, price controls. For instance, many cities in the United States have statutes that prohibit the rental of residential property for periods of less than thirty days to discourage establishment of illicit hotels. With respect to transportation, local governments have sought to prevent drivers from operating unsanctioned livery services that could put passengers at undue risk. At the same time, key players in these sectors have amassed considerable political power and influenced their respective regulatory regimes in ways that discourage the entry of new competition.[73]

Airbnb and the ride-sharing startups have challenged these provisions using a strategy that some observers have described as asking for forgiveness after the fact rather than permission in advance.[74] This aggressive—and sometimes even belligerent—posture has led to contentious and protracted wrangles with regulatory commissions in numerous cities in the United States and around the world.[75] Shared access enthusiasts have accused regulators of bowing to pressure from entrenched interests and failing to adapt to the new era of Internet-enabled commerce. The countercharge is that consumer and health protections exist for valid reasons and that appeals to inexorability are being used to subvert legitimate governmental authority. These disputes will continue to play out in different jurisdictions with inconsistent results over the next few years, but prevailing momentum seems to be on the side of "Big Sharing" because the vanguard firms have successfully positioned themselves as victims of regulatory overreach and strategically activated their customers as a political force. Though there has been grumbling about the use of exploitative pricing strategies and other heavy-handed tactics by some platforms, it is nonetheless now possible in a growing number of locales to e-hail a taxi using a smartphone, to book relatively inexpensive accommodation in a local resident's spare room, and to rent or swap designer apparel at a distance.

Second, leading advocates of the sharing economy have devised ways to avoid paying local taxes. Most cities impose a stiff tourist tax on hotel guests, but Airbnb argues that its hosts are not providing formal lodging and hospitality services and hence are exempt from collecting and remitting these payments. The ride-sharing companies treat their drivers as freelancers rather than employees and do not deduct payroll taxes. Some municipal governments and industry incumbents argue that the economic competitiveness of the sharing economy is partly attributable to tax avoidance. It is furthermore charged that tourist taxes are often used to provide dedicated funding for local arts and cultural programs. In many places it is precisely these investments that add to touristic attractiveness and that without adequate resources it will be difficult to maintain appeal in a competitive tourism market. In other words, tax dodging by the sharing economy constitutes a form of free-riding and over the longer term threatens to undermine its own success.

Third, propagation of the sharing economy poses challenges for municipal governments with respect to how they market themselves as desirable locales for both residents and visitors. Many cities invest considerable resources creating "buzz" and trying to cultivate popularity among members of the so-called creative class.[76] More specifically, place-based promotionalism these days is centered on nurturing a vibrant digital media industry, supporting a stylish arts and entertainment district, and encouraging tourism. Given that the sharing economy touches closely on all of these objectives, cities are—despite the counter-vailing obstacles mentioned earlier—under a great deal of pressure to accommodate such activities.[77]

Finally, arguably the most controversial debates pertaining to the economic sustainability of the sharing economy revolve around its labor force.[78] Proponents regularly highlight that renting out an extra bedroom, becoming a casual driver, parsing out portions of one's ward-robe, caring for pets, assisting with grocery shopping, or taking up all manner of odd jobs, are forms of "opt-in employment." In other words, unemployed or underemployed workers no longer need to float on the vicissitudes of the wage-based part of the labor market. The sharing economy provides people with the opportunity to work as hard as they are inclined and to generate an income on a fully flexible basis, all while being their own boss.[79] Moreover, it is alleged the compensation can be duly rewarding. Airbnb calculates that the typical New York City host earns $7,530 per year and Uber contends that its drivers in the city working 40-plus hours per week are able to reach a median annual income (before expenses) of $90,766.[80] Given that the federal minimum wage in the United States is presently $7.25 per hour (in New York City the amount in 2016 was $10.50 for workers in the fast-food industry and $9.00 for others), these would seem to be heady sums of money. And, it is claimed, the sharing economy enables hospitality providers to access interesting opportunities for cultural exchange that are not only finan-cially remunerative, but fun and stimulating as well.[81]

To a more critical eye, it is no surprise that shared access first emerged into popular view in 2008 and its early development paralleled the Great Recession and its aftermath. From this perspective, the sharing economy has been scornfully termed the "servant economy," the "gig economy," the "1099 economy" and characterized as "neoliberal solutionism" and "disaster capitalism."[82] Most Airbnb hosts are not compelled to wake up at six o'clock in the morning to make pancakes for guests because they are inherently hospitable. They do not regard themselves as the shock troops of a new economy. Rather, it is for most people financial need and the fact that they are fraught about the next rent or mortgage payment that prompts immersion in the sharing economy. Moreover, failure to fulfill certain obligations as a lodging provider could trigger an unfavor-able online review from a recently departed visitor, thus jeopardizing future business. There is moreover little support for contentions that ride-share drivers avidly embrace the opportunity to ferry strangers around town. They, too, are motivated to perform an oftentimes stressful and boring job by a need to make ends meet. Though the evidence on clothing-swappers is less clear, we can presume that at least some of the people attracted to these exchanges are seeking to maintain social or professional appearances in the face of tight budgetary constraints.[83]

The sharing economy extends and deepens developments that have been accruing in significant segments of the customary economy for the past two decades. A range of occupational categories—from editing to graphic design to accounting—are increasingly being performed by independent contractors (see Chapter 6). Economist Guy Standing characterizes people laboring under conditions of extreme insecurity as constituting a new class that he terms the "precariat."[84] When one's livelihood is dependent on completion of short-term outsourced tasks it is necessary to be perpetually on the lookout for new assignments so the imputed flexibility of this mode of work is typically unrealizable for all but a very few extremely successful individuals. In addition, time spent searching for the next job (or "gig") is uncompensated and casual workers are continually at risk of being undercut by others even more desperate for opportunities that arise. When business slackens, service and goods providers are left to fend for themselves. There is no security, no chance for career advancement and—at least in the United States— freelancers must shoulder the cost of their own medical insurance, fund their own retirement savings, and set aside personal reserves in case of injury or more permanent disability.[85] Furthermore, in the sharing economy service and goods providers are typically deploying their own assets in the form of houses, vehicles, clothing, and tools.[86] This is advantageous for the platforms because it obviates the need to invest in capital stock or inventory and places them at arm's length distance when mishaps arise. Though it has recently become common for the online companies to carry indemnity insurance (typically up to $1 million per incident), the contested legality of the associated activities is likely to make pursuing a claim a murky undertaking for the foreseeable future.

To counter impressions of disagreeable working conditions in the sharing economy some of the platforms have devised jocular routines or emotional narratives. Lyft, for instance, initially encouraged its drivers to adorn the front grill of their vehicles with a large and fuzzy pink mustache and to greet passengers with a ceremonial fist-bump. Airbnb strives to recast the activities of its hosts as contributing to the heart-warming idea of "belong anywhere." A posting on the platform's blog conveyed the following message to hosts and prospective guests:

We used to take belonging for granted. Cities used to be villages. Everyone knew each other, and everyone knew they had a place to call home. But after the mechanization and Industrial Revolution of the last century, those feelings of trust and belonging were displaced by mass-produced and impersonal travel experiences. We also stopped trusting each other. And in doing so, we lost something essential about what it means to be a community.[87]

Converting one's apartment into a hotel may not entail the most degrading labor, but it is work and to describe it as "sharing" or something similar propagates a deceptive fantasy. It is a charitable and legitimate gesture to make breakfast for a friend in the morning darkness, but something altogether different when performed for a paying houseguest. It is almost as if Airbnb is trying to wish away the transactional nature of the exchange, or to conveniently ignore the reasons why most hosts got into the business in the first place. There is also a failure to get to grips with the essential asymmetry in the way in which shared access is delivered. For recipients it is a low- (or at least lower-) cost way to access a desired service or good, but from the standpoint of the provider it is, to use Susie Cagle's evocative terminology, a "side hustle."[88]

The popular supermarket-shopping platform, Instacart, is frequently deemed to be part of the sharing economy and comprehensively conforms to this appraisal.[89] The website enables customers to upload shopping lists where they are retrieved by "pickers" who then fulfill the order, pay for the groceries, and then make delivery using their own car. In its early incarnation, Instacart did not notify supermarket managers that it was essentially using their stores as a free warehouse and final prices included a 10–20 percent markup on each item plus a delivery charge. After operating for one year on the basis of this strategy, the startup realized that customers resented paying the premium and that supermarkets experienced an incremental increase in sales. On the basis of these insights, Instacart changed its initial pricing formula, eliminating the surcharge and entering into collaborative agreements with supermarkets where some food retailers now allow pickers to use in-store refrigerators to hold completed orders prior to delivery and to speed through dedicated express checkout lanes. According to the platform's founder and CEO, "Instacart was adding so much more volume and new dollars to the store that it made sense for them to partner with us."[90]

Conclusion

Enthusiasts have made many claims to encourage proliferation of the sharing economy and to recruit participants into its ranks. This chapter assesses the performance of several of the more prominent platforms from the standpoint of the three dimensions of sustainability. From each of these perspectives, the sharing economy falls significantly short of what its champions contend. There is serious reason to question the efficacy of currently dominant modes of shared access as a new system of social organization—one that advances social inclusivity, reduces resource throughputs, and fosters economic stability and diversity. What accounts for the wide gap between the promise and the reality of the sharing economy?

The concept of "diversionary reframing" offers some suggestive insights. Formulated by sociologists William Freudenburg and Robert Gramling, it describes the social and political processes that recast disreputable activities in affirming terms.[91] Practitioners of this art strive to divert public scrutiny by fashioning narratives that shift the focus of attention—the frame—away from questionable aspects of particular pursuits and toward more redeeming ones. They also work relentlessly to undermine the legitimacy of critics. While diversionary reframing does not suggest overt duplicitousness, we do see consistent efforts on the part of the proponents of shared access to create a simulacrum of cooperation to assuage palpable public anxieties associated with these activities.

The reassuring narrative that has been constructed around the sharing economy has been excitedly taken up by both the mainstream media and public officials fearful of missing an opportunity to spur economic growth. Anyone who does not agree with the prevalent view tends to be treated as a technological reactionary too obtuse to comprehend the inevitability of a future of ubiquitous mobile communications and near-instantaneous satisfaction of consumer demands. Evidence that draws attention to the multifarious shortcomings of the sharing economy—

most notably its tendency to compound precariousness and to fortify deepening patterns of inequality—is dismissed as the growing pains of a transition still moving through its formative stages.

This chapter challenges this fervor and demonstrates that serialized rental and brokered micro-entrepreneurship are poor approximations for more genuine modes of collaborative exchange and fail most tests as credible sustainability strategies. In short, "Big Sharing" is a Trojan horse. Advocates have mistakenly maintained that the sharing economy is a way for the imperiled middle class to stabilize and hopefully reverse its declining fortunes. While putting slack assets to profitable use can be a valuable way to generate supplementary income, it all too often becomes a measure of desperation and further locks into place a decidedly two-tier economy where less-affluent "sharing" providers put themselves at the disposal of better-heeled clients.

The next chapter considers a related development, namely the incipient "Maker Movement" which offers a vision for a future shaped by cottage-scale producer–consumers deploying an array of high-tech digital fabrication machines and creative artisans renewing interest in underappreciated handicrafts.

4

The Mass-Market Maker Movement

Introduction

The last several years have given rise to an explosion of interest in self-provisioning—from knitting to winemaking to fashioning replacement car parts on 3D printers—and everyone seems to be involved in a do-it-yourself (DIY) undertaking of one kind or another. Often referred to as the Maker Movement, this assemblage of activities is fascinatingly diverse and various facilities have sprouted up in the United States and other countries to support a veritable wave of creative ingenuity.[1] Community-fabrication laboratories ("fab labs"), shared machine shops, and commercial makerspaces have taken root in a growing number of cities around the world.[2] Public policymakers are embracing the Maker Movement as a way to reinvigorate former industrial districts and to bring manufacturing employment to communities in need of jobs.[3] Even in locales where industrial production remains viable, small-scale making is being heralded as a way to encourage economic diversification and to prepare for future uncertainty.[4] For instance, the municipal government in Shanghai is constructing more than 100 "innovation houses" and other clusters of maker activity are cropping up in Beijing, Shenzhen, and Hangzhou.[5]

Making is also sweeping through educational circles as a way to cultivate enthusiasm among students and to steer them toward STEM (science, technology, engineering, and mathematics) fields, as well as to fill in curricular gaps left by the evisceration of home economics and manual arts programs.[6] Over the past few years, 3D printers have supplanted iPads as the new "must-have" instructional device and administrators have been rushing to purchase equipment and to recruit qualified teaching personnel. In addition, science museums, public libraries, and summer camps have developed tailored programs to encourage children to join the Maker Movement. Some churches and community centers have turned their basements into makerspaces so that youngsters can fabricate, assemble, build, and co-create in their spare time. A regular calendar of so-called Maker Faires provides yet more opportunities for students to cultivate their creativity working with fabric, wood, electronics, and more. Coordinating much of this activity are newly launched organizations like the Maker Educational Initiative that provide instructional materials, organize competitions, and facilitate communication among a cadre of energetic teachers committed to overturning conventional pedagogical wisdom through development of innovative design-build curricula.[7]

Champions of the Maker Movement are notable for their contagious passion and excitement. Some of the most ardent and publicly visible spokespersons contend that we are on the threshold of "the next Industrial Revolution" and encourage everyone, regardless of creative proclivity, to get on board or risk being left behind by a groundswell of historic significance.[8] Their fervent promotionalism has had marked effect and making is no longer confined to devotees with trained expertise or hobbyists with extra time on their hands. One estimate claims that there are currently 135 million makers just in the United States.[9] Noteworthy is the fact that the movement is recruiting novices who are fashioning products for personal use (so-called prosumers) as well as for sale via popular websites like Etsy or CustomMade.[10] Moreover, it is alleged that making provides a way for people to satisfy latent cravings for artful expression that normally find few outlets while toiling for a weekly paycheck in a perfunctory job. Even the White House has joined in with President Obama declaring June 17, 2014 to be the National Day of Making.[11]

All of this activity has prompted a flurry of reports boldly announcing that consumers are finally overcoming their fixation with mass-produced goods and that we are at an incipient stage of a process that in due course will radically reconfigure familiar modes of production and consumption.[12] Rendering contemporary interest in making still more compelling is that it revives a number of appealing proto-sustainability ideas dormant since the days of the Arts and Craft Movement during the early twentieth century.[13] How might we begin to make sense of the zeal that newly surrounds small-scale provisioning and, more specifically, what might be its prospects as a pathway toward a more sustainable future? It is the task of this chapter to take up these questions. We first begin by considering the societal dynamics that are contributing to recent growth of the Maker Movement.

Why the Upsurge in Making?

As noted earlier, the Maker Movement constitutes a wide range of activities spanning from the hand sewing of clothing to the precision manufacturing of airplane components. It is thus first and foremost important to distinguish between, on one hand, making that has long been—and continues to be—performed as an individual and largely solitary activity and, on the other hand, making as it has come to be institutionalized over the past few years on a more formalized—and oftentimes commercial—basis. As suggested by the notion of a "movement," it is the organized manifestation of making that is the primary focus of this chapter. Unquestionably, as a practical matter, the two domains bleed into one another, and this is especially the case in terms of how the profit-seeking facets of making appropriate and redeploy the evocative narratives of more autonomous practitioners.[14]

Proponents contend that interest in making "has come about in part because of people's need to engage passionately with objects in ways that make them more than just consumers."[15] Such an interpretation suggests that the phenomenon has emerged out of spontaneous grassroots impulses. While appealing to observers who regard discovery of industrious design as a station on a personal journey, more careful analysis suggests that another, more systemic and socially constructed, process is at work.

A useful way to proceed in developing this understanding is to divide the Maker Movement into two spheres based on relative degrees of technological rigor. The less technically demanding end of this spectrum has been built up over the last couple of decades by mass-market stores and online distributors selling low-cost crafting supplies (typically pre-fabricated by Asia-based manufacturers) to consumers interested in fashioning customized housewares, décor, and gifts. By contrast, more technologically intensive making activities are apt to rely on power tools, laser cutters, and various computer-numerical control (CNC) machines that, in some cases, have been adapted to fit the needs of small-scale producers. For instance, hobbyist makers can now buy a 3D printer for their kitchen countertop or basement workshop for a few hundred dollars. The point here is that favorable economic and technological developments have enabled the Maker Movement as a novel means of production *and* an innovative form of consumption. Expanding on the insights of sociologist Colin Campbell, the discussion considers three interrelated reasons for the rising popularity of making as a new way to consume: a counterbalance to increasing commodification, a consequence of the deprofessionalization of white-collar jobs, and a means for ongoing status differentiation.

First, it is specious simplification to regard greater individualization of consumption as a mere response to evermore stultifying processes of commodification. Despite the countercultural tendencies of some intrepid renegades (in certain cases even expressed as anti-consumerism), most people today simultaneously accede to the commercial barrage to which they are exposed and try to seek out opportunities for more personally tailored experiences. Campbell writes that "the progressive strengthening of the one serves not so much to eliminate the other, but rather to stimulate an equal and opposite reaction."[16] In other words, it is more appropriate to regard interest in the Maker Movement not as an overt strategy for countering mass marketization but rather as a way to renegotiate its homogenizing tendencies. He further contends that:

As more and more aspects of modern life become subject to this economic imperative, so more and more individuals might come to experience the need to escape from, or even counteract, this process. That is to say, they might come to desire some small corner of their everyday existence to be a place where objects and activities possess significance because they are regarded as unique, singular or even sacred. Seen in this light, the arena of craft consumption could become highly valued because it is regarded as an oasis of personal self-expression and authenticity in what is an ever-widening "desert" of commodification and marketization.[17]

Second, the manufacturing heartlands of many post-industrial countries went through some extremely difficult times during the 1970s and 1980s as large numbers of jobs disappeared due to the relocation of production to regions or nations with lower labor costs.[18] It was for the most part lesser-skilled manufacturing workers that suffered the brunt of this wrenching process and in response policymakers designed initiatives to shift the displaced manpower into fields that were at the time part of an expanding service economy.[19] During the intervening decades, the Internet has claimed its place as a preeminent tool of commerce and work routines have become more geographically dispersed. As journalist Thomas Friedman metaphorically observes, the world has become flatter and a similar process of employment attrition has more recently begun to sweep away thousands of white-collar jobs once thought to be secure from the effects of offshoring.[20] Moreover, it is not only clerical work that is being deskilled or rendered redundant by increasing digitization; attorneys, lawyers, physicians, architects, and others are discovering that their services can be performed for a fraction of the cost in Manila or Bangalore or discontinued altogether (see Chapter 6).[21]

Many of the skilled jobs that have escaped displacement or elimination have nonetheless been drastically narrowed in scope and today allow for far less personal autonomy than was previously the case.[22] Campbell asserts that these positions have been subject to a process of "deprofessionalization" entailing increased bureaucratization, external monitoring, and formal performance assessment. He further argues that this experience has undermined prior sources of identity and prompted affected individuals to seek out alternative ways to foster a sense of self:

Could it be that, as a result, these people are increasingly retreating into a privatized world of self-expression as a direct consequence of the decreasing opportunities for independent creative and expressive activity available in their occupational roles? For these are just the people whose work has traditionally had many of the attributes of a "vocation", which is to say that it has not merely been viewed as a "life task", but also that it has been regarded as offering both a clear sense of identity and profound personal satisfaction. However, as their occupations have progressively lost their professional character . . . then this might explain their tendency to seek in the private sphere just those satisfactions that they find are no longer available to them in the public one.[23]

Campbell is not alone in recognizing the linkage between deprofessionalization and making.[24] Craft memoirist Peter Korn writes that "without romanticizing preindustrial society, it is still possible to say that craft offers a holistic experience many contemporary Americans find lacking in their occupations and personal lives . . . particularly those who work in corporate environments where individual effort is engulfed in a collective enterprise, where results are often as ephemeral as numbers on a computer screen, and where the work of the mind is generally segregated from the work of the hand."[25] The upshot here is that as systems of accountability become more confining and internal regulations make it increasingly difficult for people to derive a satisfactory identity from their roles within prevailing systems of production, they will seek out spaces that afford opportunities to regain a measure of personal control. For many affected individuals, the various pursuits that comprise the Maker Movement seem to provide a refuge that fulfills this need.[26]

Finally, it is not practicable for the vast majority of upper- and middle-class consumers to completely escape an alienating world of com-modified consumption. By appropriating consumerist goods and processes, and imbuing them with their own creative capabilities, what are other-wise mass-market products can be redeployed in novel ways to confer distinction and communicate social superiority. Campbell observes that

Instead of merely bemoaning . . . rampant consumerism (something which, in their eyes, has become all too pervasive, largely as a consequence of the unin-hibited greed and hedonism of their social inferiors) or alternatively attempting to escape the worst effects of a materialist and consumerist society by downsizing or joining the simple living movement, they have co-opted and adapted con-sumerism in such a way that it can give expression to their own distinctive cultural values and traditions.[27]

In other words, rather than offering a pathway to move beyond con-sumer society, the Maker Movement is actually situated at its very heart and strengthens already dominant practices, especially with respect to identity- and status-striving. Instead of transcending consumerist sens-ibilities, particular modes of making—and in this sense not all forms of handwork are equal—paradoxically become a means for reproducing and reinforcing them. The following section introduces a taxonomy for distinguishing these different expressions of making and highlights how proponents of the Maker Movement have exploited popular fascination with hacking to useful commercial advantage.

From Hacking to Making

The large variety of activities, and the different skills that they entail, pose challenges for development of a comprehensive conception of the Maker Movement. It initially seems to engender so many incommensurate endeavors that trying to impose order on all of it is a futile exercise. One strategy for beginning to tackle making in a more systematic way is to envisage a continuum that extends from *crafting* at one end to *micro-engineering* at the other. On one hand, archetypal forms of crafting include sewing, knitting, cheese-making, and other undertakings premised mostly on handwork and relatively simple tools. On the other hand, exemplary types of micro-engineering involve the use of digital fabrication equipment such as CNC routers, laser cutters, and electronic compilers. Against this broad background, it warrants acknowledging that most making activities these days (in terms of both labor hours and materials utilization) are more closely akin to crafting than to micro-engineering. This characterization, of course, flies in the face of the image constructed by a credulous media which favors fantastical accounts about self-replicating machines and homemade jetpacks over more mundane maker activities like backyard gardening and the baking of artisanal bread.

Most craft-type forms of making require the maker to secure the necessary equipment from proprietary sources (often available in partially assembled kits) and to configure the materials into an ultimate form using a proven set of instructions. Acquisition of rudimentary competence for these making modes can typically be acquired through some basic training and practice.[28] Achievement of higher orders of proficiency requires the maker to develop refined skills premised more on aesthetic elegance than on precise functional performance.

By contrast, expressions of making oriented toward the micro-engineering end of the continuum generally involve first separately fabricating the constituent components before experimentally fashioning a final product. Expertise often depends on technical rather than stylistic competence and is attained through a combination of formal instruction, immersive experience, and cultivated intuition. Hacking, or the constructing or repurposing of artifacts to meet either superior or ulterior standards of functionality, is the most challenging and widely venerated form of micro-engineering. At the extreme, hacking can closely approximate inventing.

With the basic terms of this framework established, we can now redefine crafting and micro-engineering, respectively, as "soft making" and "hard making." Again, it is reiterated, that the most widely practiced types of making fall into the realm of soft making and hard making is more exceptional, in part because of the obstacles one must overcome to acquire initial familiarity and the high costs of developing the necessary set of skills.

Before further elaborating this Maker Movement taxonomy it is necessary to digress briefly to distinguish the different ways in which making services are delivered to practitioners. Particularly in the case of hard making, it is unusual for people to have personal access to the required ensemble of equipment and they must first arrange for admittance to a pre-equipped workspace. There exist today both for-profit and nonprofit making facilities and, perhaps not surprisingly, there is palpable tension between these two organizational forms. On one hand, commercial ventures like TechShop and Stratasys are striving to develop angles that profitably tap into popular interest in making and these circumstances necessarily require keeping a close eye on the bottom line.[29] On the other hand, university-affiliated fab labs and community-based machine shops are not directly impelled by the same financial considerations and are hence able to maintain greater adherence to the defiant commitments conceived by the progenitors of the contemporary Maker Movement.[30] These latter maker venues continue to be more acutely devoted to perpetuating the rebellious hacker spirit that celebrates activist innovation, creative reinvention, and the diffusion of knowledge through open-source networks.

We can now return to the main line of discussion premised on delineating the differences between soft making and hard making. The success to date of the commercial side of the Maker Movement is largely attributable to an ability to assist clients in acquiring modest proficiency while simultaneously giving them the opportunity to experience a pretense of hacking (perhaps best understood as "lite hacking"). In other words, resourceful entrepreneurs have deployed user-friendly machines and enlisted instructional personnel (TechShop calls its trainers "Dream Consultants") to create a new kind of enterprise that successfully "softens" relatively hard making activities to render them accessible to novice makers.[31] TechShop CEO Mark Hatch describes the process in the following terms:

In the past, if you wanted to personally learn how to make something out of plastic using molding machines, you could choose the trade school and apprentice route, maybe a junior college, or go through a full four-year bachelor's degree in mechanical engineering (and risk not actually getting to use mills and lathes or an injection molder). Both of these could easily take years. Now, you would sign up for a few specific software classes (two or three class sessions) and an injection molding class (one class session). You would then have enough skills to at least get started—this month.[32]

Hacking (or at least its simulacrum) has been transformed into a commodified experience and, in doing so, converted from a furtive and quasi-clandestine activity into a mass-market pursuit. Technology researcher Stephen Fox highlights this process by observing that:

The traditional trade-off between aesthetic creativity and production efficiency is reduced by additive manufacturing (AM) machines such as 3D printers. This is because, unlike industrial machinery that is product-specific and efficient (e.g. moulds and presses) or is general-purpose and less efficient (e.g. saws and drills) AM machines are general-purpose and efficient. Thus, they can enable the traditional trade-off between esthetic creativity and production efficiency to be transcended . . . Hence, manufacturing complicated aesthetics becomes much simpler.[33]

Social philosopher Richard Sennett makes the same point when he remarks that computer-aided design (CAD) programs enhance efficiency by dispensing with the need for makers to engage in the painstaking process of iteratively producing hand-drawn sketches. He contends that computer-facilitated design has become a "disembodied design practice" that is used to "repress difficulty." Once the user has acquired some basic familiarity with the operational manipulation of the software little active learning is required.[34]

The paradox of making on a commercial basis should then be clear. If all it takes is a subscription to a makerspace and few classes to establish a financially viable foothold as a micro-entrepreneur in the maker economy, it will be just a short time before the associated price premium dissipates and makers become just another layer in the inadequately compensated underclass of craftworkers.[35] Jathan Sadowski and Paul Manson put their fingers precisely on this tendency: "The maker movement is not ushering in a decentralized, noncorporate, democratized world. Rather, what it will be adept at doing is serving as a convenient veneer, which hides the gears of corporate capitalism that have been turning all along. Instead of manufacturing jobs, we get manufacturing as a hobby. There's no financial security and no time for rest when everybody is constantly working the maker hustle."[36]

Assessing the Maker Movement

Another way to get a handle on the Maker Movement is to focus attention on the small cadre of proponents that has assumed a foremost position in advocating on behalf of these activities. Most notable in this regard is Chris Anderson, former editor of *Wired* magazine and most recently author of *Makers: The New Industrial Revolution*, and Mark Hatch, presently CEO of TechShop and author of *The Maker Movement Manifesto*.[37] By no means are these two champions of the Maker Movement the sole spokespersons on the subject (and we should not discount that both of them have explicit financial stakes in its future), but they are highly visible leaders and their views on unfolding developments are regularly featured in both specialized publications and the general media.

In advancing this assessment of the Maker Movement, the following section takes up four salient issues: the efficacy of micro-entrepreneurship in light of historical experience, the potential of making to displace current modes of industrial production, the commercial contradictions of making, and the promise of making as a pathway toward a more sustainable future.

Efficacy of Micro-Entrepreneurship in Light of Historical Experience

Proponents of the Maker Movement contend that current interest in DIY production represents a historic break from factory manufacturing as the primary driver of economic development. They argue that the advent of relatively affordable CAD software, 3D printers and scanners, CNC routers, and other related equipment gives small-scale producers a competitive edge over outsized counterparts. Anderson, for example, confidently asserts that we are on the brink of new era of home-based production where manufacturing moves to the desktop. He enthuses that "rather than selling to factors that control the path to market, today's Maker-style cottage industries sell directly to consumers around the world online, on their own websites, or through marketplaces like Etsy or eBay."[38]

An important issue raised by this claim is to consider carefully the frequently invoked analogy between contemporary making and the cottage industries of rural England and elsewhere in Europe during the late eighteenth and early nineteenth centuries that many historians maintain were important precursors of the first Industrial Revolution.[39] Home-based production was organized around the so-called "putting-out" system where early industrialists would consign production to households and provide payment on a piece-rate basis. While crude manufacturing by countryside families was itself not a novel development

(its origins date back to the sixteenth century and earlier), rural production became more prevalent as agricultural productivity increased grain
yields and larger harvests led to lower prices. The combination of labor
redundancy and the need for auxiliary sources of income during a multi-
decade period of rising demand for cheap manufactured goods during
the eighteenth century prompted farming and former farming households to accept orders from "factors" to produce textiles, leather, gloves,
nails, and more.[40]

Historians have devoted a tremendous amount of effort to unraveling
the early phases of the Industrial Revolution, but clear explanations are
hard to formulate because the period was characterized by rapid change
due to intellectual ferment, population growth, increasing urbanization,
territorial enlargement (due to colonialism), and expanding international trade. Given these circumstances, widespread debate persists
on the extent to which each of these changes contributed to resultant
social and economic transformations.[41] The role of the putting-out
system in catalyzing urban industrialization remains an especially contested issue.[42] Anderson skirts over most of these complications and
instead conveys a partial understanding of domestic production that
seems to be largely informed by selective reading of a 1983 magazine
article by British historian Duncan Bythell.[43] Drawing directly from the
original source, Anderson observes that:

> The spinning jenny was used in the home, multiplying the work of one spinner
> manifold, and for the first time making indoor work more lucrative than outdoor
> work for much of the population. By allowing both men and women to work
> within the home, it helped cement the nuclear family, provided a better working
> environment for children, and broke the dependency on landowners. It was also a
> way for regular people to become entrepreneurs without having to go through the
> apprentice process of the guild system . . . The family members working in the home
> had more independence and control over their own economic future. Wages were
> often no better than in farmwork, but at least the workers could set their own
> schedule . . . [Cottage industries] fit into and reinforced the family structure, finding
> work for all the family members (including, like it or not, lots of children, contrib-
> uting to the population explosion that defined that period of British history).[44]

Anderson's sanguine characterization of "thatched-roof manufacturing"
is unfortunately not only incomplete, it moreover does not do justice to
Bythell's earlier account. When read in its entirety, the original source
tenders a more nuanced interpretation of domestic production than

Anderson is inclined to acknowledge. While granting that putting out conferred a measure of classlessness and provided a degree of autonomy, especially in comparison to the discipline and routinization that later came to exemplify factory work, Bythell contends that:

We must not imagine that, in a capitalist-controlled industrial system such as outwork was, relations between masters and operatives were marked by much sweetness and light. Since the main tie between them was the cash nexus, disputes about wages could be frequent and bitter. Most employers in the industries which used the domestic system operated in a tough competitive environment, and their likely reaction to a spell of bad trading conditions would be to cut the piece-rates they paid their workers. Most of the scattered rural outworkers were disorganized and docile ... But what kept the domestic system alive after the mid-nineteenth century more than anything else was the continued availability ... of female and child labour: incapable of collective self-defence, and often deliberately ignored by their better organized menfolk; accustomed to regarding any earnings, however, minute, as a worthwhile contribution to family income; and often only able to work on a part-time or casual basis—they were ideal for many employers' purposes.[45]

While the demise of cottage manufacturing proceeded unevenly across industries and regions, these arrangements were ultimately undermined by the scaling up of production, the need to deploy more technologically intensive industrial techniques, and the establishment of compulsory schooling (which took young children out of the labor market). Bythell concludes that "It is hard to escape the conclusion that the domestic system was in many ways even less agreeable [than factory production]. Even where cottage workers were not directly competing with factory workers ... most of them were poorly paid, and likely to be alternately overworked and under-employed."[46]

Anderson is by no means the first commentator to adopt an unduly nostalgic view of this era and to place home-based micro-entrepreneurship in an unjustifiably attractive light.[47] Historian E. P. Thompson argued years ago that this tendency is part of a larger syndrome that stems from the generally favorable impression of domestic manufacturing that survives because this system appears to be relatively benevolent when compared to the immiserating conditions of the industrial factories that came to supplant it.[48] The outcome of this discussion is that we should be cautious about envisioning a future that draws inspiration from a historical era premised on conscripting into the production system the most politically and economically marginalized members of society.

The Potential of Making to Displace Current Modes of Industrial Production

It is clearly apparent, as noted earlier, that making—despite its contradictions as an economic system—can be a valuable source of personal satisfaction and we should not disregard this promise. This is particularly important in an era when so many people are forced to toil in mind-numbing work routines and are actively seeking ways to reskill themselves.[49] However, it is difficult to envisage how incipient modes of making, in all of their multifarious expressions, might supplant incumbent provisioning arrangements, especially in a way that might enable countries like the United States to maintain accustomed standards of living. It is, of course, entirely possible that your neighbor will strike it rich with a new juice recipe or even that his daughter tinkering in her school's computer class will invent the next must-have mobile app. However appealing the vision of retrofitted loft spaces filled with amateur artisans and technologists avidly immersed in constructing bespoke creations might be, most of these pursuits are unlikely on the whole to amount to more than pastimes or hobbyist diversions.

Even an ardent proponent like Anderson seems to harbor reservations. Reporting on a visit to a fab lab in the gutted—but nonetheless iconic—former industrial district adjacent to today's Manchester city center, he offers the following assessment:

On a typical Friday while I was there, there was a gentle hum of activity as students from local universities worked on architecture and furniture models, and the laser cutter was in constant use making art pieces and design-school classwork . . . It is, to be honest, a little hard to see this makerspace as the seed of a new British manufacturing industry. Most of the work is being done by local students, and is the sort of modest stuff you might expect to find in any design or shop class. No hot startups have been spawned here yet.[50]

The situation in Manchester is not especially unusual given that the emphasis in most maker communities is weighted more toward the artfulness of design than the nuts and bolts of actual production. Moreover, when real fabrication does occur the overwhelming penchant, as documented in studies conducted to date, is on trinkets and novelties: stickers for Macbooks, replacement parts for vintage cars, Internet-enabled sprinklers, dollhouse furniture, photo-realistic action figures, personalized birthday cakes, jellyfish aquaria, backpack-mounted cameras, camping hammocks, towel racks, and closet organizers. And, of course, a virtually endless supply of iPhone cases. Anderson himself acknowledges that most of these items are "slightly inessential" examples of "hipster ephemera" and concedes that "you don't need it, but once you've seen it you might want it." It is difficult to square these observations with the overwrought rhetoric about self-reliance that pervades the Maker Movement or the continual references to the Homebrew Computer Club that served as the Silicon Valley launching pad for several computer-industry pioneers.[51]

This characterization is, to be sure, only part of the picture of contemporary making. The same equipment that has enabled ordinary people to become makers has contributed to lower-cost customization and led to important advances in the production of, for example, dental crowns, electrical circuits, and prosthetic limbs, as well as more exotic products like spaceplanes and open-source-designed automobiles. It is also quite conceivable that the day will arrive when medical laboratories will be able to use replicating machines to fashion replacement organs from stem cells.[52]

The question though remains whether these developments might add up to revolutionary changes in contemporary systems of production and consumption. Though he is conflicted by the prospects, Mark Hatch recognizes that the Maker Movement is likely to contribute to more rather than less contract production in Chinese factories. He indicates that:

[In China] it is possible to have just about anything made for extremely competitive prices. This is where China really does shine. It's not just that the Chinese can do it cheaply, it's that they have a very dense network of suppliers who carry almost everything and short, tight supply chains that can get the rest. The number and variety of flexible manufacturers in China with access to the hardest-to-find components means the job can be done quickly and cheaply and you can have it drop-shipped to your door anywhere in the world. This is the true competitive advantage that China has developed: there is no place else in the world where anything can be made, in volume, quickly, and very inexpensively. Some of the world's best manufacturing capabilities are now only a click away.[53]

Writing in the *MIT Technology Review*, David Rotman takes this point further when he asks, "How does sharing digital designs change the fact that most of the goods we want and depend upon, from iPhones to jet planes, still require the skills and budgets of large manufacturers?"[54] For the foreseeable future, making is likely to remain confined to diversionary amusements and niche-based manufacturing applications rather than wholesale reconstitution of global supply chains. Reflecting specifically on Anderson's understanding of the relationship between making and producing, Rotman goes on to observe that:

He has little interest in how most things are actually manufactured. He locates the real value of the subculture in the creation and sharing of digital designs for stuff. Anderson is agnostic about what should happen next: send the design to your 3D printer or upload it to the cloud and send it to a contract manufacturer in China, he suggests. While 3D printers will no doubt get more versatile—some advanced models are already able to handle an impressive range of materials— additive manufacturing will remain, at least for a while, better suited to making parts than to building entire machines or devices.[55]

It is not difficult to envision a future where makers become so fixated with the bedazzling images on their computer screens that actual production becomes a decidedly secondary consideration. Rotman is also attentive to this problem and contends that:

Many types of manufacturing require a sophisticated series of steps and processes to be done in precise sequence. Selecting the right materials and technologies is key to high-quality, low-cost results. If designers don't understand the manufacturing processes and materials that are practical they will never come up with the most advanced and compelling new products.[56]

Richard Sennett, too, is aware of this dilemma of outsourcing our creative imaginations to computers and focusing only on digital manipulations. Drawing on the insights of architect Renzo Piano and physicist Victor Weisskopf, he remarks that the problem "is that people may let the machines do this learning, the person serving as a passive witness to and consumer of expanding competence, not participating in it ... Abuses of CAD illustrate how, when the head and the hand are separate, it is the head that suffers."[57] This outcome seems to be especially probable when design files can be effortlessly transmitted for production to a factory across town, or more likely in China.

The Commercial Contradictions of Making

Proponents exult in portraying the Maker Movement as comprising irrepressible crafters and professional-amateur engineers, but more detailed examination reveals that all of this making activity rests on an extensive infrastructure of suppliers and equipment purveyors primarily interested in increasing turnover and maintaining sales to a dedicated clientele (sometimes referred to in promotional materials as "fans"). The much-heralded Maker Faires, a sort of cross between a high-school science fair and a trade show, have evolved from public celebrations of innovative manufacturing into improvised shopping malls. These physical embodiments of making are only one facet of the movement and its Internet-based expressions are at least equally as extensive. Reflecting on how the online marketplace for maker goods functions as a kind of virtual superstore, geographer Doreen Jakob finds that:

Tracing some of the numbers and growth statistics back to their original sources and examining what those crafts businesses actually produce and sell, reveals that most growth and success within the crafts industry stems from supplies and not the crafters themselves . . . Looking at the products of each month's top 25 sellers [on the website craftcount.com] reveals that most handmade businesses are in fact craft supply businesses selling crocheting and fabric patterns, appliqués, paper, beads, personalized postcards, t-shirts, and so forth.[58]

Jakob further reports that financial success for individual "crafts entrepreneurs" typically requires making the jump from hawking handcrafted products to selling the associated services in terms of seeking to "manage craft boutiques, organize festivals, markets and conferences, work as craft business consultants, publish profitable blogs, craft technique and craft business books."[59] A cursory Internet ramble reveals the manifest truth that there is a seemingly limitless proliferation of podcasts, YouTube videos, and DIY manuals aimed at capturing a slice of the Maker Movement pie.

The conflicting commercial dynamics of making become more clearly apparent when movement adherents get caught up in protracted spectacles over authenticity regarding, for example, the outsourcing of production to subcontractors or the use of materials of questionable provenance.[60] These dramas also demonstrate how maker products have become important cultural tools for creating identity, establishing distinction, and communicating social status and their ability to fulfill these functions is compromised when producer-vendors violate tacit understandings and transgress prevailing norms of appropriate conduct.[61] And this points to an obstinate contradiction in the economics of the Maker Movement, namely to be financially successful in this domain it is virtually impossible to comply with strict performance standards regarding the personalized handcrafting of goods.

The Promise of Making as a Pathway toward a More Sustainable Future

We now arrive at what is from the perspective of this book the most critical test for the Maker Movement: the degree to which it might help to pave the way toward a more sustainable future by reducing demand for energy and materials and reorganizing provisioning systems to achieve more equitable outcomes. Though inextricably interlinked, let us take each of these challenges up in turn.

Originating in the work of Buckminster Fuller and his numerous protégés, the supposition that creatively minded self-provisioning enables less resource-intensive modes of living is a prominent tenet of contemporary sustainability paradigms.[62] This school of thought has co-existed in an uneasy relationship over the last several decades with more mainstream environmental ideas rooted in the conservation of valued landscapes and the protection of endangered wildlife.[63] The public embrace of the Maker Movement, and for creative expression more generally, is a laudable development. It is, though, difficult to get past apprehensions that current interest in making derives primarily from two wellsprings: entrepreneurial enthusiasm and recreational diversion. Despite lots of emphasis on transforming passive consumers into active producers, the commercial dimensions of the Maker Movement have evinced little tangible concern for reducing consumptive throughput and success relies largely on perpetuating consumerist sensibilities. In an article on the technology-savvy website *Medium*, designer and journalist Allison Artieff exposes the issue in unambiguous terms and asserts that she is "struck by the absence of sustainable discourse in the maker movement."[64]

For instance, Chris Anderson devotes only a single paragraph of his monograph to the issue noting merely that:

As 3D printers proliferate and are used for small-scale bespoke or custom-made manufacturing, they can provide a more sustainable way of making things. There are little or no transportation costs, because the product is made locally. There is little or no waste, because you use no more raw material than you need. And because the product is custom-made just for you, you're more likely to value it and keep in longer. Personalized products are less disposable; you simply care about them more.[65]

Mark Hatch raises a related point, specifically that the Maker Movement has created a situation where "failure is free," and writes that "a critical by-product of this new reality is that this means almost anyone can afford to innovate."[66] It is nonetheless important to ask whether we really want to live in a world where supposed originality entails little cost and all manner of ideas can be pursued, and potentially brought to fruition, as long as they generate a private income stream that is, for all intents and purposes, greater than zero? In addition, as part of their efforts to encourage widespread participation, Maker Movement proponents suppress the reality that non-trivial breakthroughs are extremely difficult to achieve. It is for this reason that most making concentrates on the production of playful consumer knickknacks. Given these circumstances, a system of obstacles to distinguish socially useful invention from dubious novelty is not without utility. This does not mean to suggest that as a society we have achieved an Aristotelean golden mean on the management of innovation, but rather to point out that enabling every aspirant inventor to embark on a heedless rush to the patent office would likely be less than optimal from a societal perspective.[67]

When product development is extremely inexpensive it is just as easy to envision a future typified by the proliferation of tchotchkes and the hyper-replication of multiple, or roughly similar, versions of the same object. This is the society-wide version of when a teenager acquires a drawer full of iPhone cases and then treats them as revolving fashion accessories. In more technical terms, the phenomenon has come to be referred to as the "zero marginal cost society" and most commentators perversely extol it as an unambiguous source of human betterment.[68] This dynamic points to another contradiction at the heart of the Maker Movement that proponents have yet to actively consider: from the standpoint of environmental sustainability declining production costs are not singularly advantageous.[69] Without a way to proportionately reduce income (perhaps by cutting working hours), lower financial outlays for fabrication will almost certainly increase the volume of aggregate output. While the substitution of services for material goods holds some potential to relieve this problem, it is a mistake to presume that so-called ephemeralization affords a straightforward solution. As discussed in Chapter 3, services are invariably a constituent part of larger and otherwise tangible provisioning systems and it is a mistake to presume that virtuality always affords a more sustainable outcome.[70]

Let us now turn our attention to the social dimensions of sustainability which concentrate attention on issues of equity and inclusion with respect to gender, race, ethnicity, age, and class. While data are sketchy, the commercial facets of the Maker Movement in the United States appear to be comprised overwhelmingly of relatively wealthy (middle-class and above) white and Asian males holding college degrees.[71] The picture regarding social sustainability widens slightly when we focus specifically on attendees of Maker Faires (and scaled down mini-Maker Faires). These events have become popular destinations for family out-ings where children are encouraged to interact with the exhibits. Formal embedding of maker training in schools remains at this point largely confined to relatively affluent communities that have the resources to purchase equipment and to hire dedicated personnel.

Most Maker Movement spokespersons recognize that they could be doing a better job to enable broader participation and have sought funding for more comprehensive outreach and program development. One approach has been to expand financial support from philanthropic foundations as well as government agencies like the Defense Advanced Projects Research Agency (DARPA). Another strategy has involved enlisting prominent corporations, and in particular firms such as Google, Ford, and General Electric, which intuit that associating themselves with various maker initiatives confers valuable promotional benefits. While these collaborations may initially seem to be effective in augmenting the social sustainability of the Maker Movement, there is palpable risk that the initiatives will in due course be captured by their sponsors. Indeed, some critics claim that this process is already well underway and that making has become in recent years less of a social movement and more of a branding strategy.[72]

A final point pertaining to the social sustainability of the Maker Movement is relevant. Proponents seem unable—or unwilling—to recognize that interest in making is simultaneously a byproduct of economic hardship and a means to overcome it. Many people are attracted to making because it provides a way to acquire marketable skills or to supplement incomes (what TechShop terms a "lifestyle business"). Accordingly, the recent popularity of the Maker Movement could prove to be economically countercyclical. In other words, once more conventional employment opportunities have again become consistently available we would expect to see a waning of interest in the commercial facets of making. How plausible is such an outcome? If the shifts that we have seen in labor markets over the past few years are indeed evidence of a pervasive societal transition, the Maker Movement will likely continue to fill a role in enabling micro-entrepreneurs and others to acquire new technical competencies, to forge new identities, and, in some instances, to develop more diverse income streams. This suggests that making, provided proponents are inclined to open up to a broader base of participants and modulate their transactional proclivities, could usefully temper the effects of ongoing economic dislocation while simultaneously contributing to improvements in social equity.

Conclusion

It seems extremely unlikely that we will in the short- to medium-range future be making our own dishwashers, toasters, or most of the rest of the welter of consumer goods on which we rely. Maker Movement proponents seem to acknowledge this situation. After venerating the virtues of 3D printing, Mark Hatch concedes that "the amount of 'things' made by traditional means will continue to expand for a long, long time." This does not mean to suggest that all maker products will be commercially impracticable. Especially in a world where there is demand for goods that can confer status, and a population of consumers for which price is at best a secondary consideration, there will be a market for small batches of customized products that communicate individuality and distinction.

The potential of the Maker Movement as an efficacious pathway beyond consumer society is much less assured, in part because of a lack of both political engagement on the part of proponents and willingness to challenge prevailing economic prerogatives (and the technological determinism that underpins them).[73] In particular, it is striking how little interest publicly prominent makers have in rekindling debates from the 1970s about appropriate (or alternative) technology, socially useful production, and participatory decision-making about technological choices.[74] All of the talk about "revolution" becomes anodyne when there is no real impetus to reorder existing priorities and Fortune 500 companies and the Department of Defense are the primary source of patronage.[75] Advocates invoke insurrectionary slogans mostly to induce discontented professionals, earnest micro-entrepreneurs, exasperated educators, and anxious policymakers to rally behind a common banner of purportedly noble objectives. Efforts to provide people with training in digital control technologies and advanced manufacturing—especially when public commitment to such upskilling is far less than it should be—deserve active encouragement. However, we need to keep making in perspective. The Maker Movement is not a force of ruptural transformation but rather a means of ameliorative reform that will, at best, enable the average maker to derive a partial livelihood.[76] This does not mean to say that some number of innovations that spring out of organized making will not have disruptive potential, but these cases will be the very rare exception.

An unfortunate paradox of consumer society is that over time it alienates people from their material possessions and they lose capacity to apprehend their televisions, computers, handheld digital devices, and so forth. The technological underpinnings of consumption become a dark mystery. Even persevering individuals face an uphill struggle carrying out basic repair work because products are explicitly designed to discourage it. It was not always this way. When everyday items were comprised of mechanical subassemblies, tinkerers with relatively modest proficiency could often complete routine fixes with a few common tools and a little ingenuity. A direct outcome of the electronics revolution—where even simple appliances now have embedded computerization—is that these undertakings have become much more difficult and, in many cases, impossible for the average person. In many cases, it is not maker-conceived innovations that we need but rather more reliable ways to ensure the ongoing functionality of what we currently have on hand.

It is for this reason especially unfortunate that a chasm exists between the Maker Movement and ongoing efforts to increase accessibility to rudimentary repair services through, for instance, pop-up fix-it clinics.[77] There is, moreover, no indication of interest in integrating organized making with emergent initiatives that foster the transfer of skills through collaborative learning and delivered these days by proprietary companies like Skillshare (which, in its own words, seeks to become the Airbnb of learning and education) and community-based "how-to" programs.[78] These instructional models have been expanding rapidly in recent years, particularly in areas that are popular residential locales for urban millennials. Courses span the gamut, from jam-making to soldering, and typically run for just a few sessions at reasonable prices in face-to-face, hybrid, and online modes. It is even possible to pay a nominal monthly subscription that allows unlimited access to a full range of course offerings.[79]

Active collaboration with these allied ventures, however, will require Maker Movement proponents to develop a vision of social transformation that goes beyond gee-whizz wonderment and unrestrained ardor for "the next big thing." It will entail disavowing expedient partnerships (especially with military contractors and the defense industry) and rejection of overexcited promotional practices (particularly ones that unreservedly celebrate the founders of Silicon Valley technology firms). On the educational front, a more enduring—albeit more difficult—pursuit would be to embrace not just trend-chasing charter schools, but to engage as well with civic-minded reformers working to reinvent the home economics and manual arts programs of conventional public schools.[80] There are indications that some Maker Movement proponents understand the importance of this reorientation, but this sensibility is far from widespread.

Finally, makers of all stripes, but especially the movement's commercial manifestations, will need to redouble their resolve to common access and use rather than retreat from these commitments when compelled to do so by their investors. This will be a major challenge because it will require operationalizing new business models that can legitimately contribute to a more sustainable future. Such discussions are today very much on the margins and progress on this front will require reversing commitments that have become quite deeply entrenched in the institutions of the Maker Movement.

Chapter 5 turns attention to economic localization, the third potential pathway for facilitating a transition beyond consumer society in the new economy.

5

Localization Fallacies

Introduction

Environmentalism has long valorized local provisioning and a growing number of advocates earnestly embrace this idea as an effective way to curtail the social and ecological impacts of contemporary lifestyles. Indeed, in supermarkets and other retail venues the appellation "local" has supplanted the more amorphous concept of "sustainable" as a way to give precision to how, in an overtly practical sense, we can realign our lives as consumers with biophysical limits.[1] Within the realm of food localization often fuses with "organically grown" in the ongoing societal conversation about achieving reductions in material throughput and fostering more equitable and ethical commercial relationships. It moreover merits recognizing that this tendency to embrace proximity as tantamount to sustainability is not confined to individual consumers but it is also a prominent feature of sustainability scholarship and arguably an inclination across academia more generally. In recent years proponents of localism have become increasingly adamant in asserting that immediate provenance constitutes an unambiguously efficacious sustainability strategy.

Due to the tireless efforts of localist champions, consumers have adopted geographic proximity as the preferred strategy for ameliorating the manifold problems of industrial agriculture and for reorienting the priorities of the prevailing production system in favor of safe and nourishing food.[2] Despite generally higher prices, farmers' markets are now common fixtures in many cities and in some locales, community-supported agriculture (CSA), where consumers make a pre-season payment to a nearby farmer in exchange for a weekly produce basket, has become a popular way to procure locally grown fruits and vegetables.[3] Community gardens, once largely conceived as a way to improve food security in poor urban neighborhoods, are experiencing new popularity as a social enterprise of wider significance.[4] More controversially, the school cafeteria has acquired new status as a pitched battleground for the contestation of political debates over the traceability of food and the preparation of healthy meals for children.[5] Prompted by similar impulses, some municipal governments, civic organizations, community groups, and individual farmers have endorsed commercial-scale urban farming to shrink the distance from farm field to table and to enhance access to wholesome produce.[6] Other novel forms of food localism include vertical farms (intensive agriculture on floors of multi-level buildings), geographically circum-scribed food-sourcing like small-plot intensive (SPIN) farming, and yardfarming (conversion of suburban yards into mini-farms).[7]

We should not, though, regard food as the limit of localization. Another prominent expression is impelled by the combined concerns of resource scarcity and climate change and centers on the community-scale generation of renewable energy.[8] Some of these initiatives have grown out of grassroots stimuli in discrete communities and others have been driven by so-called glocalist phenomena like the Transition Towns movement.[9] Still other localization projects center more explicitly on enhancing economic resilience through, for instance, the creation of local exchange trading schemes (LETS) that typically rely on barter or spe-cially designed currency. More recent variations on this idea entail community time banks and neighborhood clothing swaps that are gen-erally recognized as components of the so-called sharing economy discussed in Chapter 3.[10] The aim of these endeavors is often to create more robust and interdependent social and economic linkages within a demarcated locale that attenuate the need for long-distance transactions between anonymous sellers and buyers. Even more ambitious have been efforts to import the notion of localization into the purchase of building materials and the production of manufactured goods (sometimes termed "eco-industrialization").[11]

The widespread view among proponents is that localization is an effective strategy for reducing material throughput, for forging more resilient communities, and for enhancing social equity. The cultivation of proximate economic relationships is also endorsed as a way to temper consumerism. The aim of this chapter is to interrogate this conventional wisdom and to offer a critical review. We first begin with a brief history of localization in sustainability thought and activism.

A Brief History of Localization

While interest in localist modes of social organization traces back to the classical Greek city-states, it was during the middle of the nineteenth century that a loose assemblage of French and Russian economic geographers with strong anarchist or libertarian leanings—among them Charles Fourier and Peter Kropotkin—began to infuse the notion of localization with modern meaning premised on autonomy, proximate governance, and decentralization.[12] These ideas received expression during the short-lived days of the Paris Commune in 1871 and then again during the revolutionary upheavals in Russia in 1905 and 1917. Indeed reviewing the historical record from early Medieval Europe through the twentieth century, the bioregionalist Kirkpatrick Sale argued that:

> Everywhere it seems to be the case that the absence of government does not lead to bewilderment and confusion and disorder, as might be imagined if all of government's claims for itself were true, but rather to a resurgence of locally based forms, most often democratically chosen and scrupulously responsive, that turn out to be quite capable of managing the complicated affairs of daily life for many months, occasionally years, until they are forcibly suppressed by some new centralist state less democratic and less responsive.[13]

The nineteenth century's robust political ferment gave rise to several prominent social reformers who further developed these planning ideas centered on small-scale and distributed governance. Particularly notable was the socialist Robert Owen who was an important figure in the establishment of the cooperative movement in the United Kingdom and went on to found two cooperative communities, Orbiston in Scotland and New Harmony in the United States.[14] Both the conceptual and practical insights of these experiments influenced the town planner Ebenezer Howard who incorporated localist principles into the design plan for his utopian Garden City which, in a number of paradoxical ways, became an influential template for the American-style suburb.[15]

Localism as a political philosophy continued to develop during the twentieth century due to the work of the pioneering Scottish sociologist-planner Patrick Geddes and his protégé Lewis Mumford.[16] Other important proponents of localization during the latter part of subsequent decades were Murray Bookchin, Ivan Illich, Gerry Mander, and Edward (Teddy) Goldsmith.[17]

While interesting as a matter of intellectual history, from the perspective of socio-environmental planning (and eventually sustainable development) it was the 1973 publication of E. F. Schumacher's *Small is Beautiful*, and the ensuing debates that it triggered, that gave the issue of scale, and localization in particular, prominence in both scholarly and public consciousness.[18] The book gave voice to palpable misgivings over what seemed to be, at least to more critical or countercultural observers, a relentless emphasis on dehumanizing bigness and "super-technologies."[19] Nuclear power plants were the epitome of this phenomenon but other features of modern life including mega-sized residential and commercial developments, massive highways, unabated reliance on nonrenewable fossil fuels, and non-transparent supply chains for agricultural commodities and other products were part of the more general critique.[20] Schumacher described in elegiac prose the brutalizing effects of these projects that he attributed to their excessive proportion and unrepentant propensity to overwhelm accustomed sensibilities. In addition to providing inspiration to the "appropriate (or intermediate) technology" movement, perspectives informed by *Small is Beautiful* continue today to serve as counterpoints to more technologically driven sustainability strategies.[21]

As noted earlier, in the popular mind localization fused with sustainability and engendered a number of prominent voices including Bill McKibben, Wendell Berry, Richard Heinberg, and David Korten.[22] Distinguished novelists, perhaps most notably Barbara Kingsolver, have also integrated localist themes into their work, thus bringing these ideas to a readership that might not normally be exposed to them in such an intimate way.[23] A number of institutions have also formed over the past several decades to advance a localization agenda with prominent examples being Schumacher College, the Schumacher Center for New Economics, the Post-Carbon Institute, and the Business Alliance for Local Living Economies.[24] *Small is Beautiful* continues to resonate in contemporary debates regarding economic growth, renewable energy transitions, alternative agro-food systems, work–life balance and human well-being, sustainable consumption, and technology assessment.[25]

What Does "Local" Really Mean?

While localization may be appealing in many respects, when we begin to push a little harder on the concept it turns out that "the local" is more difficult to pin down and the pursuit of relevant priorities is not as direct and unambiguous as proponents contend. For instance, how do we distinguish whether a particular product is local? Should we subscribe to a strict definition of localness or does the determination depend on the inherent features of specific items? Are products best understood as being local or nonlocal or, alternatively, are progressive gradations of localness arrayed along a spectrum? Moving from the abstract to the practical, how do we determine when a particular tomato is locally grown or when a piece of lumber is locally harvested? Should, say, a ten-mile radius between the site of production and the site of consumption hold for localness to be apparent? Is ten miles too far or too short a distance for something to be genuinely local?[26]

Further complicating such appraisals is that small-scale retailers and economic development boosters have in many communities embraced localization (sometimes termed localism) as a marketing strategy and regularly deploy "buy local" schemes as a form of place-based branding.[27] This practice is shamelessly invoked even when the products on the shelves have been assembled from globally sourced supply chains and are more or less identical to alternatives available at big-box competitors on the nearby highway strip. Many people are understandably attracted to the notion of living in a neighborhood with a bustling shopping district populated with locally owned retail businesses, but there is something sadly paradoxical when most of the inventory in the shops has been imported from China. It ultimately warrants exploring whether localization constitutes a meaningful challenge to contemporary consumerism or instead represents yet another strategy for easing the anxieties prompted by excessive shopping.[28]

An instructive way to proceed is to pose the question "What is local?" and to begin to formulate a response that draws on the thinking of geographers who contend that scale is a socially constructed phenomenon.[29] While most people would assert that they have an intuitive understanding of scale that differentiates in a straightforward manner among, say, local, regional, national, and global, adherents of a constructivist perspective credibly emphasize that this is not the case. These scholars assert that scale is not an ontologically determined hierarchy but rather is contingently premised and shaped by social context and historical experience. For instance, Sally Marston maintains that the factors generally regarded as responsible for constituting and reconstituting scale include "the state, capital and nonstate-level political actors such as labor, political parties and political activists with an emphasis upon the interactions among them."[30] She persuasively argues that the customary emphasis on production—and capitalist relations more specifically—fails to adequately consider social reproduction and consumption which are essential to a comprehensive appreciation of how scale is both disputed and constructed.[31] There is, moreover, a great deal of fluidity as various actors adjust their strategies in accordance with efforts to overcome constraints and exploit opportunities across different geographic levels. These dynamics lead to an inevitable blurring between local and global systems of exchange that, ultimately, mutually constitute one another and become extremely difficult to isolate and assess.[32]

Consumers socially construct scale by assembling a complex array of factors including scientific rationales, tacit intuitions, and experiential evidence into a set of malleable heuristics. Brídín Carroll and Frances Fahy describe, for instance, how shoppers enlarge their understanding of local as a particular product becomes less readily available.[33] There are furthermore indications that general conceptions of the local are highly elastic and often dependent on different spatial frameworks. In the United States, for instance, the notion is typically associated with a specific state and this tendency derives from how it is used for promotional purposes. However, as a practical matter claims of state-produced mean quite different things in, say, super-sized Montana and Lilliputian-scaled Delaware. To get around this problem, some advocates of localization subscribe instead to a stricter linear delineation of, say, 100 miles.[34]

Other researchers have drawn attention to how some consumers confuse local provenance and organic production and use a liberal dose of personal discretion to operationalize their own idiosyncratic locally oriented routines.[35] While perhaps unnerving to more discerning locavores, this melding is understandable. Local produce is typically cultivated on small farms within the proximity of major metropolitan areas and these growers are more likely to have adopted chemical-free practices. However, as large retailers like Wal-Mart increase their organics inventory—much of it from distant sources—the conflation of local and organic becomes less tenable.

The upshot here is that we need to acknowledge that local alternatives often lack both specificity and objectivity. Localization, like many of the normative commitments that are salient in sustainability science, is a contested concept.[36] In other words, it is not an impartial referent but rather a plastic idea that is deployed to galvanize support for explicit moral appeals. This does not mean to suggest that local claims are disingenuous or duplicitous, or that they lack scientific foundation. We do, though, need to be attentive to the fact that invocations of the local seek to reinforce certain economic interests at the same time that they challenge others. Because such claims are being refracted through a political lens, the efficacy of spatially circumscribed systems of commercial exchange needs to be carefully scrutinized.

The subsequent discussion interrogates three facets of localization. This chapter first reviews the argument that shorter supply chains are beneficial from the interrelated standpoints of reducing energy use and cutting carbon emissions. The second facet subjected to critique asserts that proponents of localization run the risk of falling into a "local trap," which occurs when there is confusion between the means and ends of a particular project. In the final instance, this chapter considers the Marxist contention that efforts to venerate the local lack a sufficiently radical edge because they aim to accommodate rather than overturn capitalism. Because food provisioning casts a long shadow over current debates about the credence of localization as a sustainability strategy much of the following discussion focuses on the production and consumption of agricultural goods.

Assessing the Sustainability of Localization Strategies

As the conversation about localization has expanded over the last few decades, new concepts like ecological footprints, food miles, and embodied carbon have become prominent additions to the lexicon. Concomitantly, locally procured products have become increasingly important resources for identity formation and social communication and it is not unusual for consumers to engage in passionate and extremely complicated debates about their provisioning practices.[37] A widely held presumption exists that, virtually across the board, products from local sources are environmentally preferable to alternatives shipped over longer distances. Unfortunately, such determinations are not so easy to make and, in a sizeable number of cases, probably incorrect when evaluated on the basis of scrupulous scientific calculations. Problems arise because often lost in these appraisals is the fact that transportation typically constitutes a relatively small part of overall energy inputs and carbon emissions of most food products account for less than 20 percent of their total effects.[38] In addition, if we conceive of ecological implications as extending beyond fossil fuels, it becomes a tricky business to sum up the different—and typically incommensurate—impact categories. For instance, we lack an adequate framework for reconciling the adverse effects of greenhouse-gas releases and the consequences of exposure to toxic chemicals.

Despite these complications, life-cycle analysis (LCA) has become a popular methodological tool for measuring the environmental sustainability of consumer goods.[39] The technique involves identifying and measuring the direct impacts (generally calculated in terms of energy units) of a particular product across the various phases of its lifespan including extraction and processing of raw materials, fabrication and assembly of components, deployment by consumers during use, and final disposal (or material recovery in cases of partial or full recycling). It is also necessary to account for the transportation-related inputs connected with each of these phases. More comprehensive LCAs consider the indirect impacts that accrue as one widens the arc of analysis to also consider secondary and tertiary activities. In the case of agricultural products, this more thoroughgoing inquiry would require assessing the life-cycle affects that accrue not only on the farm but also at, say, the fertilizer plant and the factories that manufacturer the machinery used for cultivation and harvest. An extremely fastidious analyst would also want to include the fuel used to power the farmer's car when she drives into town to consult with her accountant and the occasional trip by a mechanic to repair a malfunctioning tractor in a distant field. Because a sizeable professional industry has developed around the preparation of LCAs, and the technique has acquired a pretense of authoritative soundness, analysts have been reticent to fully disclose the subjective judgments that are required to perform this work. The truth is that the methodology, like all forms of quantitative sustainability assessment, is equal parts art and science and the results that it generates should be interpreted in this light.[40]

As important as these caveats are, most localization proponents are generally less concerned with LCAs than they are with food miles. The measurement of food miles can also involve elaborate computer-driven procedures to determine the embodied energy in discrete products, but locavores typically deploy the concept tacitly rather than algorithmically. Accordingly, consumer goods that originate from more proximate sources are intuitively favored over similar items transported over longer distances. However, as noted, an exclusive focus on shipping mileage oftentimes fails to adequately account for the full measure of a product's environmental profile. In many instances, the impacts that accrue during production or use can overwhelm the effects arising from other life-cycle stages. At minimum, a more complete understanding requires consideration not only of distance but haulage mode (i.e., semi-trailer truck versus airplane).

It is moreover critical to investigate the broader conditions under which an item has been produced. For instance, cucumbers grown in artificially heated greenhouses in cold-weather climates require significantly more energy than when they are cultivated outdoors in a temperate region.[41] In addition, the eating practices of specific populations will lead to differential impacts. Especially problematic from the perspective of environmental sustainability are the effects of diets heavy with beef and dairy products, which studies have found account for upwards of 60 percent of food-related greenhouse-gas emissions.[42]

Despite the casual and oftentimes selective way in which localists apply sustainability science, transactional proximity—and this is a key feature of research on farmers' markets and other alternative agro-food systems—holds important potential for certain social benefits in terms of closer interpersonal relationships and enhanced political attentiveness.[43] These outcomes are obviously desirable in the civic sense (indeed the term "civic agriculture" is applied to describe these activities), but more robust participation in the life of a community can have important ancillary environmental outcomes. The plausible expectation is that the embedding of production and consumption in communal relationships reduces the likelihood of deviant behavior that undercuts both individual and collective well-being. Economic exchange under such circumstances becomes part of a wider network of social commitments that enhance opportunities for oversight and informal surveillance. In the case of local food, proponents contend that it becomes less tenable for agricultural operations to rely with impunity on questionable labor practices or ecologically harmful routines when farmers and consumers are engaged in relationships that extend beyond the occasional transaction. For instance, a vendor at a local farmers' market has less incentive to pass off adulterated produce than someone half a continent away who is only accountable to formal regulatory controls and has no liability for what occurs after he delivers his harvest to a regional depot.

It additionally merits recognizing that because all locales do not have the same resource endowments, a shift toward more proximate provisioning will not hold the same sustainability implications for all geographic regions. For instance, South Dakota has considerable advantage for the production of wheat and residents would face great difficulty transitioning to a more geographically circumscribed agricultural economy. By contrast, a North Carolinian, owing to the state's generally moderate climate and varied agronomic conditions, is able to access a wider-ranging supply of locally grown produce.

By way of further contrast, a resident of California's Central Valley is able to enjoy a vast bounty throughout most of the year. The rest of the country is considerably less fortunate. In the absence of very substantial investments in climate-controlled production facilities and other ancillary equipment most consumers would need to forsake oranges, grapes, nuts, and much more. Indeed, it is an awareness of this situation that has led to the prevailing situation where localization is pursued on an extremely strategic and selective basis. Most locavores purchase goods from nearby sources when they are seasonally available and supplement at other times with products arriving via long-distance supply chains. To do otherwise would entail, for a large majority of consumers, having to adjust to a much less diversified diet.

It would be remiss, finally, not to consider the macroscale implications of a large-scale adoption of localization. Movement beyond prevailing spatially extensive patterns of procurement and adoption of more thoroughgoing commitments to localized sourcing would likely trigger massive migration as people sought to take advantage of regional variations in productive potential. The associated resettlement would entail extraordinary upheaval and probably be the premise for protracted and conflictive processes of social reorganization. A large-scale shift toward more locally situated economies would furthermore increase the cost of food due to the allocation of more expensive land to agriculture and downward adjustment in farm size. If implemented on a widespread basis, we would also likely see an increase in agro-environmental impacts as more acreage in close proximity to major population centers was drawn into intensive agricultural use.[44] It is currently difficult for most locavores to comprehend the consequences of a transformation of appreciable magnitude because the current scale of local provisioning is miniscule. In the United States, direct-to-consumer transactions presently constitute less than one half of one percent of total food sales and the marketing focus, especially in urban locales, is on catering to the specialized preferences of relatively affluent consumers.[45] In sum, it is incorrect to presume that localization constitutes a straightforward sustainability strategy and active encouragement of such policies on a broad basis would lead to differentiated impacts. Presumptive winners would embrace such a shift in provisioning practices while losers could be expected to mobilize stiff resistance.

Confronting the Challenges of the "Local Trap"

As described earlier, localists frequently presume that the devolution of responsibility and the performance of production and consumption activities at more proximate scales are more effective than the alternatives. Whether the prevailing issue is ensuring the wholesomeness of food supplies, protecting water resources, or generating energy, more localized scales are typically regarded as having the capacity to ensure more socially desirable and ecologically responsible outcomes. This chapter describes how this penchant to privilege propinquity is a foremost tenet of contemporary sustainability scholarship and policy, despite considerable evidence that the localist case tends to rely on oversimplified heuristics.

A second avenue of critique has been formulated by geographers, political ecologists, and planners who contend that researchers and practitioners have developed a "habitual preference for local scales."[46] For instance, J. Christopher Brown and Mark Purcell observe that:

No scale has any inherent and eternal qualities that make it particularly suited to a specific social or ecological process . . . [and] the characteristics of a given scale or scalar arrangement cannot be assumed a priori; rather the social and ecological outcomes of any particular scalar arrangement are the result of the political strategies of particular actors, not the inherent qualities of particular scales.[47]

The pitfalls associated with this inclination of assigning preference to goods that derive from proximate locales and to instinctively encourage a shift toward more localized provisioning has been termed the "local trap."[48] This situation arises when localists presume that provenance is synonymous with other objectives to which they aspire—sustainability, equity, food security, nutritional quality, and so forth—when there is little evidence that it systematically enables these capacities. For instance, it is frequently inferred that there is strong linkage between localism and social justice and such assertions are an especially prominent feature of many alternative agro-food projects. The argument advanced here is not that local scale is innately imprudent, but rather that it is a neutral and unbiased characterization. As Branden Born and Mark Purcell observe, "Local-scale food systems are equally likely to be just or unjust, sustainable or unsustainable, secure or insecure. No matter what its scale, the outcomes produced by a food system are contextual; they depend on the actors and agenda that are empowered by the particular social relations in a given food system."[49] In short, unreflexive localism confuses ends and means. Rather than regard localization as a strategy for pursuing a defined planning goal for, say, reducing greenhouse-gas emissions, it oftentimes gets invoked as an objective in and of itself.

Proponents of the local-trap thesis assert that it is not that emphasis on localization will fail to generate intended outcomes, but that there is a surfeit of evidence suggesting that this strategic preference will often have the opposite outcome. For instance, case-study research suggests that localism in the case of agro-food systems can lead to the empowerment of oligarchic structures because of inadequate competition, higher retail prices due to captured markets, and environmental degradation attributable to insufficient expertise or productive scale.[50] Some observers also contend that localism is tantamount to protectionism, insulating inefficient producers and perpetuating a kind of reactionary parochialism.[51] Still more critically, certain scholars argue that the turn toward local provisioning is in no way a form of resistance to consumerism but rather reinforces neoliberal prerogatives and inculcates customary instrumentalist commitments. The emphasis on individual responsibility and consumer sensibilities further entrenches patterns of economic inequity, social injustice, and political inequality.[52] Roberta Sonnino sums up the prevailing situation when she writes, "The celebration of the local is beginning to be replaced by its detraction. What was only a few years ago considered as a site of resistance to the destructive neoliberal logics of globalization is now increasingly seen as so embedded in these logics to become a potential obstacle in the pursuit of sustainable development."[53]

The local-trap critique proceeds to observe that just because there are often obvious and widely acknowledged problems associated with global supply chains in terms of transparency, labor practices, environmental degradation, and so forth does not automatically mean that proximate alternatives offer more effective solutions. Born and Purcell, drawing on the social constructivist argument outlined earlier in the chapter, contend further that:

> Scale is not ontologically given but socially constructed; therefore, there can be nothing inherent about any scale. No scale can have an eternal extent, function, or quality. In this view, scale is not an end goal itself; it is a strategy. Scale is a means that may help achieve any of many different goals. Which goal is achieved will depend not on the scale itself but on the agenda of those who are empowered by the scalar strategy. Localization, therefore, does not lead inherently to greater sustainability or to any other goal. It leads wherever those it empowers want it to lead.[54]

It also merits noting from a historical perspective that current enthusiasm surrounding localization is a relatively recent phenomenon. Consideration of the experience of American social and environmental policy reveals that for most of the twentieth century governance institutions at the national scale were viewed as the most effective way in which to advance a progressive agenda. The widespread—and largely accurate—understanding was that local officials were either too corrupt or irrecoverably captured by parochial business interests and hence disinclined to advance an expansive understanding of the common good.[55] This was clearly the case with respect to racial politics where it took, in many parts of the country, federal legislation and enforcement to create more tolerable conditions. In the environmental realm, some states did serve as laboratories for policy experimentation prior to the 1970s, but significant steps to create and deploy meaningful controls only became possible with the passage of sweeping national laws establishing new regulatory authority. The election of President Reagan in the 1980s marked the beginning of a multi-decade period of neoliberal ascendency and the national scale has tended over the years to lose stature as a catalyst for reform. It should, therefore, not be surprising that it is precisely during this era that localism began to gain credibility as an alternative way forward.

Such an observation prompts consideration of how and why localization has taken hold and diffused so widely in a relatively short period of time. Three reasons for its popular appeal seem paramount. First, the rising tide of globalization, especially over the past thirty years, has prompted dissenters to this multifaceted phenomenon to look to the local as a source of resistance.[56] For instance, the food-sovereignty movement and efforts to create more proximate substitutes to international agro-food supply chains controlled by large corporations have offered useful foci to enact this oppositional politics.[57] Second, propinquity is attractive to a wide range of political orientations. Localization resonates with communitarians on the left side of the political spectrum and taps into deeply seated conceptions celebrating back-to-the-land lifestyles, retreatist philosophies, and nostalgic idealizations.[58] At the same time, localism, as Simin Davoudi and Ali Madanipour correctly contend, resonates with libertarians who are drawn to its principles of political devolution and decentralized control and responsibility.[59] Finally, the rise of localization is attributable to its effective deployment as a bulwark by small, independently owned businesses (many concentrated in retail trade) seeking to protect themselves from competitive encroachment by much larger competitors. Campaigns to "buy local" have had remarkable success, especially among affluent consumers, who have appropriated the idea of imputed provenance as a way to communicate social distinction.[60]

So the question becomes, if the local trap in its various manifestations is seemingly so pervasive, how might proponents of localization avoid its consequences? Stepping clear requires maintaining focus about the ultimate objective of a particular initiative and keeping that goal firmly embedded in project planning and implementation. If the aim of a stipulated undertaking is, for instance, to reduce the amount of energy associated with food production, it is important to keep this intention in mind rather that to allow certain proxies like local production to take priority. More generally, sustainability entails developing a complex assemblage of strategies with some interventions privileging provisioning from proximate supplies and other aspects favoring appropriation from other scales. To reiterate the point made earlier, there is nothing inherent about a specific scale and comprehensive efforts to enhance sustainability should be careful not to assign unwarranted credence to localist schemes.

Marxist Critique of Localization

The appraisal of localization from a Marxist perspective has been exten-sively elaborated by Greg Sharzer in a provocative book.[61] As described earlier, proponents of localism seek to create spaces in which to embed economic exchange in spatially circumscribed contexts and to anchor these transactions in more solidaristic relationships between producers and consumers. In certain cases, locavores are committed to ideals of "small is beautiful" and advance a persuasive moral argument that bigness embodies a host of problems. The core dilemma for Marxists is that localization constitutes incremental reform and does not try to overturn capitalism; campaigns to encourage proximate modes of com-merce instead strive to develop protected corners within the capitalist economy and to co-exist with it. Though these efforts are championed by well-meaning enthusiasts, this critique contends that they are destined to lead to disappointing outcomes because of a failure to acknowledge the capitalist laws of motion. As Sharzer observes:

> While small-scale alternatives can survive and occasionally flourish, they won't build a new, equitable society. Their prospects are severely limited by the power of capital. The problem with localism is not its anti-corporate politics, but that those politics don't go far enough. It sees the effects of unbridled competition but not its cause . . . if localists had a greater understanding of how capitalism works, they might not be localists.[62]

Marxist authors have long contended that the economic directives to which capitalists are required to conform are unforgiving and severe. To survive and to grow, businesses must sell their commodities in the face of relentless cost-cutting competition from other capitalists. This means underpaying workers and externalizing the environmental effects of production. Sharzer proceeds to remark that:

> If the goal is to stop ecological degradation and runaway growth, then the stakes are higher, and localists need to ask whether small projects will create long-term change. In practice, building those alternatives takes a lot of time and energy; projects can become self-justifying, not the means to build broad movements for social change.[63]

Sharzer differentiates pro-market and anti-market localists. Pro-market localism seeks to work with capitalism, but to reduce the scale of operations and to root them in particular locales as a way to enhance opportunities for proximate transactions premised on interpersonal familiarity and ethical and fair exchange. It is asserted that under such circumstances greed can be kept in check through self-regulation and the potential for outsized profits eliminated. Sharzer regards these goals as unrealistic because "in the long run, small capital loses: since capitalists compete to undersell each other, the scale of ownership constantly increases."[64] The standard response to this argument is that local producers are not geared to mass-market production, but rather can survive by securing space on the periphery of the dominant economy and selling specialized products at premium prices. This strategy has, in fact, been widely applied, but Sharzer is skeptical about its ultimate viability. He writes, "If they rely on high-cost, niche markets to sell their products, firms shrink their customer base to wealthy consumers."[65] Of course, this may not be a problem at the retail level if profit margins are high and there is an ample number of affluent patrons. However, in the case of local manufacturing, producers are less likely to employ best practices to manage the environmental effects of their operations due to their sub-optimal size, prone to fly under the radar of regulatory controls, and apt to encounter continual pressure from larger firms able to realize more cost-effective economies of scale. On account of their ownership structure most local businesses are, virtually by definition, small enterprises and any competitive edge that they are able to marshal likely derives from the long hours that proprietors invest in fostering the success of their ventures.

By contrast, anti-market localists evince a combination of socialist, anti-capitalist, autarchic, and anarchist inclinations. Rather than endorse micro-scale market solutions to the dilemmas of global capitalism, they call for decentralized retreat from the hegemonic economic system. The obvious challenge here is that in most parts of the world it is extremely difficult to maintain anything approaching a contemporary quality of life by relying on local production. Urban farming, community kitchens, and other local endeavors all depend on remote inputs—if not for essential components, certainly for the supplementary supplies like shovels, cooking pots, and energy resources. Sharzer describes anti-market localism as being predicated on the so-called Robinson Crusoe theory of history (as originally formulated by Marx) and notes that:

Even the things that Crusoe used to survive, stuck on his island far from anyone, were the product of a widespread social division of labor. In fact, from the

Neolithic era onwards, individual communities have never been self-sufficient economically, and farmers and artisans have relied on outside resources for tools and raw materials . . . Production has *never* been entirely local; trying to force it to become so creates serious problems.[66] (italics in original)

In short, the practical obstacles of anti-market localism are overwhelming. Without massive change—and likely severe diminution—of living standards it would be infeasible for communities to effectively produce a suitable array of goods and certain items—heavy machinery comes most readily to mind but also relevant are photovoltaics and wind turbines—would be impossible to manufacture because the scale of production would be inadequate to justify the required investment. Geographic patterns of inequality would also likely become more perverse as regions with plentiful resource endowments exploited their comparative advantages. In the absence of strict controls on migration, population movement would reach untenable proportions.

To work around these issues, anti-market localists have proposed a variety of interventions premised on building more cooperative forms of economic exchange. Popular strategies include the implementation of community currencies, the establishment of time banks, and the creation of various bartering and trading networks. According to Sharzer, these ethical projects—however noble they may be—do little more than forge "tiny alternatives at the margins."[67] They sidestep the issue of class struggle and are less a political challenge to capitalism than a withdrawal from it.

The Marxist critique of localized agriculture, especially as a strategy for addressing issues of food insecurity, is particularly pointed. Sharzer speculates why poor people should be urged to grow their own food when they are already required to toil for substandard wages and to subject themselves to all manner of social indignities.[68] Adherents of this perspective further contend that such strategies give government a free pass from attempting to resolve issues that contribute to poverty and from diffusing pressure on capitalists to raise wages because the subsistence needs of workers are being satisfied through alternative modes of provisioning.

So the question that then emerges is, who are the champions of localism and why do they persist in nurturing small-scale projects of arguably limited significance? From the Marxist perspective, it is the petite bourgeoisie that has been pivotal to the development of local responses to contemporary sustainability challenges. In the contemporary economy, this class is heavily populated by mid-level personnel in financial companies, computer-systems experts, and "cultural creatives" working in the arts, advertising, marketing, and other related fields. The petit bourgeoisie stand apart because its members lack the resources (and perhaps the inclination) to be full-scale capitalists and occupy more ambiguous—and sometimes contradictory—positions in the contemporary system of value appropriation and labor exploitation. They are situated in occupational classifications that require the regular and ongoing cultivation of individualism as an economic asset.

This need for the petit bourgeoisie to thrive through personal resourcefulness clashes with the circumstances that this class encounters at work on a daily basis. On one hand, they are impelled to build a professional identity that emphasizes independence and autonomy while, on the other hand, they are forced to endure occupational cultures that require obsequiousness to complex managerial systems of authority (see also Chapter 4). Sharzer characterizes this paradox in the following terms:

This means that [the petite bourgeoisie] have a collective identity, but one based on a shared experience of a lack of collectivity. Like the bourgeoisie, the petite bourgeoisie is structurally prevented from seeing its relationship to the division of labor. It operates around the edges of the capital-labor relation: unlike the working class, it helps circulate small amounts of capital through its small businesses, or it helps coordinate production as technical staff. It encounters commodities as part of their distribution, not production. Because of this, the petite bourgeoisie can see the symptoms of capitalist growth but not the causes. Therefore it tries to alleviate those symptoms, not overcome capitalism.[69]

Given this incongruity, the petite bourgeoisie advocates for interventions to ameliorate surface-level problems rather than to stoke class conflicts. Accordingly, the production and consumption of local goods has emerged as a popular strategy for resolving moral anxiety about the ethical quandaries associated with global supply chains. Consistent with Pierre Bourdieu's concept of habitus, veneration of localization has supplementary advantage for the petite bourgeoisie in that it enables them to use provenance (and the price premium that local products engender) to culturally communicate their distinctiveness and to define themselves against other social classes.[70] As Sharzer summarizes, "control over consumption substitutes for real social power . . . Members of the petite bourgeoisie assume that the sum of their voluntary choices creates

social change . . . By substituting lifestyle for politics, the petite bourgeoisie is drawn towards personal, rather than collective action."[71]

The diffidentness of this response is not entirely unexpected and derives
from the political repertoire that the petite bourgeoisie bring to the task,
one in which there is a strident and hopeful confidence that progressive
change will emerge from the aggregation of individual commitment
and effort. To borrow phrasing from political scientist Michael Maniates,
such initiatives embrace "the notion that knotty issues of consumption,
consumerism, power, and responsibility can be resolved neatly and cleanly
through enlightened uncoordinated consumer choice."[72] He proceeds to
observe that "[w]hen responsibility for environmental problems is individualized, there is little room to ponder institutions, the nature and
exercise of political power, or ways of collectively changing the distribution
of power and influence in society."[73]

A visit on Saturday morning to a farmers' market in a relatively affluent
community in the United States is likely to reveal the extent to which the
localization movement has embraced a largely fatuous epicureanism.
Whether it is about chocolate, coffee, beer, or heirloom tomatoes, distinguishing provenance has become a consumerist strategy for making
gratuitous distinctions and demonstrating a type of connoisseurship
that at times is tantamount to commodity fetishism.[74] Sharzer puts an
especially acid touch on this point when he writes that "doing your part
for the planet where friendly farmers are happy to sell you $6 eggplants
can become the latest marker of habitus in a never-ending battle for status
and mobility."[75]

While captivating in parts, and perhaps strongly seductive for some
readers, in the final appraisal the Marxist critique of localization is a
polemic. The most awkward problems arise when Sharzer holds up a
small cadre of localist theoreticians including Schumacher, McKibben,
and Kingsolver as paragons and fails to interrogate more than a small
handful of tangible initiatives. In this sense, his book is more of an
academic exercise in textual deconstruction than an analysis of explicit
locally inspired projects. Moreover, his tendency to ridicule the political
naiveté of those championing localization loses some of its vigor when
read against a wider background of nostalgic veneration of working-class
solidarity.[76] The truth is that localization is not exclusively about easing
the anxieties of a desk-bound and alienated professional class (though
these factors are not unimportant in certain locales). There is, to be sure

no shortage of escapism, status striving, moral boundary drawing, and muddled strategic thinking undergirding localist conceptions. Nonetheless, it merits recognizing that there are plenty of local efforts that genuinely challenge existing capitalist prerogatives, give participants opportunities to develop political organizing skills, provide alternative livelihoods, and serve as transferable and scalable models. Some of the more notable examples are focused on recovering the vitality of deindustrialized cities while others aim to operationalize alternative business models.[77] As Francesca Forna and her colleagues recently asserted when characterizing the activities of Italian solidarity purchase groups (known as GAS or *gasistas*):

[The *gasistas*] represent new spaces for people who not only view the consumer society as unjust, but also want to search for practical alternatives. Although GAS members may hold different political and religious convictions, they come to these groups with various motivations and are impelled by a desire to share a critical approach to the global economic model and consumerist lifestyles. Within their GAS groups, members find not only information and reciprocal support. The ongoing networking among *gasistas* facilitates social learning, building social capital, and multiplying the potential of individuals to act. The emerging picture thus seems to highlight that GAS are not simply a new type of consumer organization, but rather an innovative form of political participation.... Although their overall economic impact seems to be limited ... people do more than satisfy "liberal guilt" by shopping ethically; they join together to try to make a difference to environmental and social justice issues.[78]

It is extremely doubtful that these local initiatives have the potential to overturn capitalism, but that is a tall and probably unrealistic order. This modesty, however, should not be underestimated. Extrapolating from the concept of strategic niche management and studies of socio-technical transitions, what politically charged forms of localism can do is to create liminal spaces that serve as protected incubators for new ways of understanding and novel social practices.[79] By imposing a totalizing theoretical construct on the messiness and disorder of contemporary economic organization, orthodox Marxists are guilty of the same conceit as their neoliberal rivals. The emphasis on relentless competition to drive down prices, uncompromised instrumentalist behavior, perfect information, and so forth that inform competing textbook formulations are far removed from the real world. When we liberate ourselves from these treatments it becomes apparent that people and organizations are not the caricatures that they are doctrinally portrayed to be but rather multi-faceted agents that act for all kinds of reasons.[80] Their motivations may spring from impetuousness, or even occasionally from altruism and solidarity. The overarching structures that shape and give form to conduct are unquestionably powerful, but they are not indomitable and utterly unyielding and capitalism is certainly not a spatially standardized construction. Or to put it differently, the capitalist laws of motion are not universal.[81] In coming to informed conclusions and conceiving strategies for action, we do better to rely on empirical evidence and grounded insights pertaining to how humans actually conduct themselves and pursue their ambitions than on ideological exegesis.

This is not a matter of gullibly ignoring how capitalism works in the grand scheme, avoiding mass resistance, falling back on accommodationist illusions, building utopian islands and imaginary worlds, or disregarding the significance of inequality and class struggle. It is rather recognition that prevailing arrangements are neither as resolute nor pervasive as the Marxist critique contends. It is possible to find propitious cracks in which to plant experimental seeds and to encourage them to diffuse out slowly when auspicious winds blow. Given the tragedies propagated over the past century in the name of anti-capitalist revolution, as well as the horrors unleashed by more recent revolutionary upheavals in North Africa and the Middle East, a strategy that charts a way forward between, on one hand, these kinds of catastrophic alternatives and, on the other hand, fatalistic resignation may be the only viable way forward in seeking sustainable pathways beyond consumer society.

Conclusion

Despite the strenuous challenges of implementing localist ideas on a wide but discriminating basis, there is little question of the need for more geographically delimited lifestyles, especially in affluent countries of the global North where provisioning practices have become deeply dependent on the appropriation of biophysical capacity from extra-territorial locales.[82] In many respects, localization is the most ambitious of the three alternatives considered thus far in this book and arguably the most essential.[83] The unfortunate truth, though, is that few of its proponents fully appreciate this radicalness and, as currently practiced emphasis on the local is little more than a dilettantish way for egoisti consumers to toy with sustainability. Self-styled locavores pick and choose the types of experiences in which they would like to partake and act accordingly. It is probably not unduly cynical to note that for most consumers this means driving a Japanese-made car powered by oil from the North Slope of Alaska to a farmers' market to buy a basket of locally grown peaches. It is far from clear that there is willingness among consumers—short of an epic-scale disaster—to reorient their lifestyles in the ways that a sincere commitment to localization would entail. Just in terms of diet, this would require in many affluent countries a thoroughgoing redesign of food practices toward more austere menus with substantially less variety than is customary today.

Current conceptions of localization, though, are severely limiting and problematic, in part because proponents have disregarded the fundamental importance of creating economically, politically, ecologically, socially, and culturally viable regions and have instead primarily deployed the local as yet another way to convey social distinction through curated consumption practices. Current strategies demonstrate little understanding of regional planning, especially as conceived by visionary regionalists during the first half of the twentieth century.[84] Particularly notable in this regard was the work of the social critic Lewis Mumford who wrote, "Regional planning asks not how wide an area can be brought under the aegis of the metropolis, but how the population and civic facilities can be distributed so as to promote and stimulate a vivid, creative life throughout a whole region."[85]

Genuine localization (or rather regionalization) would require significant restrictions of property rights (to ensure that land used for urban agriculture was not subsequently appropriated for other uses), recruitment of large segments of the population into farming (because mechanized equipment will not be available due to a scaling down of manufacturing capacity), high taxes on transportation fuels (to make long-distance shipment of goods cost-prohibitive), rationing of strategically important resources (to prevent hoarding of available supplies), and limits on migration (to prevent people from moving to—and overpopulating—locales with more diversified resource endowments), suppression of human rights, and other similarly draconian interventions.[86] As Greg Sharzer notes, localists delight in the example of Cuba during the 1990s and they may be right to do so because similarly harsh measures, likely implemented through decentralized eco-dictatorial decrees, would be necessary to avert rampant starvation and social chaos.[87] In short, despite manifestations of what some scholars have termed "neolocalism," contemporary consumer society remains a long way from scaling up experiments in local-living economies to required proportions.[88] Nonetheless, these loosely confederated autarkic regions may provide inspiration for the localization movement to formulate a more ambitious vision of the relationship between geographic scale and sustainability.

6

Consumption in the Era of Digital Automation

Introduction

This book, until this point, has argued that the foundational pillars of consumer society are eroding because of changes on the consumption side of contemporary provisioning routines and that emergence of the sharing economy, the Maker Movement, and the turn toward economic localization are harbingers—necessarily haphazard and inchoate—of a new system of social organization. This is admittedly a minority view and it stands in sharp contrast to more customary social theoretical formulations which assert that new societal logics are driven by shifts, typically triggered by technological innovation, in modes of production.[1] This view traces back to the eighteenth and nineteenth centuries and stresses the roles of producers, both as capitalists and workers, to determine the drumbeat to which humanity marches. In their various manifestations, these perspectives have generally regarded consumers as submissive participants in processes over which they have little ultimate control.[2] Such an outlook has only been strengthened by thirty years of deference to neoliberal prerogatives that perfunctorily advance a laissez-faire policy agenda.[3]

Recent thinking about how to anticipate and plan for a more sustainable future has not been exempt from this celebration of entrepreneurialism, deregulation, and privatization. An especially conspicuous exponent of this view is the designer Bill McDonough who has served in highly visible consulting capacities for several major consumer-product companies including Nike, Herman Miller, and the Ford Motor Company. He unabashedly asserts that "commerce is the engine of change...it is relatively quick, essentially creative, highly effective and efficient, and fundamentally honest." Implicit is this aggrandizing supposition is that other drivers of social change—for instance the campaigns of social movements, the propagation of new cultural values, and the advent of demographic ruptures—are of limited importance when trying to comprehend transitional processes.[4]

At the same time, production and consumption are inevitably bound up in tight socio-technical configurations and it is ultimately futile to unduly privilege one domain over the other.[5] To bring a more balanced perspective to bear on the prospects of consumer society, this chapter considers how several innovations currently being propagated in the realm of production are likely to reshape consumption practices. More specifically, the following discussion describes how commercial diffusion of a new wave of technologies at the interface of artificial intelligence and robotics threatens to substantially decrease the need for human labor, potentially leading to profound changes in the working lives of consumers and their ability to reproduce viable livelihoods.

The journalist Thomas Friedman has described this pending onslaught as a "technological hurricane" and the last few years have generated a steady stream of commentary on the social dimensions of these "brilliant technologies."[6] Such accounts plausibly contend that we face a "jobless future" as revolutionary algorithmic devices displace sentient workers. Because no one is exclusively a producer or consumer and we repeatedly and iteratively change roles, often numerous times during the course of a single day, it is not unreasonable to expect that it will be a decline in demand for wage labor—rather than disaffection or declining enthusiasm on the part of consumers themselves—that will bring about the end of consumer society as we currently know it.

This chapter reviews the contested claims about technologically induced unemployment and asserts that while we have managed for the past two centuries to avoid prolonged joblessness due to technical innovation, we may not be so fortunate this time around. If familiar forms of work become less readily available in the future, wage labor will decline in importance and it will become necessary to supplement household incomes through some other means. In the United States, however, the associated public policies are apt to take considerable time to garner sufficient political support and it will be essential in the short to medium term to rely on more readily implementable strategies to stave off widespread distress and privation. This chapter introduces the idea of

multi-stakeholder cooperatives—mutual associations that span both production and consumption—which could play an important role during the
twilight days of consumer society.

Technological Innovation and the Future of Work

Academic publications and the popular media have been understandably
awash over the last few years with claims that we stand on the threshold
of an era of rapid progress in artificial intelligence and robotics.[7] Compelling indications point to a future in which Siri-like devices, self-driving cars,
and a new generation of industrial automatons are pervasive and prone
to supplant human labor on a massive scale. Two prominent observers of
this phenomenon, economists Erik Brynjolfsson and Andrew McAfee,
assert that that we are embarking on a "second machine age" where
"computers and other digital advances are doing for mental power—the
ability to use our brains to understand and shape our environments—what
the steam engine and its descendants did for muscle power."[8]

Another incisive commentator, technology entrepreneur Jerry Kaplan,
observes that:

Already in commercial development are robots that can weed a garden, load and
unload randomly shaped boxes from delivery trucks, follow you around carrying
bags, and pick crops . . . Soon, just about every physical task you can imagine
will be subject to automation: painting exterior and interior spaces, cooking
meals, busing dishes, cleaning tables, serving food, making beds, folding laundry,
walking dogs, laying pipe, washing sidewalks, fetching tools, taking tickets,
sewing, and directing traffic . . . And this doesn't begin to touch on the industrial
applications, such as picking and packing orders, stocking and straightening
shelves, welding and cutting, polishing, inspecting, assembling, sorting, even
repairing other robotic devices.[9]

Importantly, it is not just minimally skilled, manual jobs that are at risk
of elimination, but vast numbers of white-collar positions are expected to
disappear as these technologies become more affordable and widely
available. The recent wave of disruption in the accounting profession
due to the diffusion of tax-preparation systems like Turbo Tax is often
seen as a precursor for what is set to occur across the legal field—from
contract preparation to estate planning.[10] The painstaking and labor-
intensive task of sifting through mountains of documents, a job once

performed by paralegals and novice attorneys, is already being carried out by pattern-recognition software that can effortlessly scan the content of a few hundred pages in minutes. Education is in the midst of being similarly upended as standardized instructional activities move, on one hand, to automated platforms that can be customized to the needs of individual learners, and, on the other hand, to massive online open courses (MOOCs) that enroll thousands of students. It is, though, in the practice of medicine that we may see the most stunning kinds of reinvention as computers with access to vast stores of scientific knowledge and comparative data are called upon to provide patient diagnoses.

Other white-collar occupations susceptible to elimination by digital automation over the next couple of decades include customer service, financial advisement, procurement, and project management. Martin Ford, another technology entrepreneur and author, describes in striking terms the disruptive software system currently being deployed by a company called WorkFusion:

The WorkFusion software initially analyzes the project to determine which tasks can be directly automated, which can be crowd sourced, and which must be performed by in-house professionals. It can then automatically post job listings to websites like Elance or Craigslist and manage the recruitment and selection of qualified freelance workers. Once the workers are on board, the software allocates tasks and evaluates performance. It does this in part by asking freelancers to answer questions to which it already knows the answer as an ongoing test of the workers' accuracy. It tracks productivity metrics like typing speed, and automatically matches tasks with the capabilities of individuals. If a particular person is unable to complete a given assignment, the system will automatically escalate that task to someone with the necessary skills.[11]

A widely cited 2013 study by Carl Benedikt Frey and Michael Osborne calculates that nearly half of all presently available jobs in the United States are vulnerable to replacement by digital technologies within the next two decades.[12] Though most economists have long dismissed the possibility of widespread and persistent technological unemployment, we may very well be facing the future that John Maynard Keynes anticipated in his renowned 1930 essay "Economic Possibilities for our Grandchildren."[13] The esteemed British economist was notably sanguine about the prospect of "three-hour shifts or a fifteen-hour week," writing that:

When the accumulation of wealth is no longer of high social importance, there will be great changes in the code of morals. We shall be able to rid ourselves of many of the pseudo-moral principles which have hag-ridden us for two hundred years, by which we have exalted some of the most distasteful of human qualities into the position of highest virtues. We shall be able to afford to dare to assess the money-motive at its true value.[14]

We may get to these hopeful arrangements, but the path will not be trouble-free. In his famous treatise, Keynes disregarded the kinds of transitional dynamics that were apparent to his frame-breaking Luddite countrymen more than a century before, as well as a long line of social theorists and political economists throughout the nineteenth century.[15] It is in fact exceedingly difficult under present circumstances to envision a prospective situation where the disappearance of work leads to leisure and unambiguous human improvement. A more realistic scenario seems to be one where large numbers of people are forced to scour for sustenance and to endure lives of tedium and poverty.

A future with less customary work—jobs that compensate employees on a salaried or hourly basis and provide reasonable health and retirement benefits—will unquestionably have sweeping impacts on provisioning practices because, after all, producers are also consumers and it is the proceeds of wage labor that invigorate and enable consumer society. Indeed, as discussed elsewhere in this book, we are already beginning to see the vivid unfolding of this process in the United States as income becomes increasingly concentrated, the middle class hemorrhages, and the livelihoods of a widening cross-section of the population become more economically insecure. Rather than rely on full-time employment for their income requirements, households are finding it necessary to develop diversified portfolios of gainful activities comprising waged work, freelancing, and household- and community-based production. It also seems probable that to avoid protracted precarity on a mass scale we will need to create a durable public program to supplement earnings.[16] Commentators have to date described several ways to achieve this objective with most recommendations premised on devising sources of non-labor income.[17] Three of the most notable alternatives are the provision of a universal basic income, the distribution of a "citizen's dividend," and the implementation of broad-based stock ownership in corporate businesses. All of these ideas have been comprehensively developed elsewhere and the following discussion is meant only to provide a cursory overview.

First, a universal basic income (UBI) entails payment of a modest stipend to members of a political community that is made without the need to work.[18] Notably, Friedrich Hayek and Milton Friedman separately championed the idea during the 1970s and at the time it found favor in the United States across the ideological spectrum—from Richard Nixon to Martin Luther King, Jr.[19] After a lapse during the 1980s, the concept was resurrected by Belgian philosopher Philippe van Parijs and an expanding circle of European political economists during the 1990s and taken up in the United States by legal scholars Bruce Ackerman and Ann Alstott.[20] More recently, UBI has become part of a progressive policy agenda as it is deemed to provide a more secure safety net during a period of stagnating wages and tenuous employment.[21] The notion is also appealing to reform-minded conservatives because it offers a less bureaucratically cumbersome approach for assuaging extreme poverty, gives recipients choice about how to spend their stipend, and could replace the current crazy-quilt of government programs that arguably do little to foster self-reliance.[22]

Beyond the United States, interest in UBI has been gathering momentum. Finland has embarked on an expansive experiment to test the feasibility of a national program and the concept is receiving consideration in Switzerland, Germany, France, the Netherlands, the United Kingdom, and elsewhere.[23] There are, to be sure, numerous unresolved issues about how UBI would work in practice with vigorous debates around the use of means-testing, the periodicity of payments, the eligibility of children and non-citizens, and numerous other policy-design features.[24] Additionally, some detractors dismiss the concept out of concern that unconditional payments would reduce the incentive to work and generate an overabundance of idle and unproductive people. This criticism is probably overwrought because under most formulations UBI would not substitute for wages but rather offer a sufficient augmentation. Most recipients would have an extremely hard time surviving exclusively on UBI, but even if 5–10 percent of the population developed lifestyles proportional to the disbursements, it is hard to see why, on a societal level, it would be an altogether adverse outcome.

Second, the idea of a citizen's dividend begins with recognition that there is a wealth of property in democratic societies that is effectively held in common.[25] Such assets include the broadcast spectrum, the natural resources accessible on public lands, and the atmosphere.

These jointly owned possessions are typically appropriated either for a relatively nominal fee paid to a government agency (as is the case for rights to harvest timber in national forests) or for no cost at all (as pertains to the emission of greenhouse gases). A citizen's dividend is predicated on the principle that exploitation of these assets should be set at a fair-market price with the proceeds being outwardly distributed to all eligible recipients of the relevant jurisdiction (generally a state/province or a country, but under some formulations the world is envisaged as the relevant geographic territory) on an equal basis as a form of non-labor income.

The most venerated application of the concept is the Alaska Permanent Fund (APF) established in 1980 and financed by a tax on oil production in the state. A portion of the revenue is retained for investment (presently valued at approximately $50 billion) and the remaining share is dispensed as an annual dividend (generally between $1,000 and $2,000 per person in a given year) to all residents living in the state for at least twelve prior months.[26] Households receive their distributions as an electronic transfer into a bank account and the money can be used on an entirely unrestricted basis—to offset expenses, to pay down debt, to fund college education, to take a vacation, or to jumpstart a business. Because disbursements are made to every qualified adult and child, the sum received by a household can be a sizeable non-labor supplement to income.[27]

The same essential idea has been promoted in recent years at the national level in the United States—thus far without success—to curtail greenhouse-gas emissions.[28] The proposal entails implementing a so-called cap-and-dividend program where the money generated by auctioning the carbon permits would be used to capitalize a trust fund to pay an annuity to compensate consumers for higher energy costs, to invest in climate-mitigation measures, and to fund research on social and technological innovations.[29] A slightly modified version of the concept, termed a "common asset trust," has been under review in the state of Vermont as a way to generate a citizen's dividend as compensation for the devaluation or appropriation of collectively held assets like groundwater aquifers.[30]

Finally, the notion of broad-based stock ownership (BBSO) originates from recognition that productivity gains across the economy have in recent decades accrued disproportionately to the owners of capital.[31] By contrast, working and middle-class households in the United States, most of which have meager savings for investment and rely largely on wages to meet consumption needs, have struggled to make ends meet. According to one widely publicized estimate, the top ten percent of earners in the country received 46.5 percent of all income in 2011 and thinner slices of the uppermost strata accrued even more outsized gains.[32] As Richard Freeman and Joseph Blasi observe, "High-rising inequality is transforming the U.S. from an economy and polity based on a broad middle class to a feudal society dominated by a small number of super-wealthy 'lords of the manor.'"[33]

To rectify—or at least begin to alleviate—the problem of increasing inequality, BBSO advocates propose enhancing the ability of workers to benefit from the proceeds of capital. This objective can be realized by allocating, preferably through options and grants, company shares to enable lower- and middle-range earners to supplement their wage income with capital ownership and capital income comprising dividend distributions and asset appreciation. In addition, evidence suggests that more democratic ownership of capital catalyzes a positive feedback loop whereby firms that give employees a financial stake through profit-sharing (or what is sometimes termed "shared capitalism") are more productive and profitable than counterparts that rely on standardized organizational structures. The United States already has approximately 10,000 companies with meaningful BBSO arrangements amounting to a trillion dollars and involving 15 million workers through employee stock ownership plans (ESOPs).[34]

While these three concepts—both independently and in combination—warrant consideration, we need to acknowledge the political obstacles in the United States that currently stand in the way of far-reaching and substantive action in the near to medium term. Despite prevailing circumstances, the country has, as noted earlier, made considerable headway creating formats for BBSOs by workers in corporations. Given these achievements, strategies premised on mutualism and shared ownership—with a solid dose of creative financing—could prove to be, at least for the foreseeable future, more practicable ways with which to respond to the contraction of conventional job opportunities and the attenuation of consumer society.

According to the Georgetown University Center on Education and the Workforce, an estimated 6.4 million jobs are "missing" from the American economy.[35] This number represents the difference between the level of employment at the end of 2015 in the United States and what it would have been if the Great Recession had not occurred. In addition, a significant number of the jobs generated in the country since 2008 have been filled by people whose qualifications and training are in excess of the skills actually required for the position.[36] Against this background, we need to be cognizant of the trends outlined in earlier chapters of this book regarding the advent of an essentially ersatz sharing economy, as well as the Maker Movement and the turn toward economic localization. These developments can be construed as early adaptation to changing labor requirements in the new economy. And this is just the preliminary wave because the artificial intelligence and robotic systems have hardly begun to arrive in their anticipated numbers.

Toward Multi-Stakeholder Cooperativism

As the next phase of digital automation sweeps through industries and picks up pace in dislocating workers across a range of occupational categories, economic insecurity is sure to rise and further undermine the coherence of consumer society. While large numbers of households in the United States have been adjusting their consumption practices for some time due to stagnating or declining incomes, the next step in the contraction of working- and middle-class livelihoods is likely to entail the large-scale retrenchment of work opportunities and the imposition of yet more acute financial challenges. Calls for social mobilization are important and well-meaning, but it is currently difficult to see them coming to fruition and, even under the most fortuitous circumstances, will take a long time to have any meaningful effect given prevailing levels of partisan fractiousness and public disillusionment.[37] While it would be shortsighted to completely discount new possibilities further down the road, there is a need for workable alternatives that leverage available institutional capabilities and opportunity structures.

As described in Chapter 3, the sharing economy, as substantially constituted at present, is predominantly organized around two transactional modes: brokered micro-entrepreneurship and serialized rental. The former entails the matching of individual assets and/or labor to irregularly scheduled tasks and the latter involves the short-term leasing of durable goods on an iterative basis. It is, though, the sharing economy's third, mostly overlooked, mode—communitarian provisioning—that can credibly and efficaciously buffer some of the instabilities created by the waning of consumer society and begin to build up new democratic and accountable social enterprises consistent with a more sustainable future.

The foundation for more communitarian provisioning is an idea initially advanced by Trebor Scholz and Nathan Schneider called platform cooperativism. Premised on the notion of worker-ownership, platform cooperativism is also notable for its emphasis on producer collaboration and vision of progressive economic transformation.[38] I uses the Internet in the same way as Uber and other contingent labor mediators, but redirects customers to worker-owned companies. As a business model, platform cooperativism enables workers to earn more than casual wages, to own shares in the company, and to acquire an additional non-labor income stream. For the concept to gain traction in practice, however, it will be necessary to move with urgency because the venture-capital-backed frontrunners in the current ersatz sharing economy are in the process of solidifying impregnable monopolies in their respective markets. The availability of open-source software that permits sponsors to easily create the electronic infrastructure for new sharing networks is a time-sensitive opportunity that will need to be seized so that each small-scale initiative does not need to invest in building its own platform.[39]

There is little question that platform cooperativism is a laudable concept and it should be pursued where there is interest and a critical mass of prospective participants. We should, though, recognize that there is an opportunity to push the basic scheme a bit further.[40] Why limit cooperation only to workers while implicitly treating consumers as little more than a preformed mass of aggregate demand? Why elevate workers over their customers when the distinction is artificial and rarely static? A Swedish political scientist Victor Pestoff observed nearly twenty years ago

Most cooperatives are defined around one, and only one of its possible membership bases. In effect, they are single stakeholder organizations. Accordingly, there are consumer cooperatives, worker cooperatives, or primary producer cooperatives. The effect of each model is to include one, and only one group—and to exclude others, which nevertheless have a significant interest and stake in them . . . Thus, a single exclusive interest is often dominant.[41]

More ambitious application of platform cooperativism would not just create Internet sites to support worker cooperatives. It would embrace workers and consumers as co-equals and seek to demonstrate the viability of novel business models that combine production and consumption in a single organization.[42] The uniting of these two domains would overcome long-persisting fractures in the cooperative movement and give rise to new predispositions that treat buyers and sellers as allies rather than rivals, prioritize full-community solidarity over return on investment, and emphasize collective enhancement instead of value appropriation.[43] Moreover, the fomented antagonism between producers and consumers that is inherent in prevailing systems of exchange and the relentless pursuit of narrow conceptions of profitability tends to amplify consumption in excess of genuine needs—often through the use of tempting volume discounts, aggressive promotionalism, and the manufacture of goods that become prematurely obsolete. By stressing their continuously shifting, and oftentimes reciprocal, relationships, worker–consumer cooperatives could bring the logics of production and consumption into closer and more mutually compatible alignment.

Fortunately, there are contemporary examples, generally known as multi-stakeholder cooperatives, to which innovative forms of worker–consumer collaboration can turn for guidance. The paragon is Eroski, a subsidiary of the venerable Mondragón Corporation headquartered in the Basque Region, which operates a chain of 800 supermarkets and hypermarkets (combination food and department stores) and a variety of other businesses including gas stations, travel agencies, liquor stores, and perfume shops in Spain (and a small number of additional establishments in France).[44] Launched in 1969 as a joint venture involving ten small groceries, Eroski grew steadily during the following years by opening new stores and absorbing a number of other cooperatives. In the 1970s, in response to a series of economic crises, the group implemented an ownership structure premised on a hybrid worker–consumer model. After further expansion and acquisition involving several smaller regional retail food companies in Spain during the 1990s and 2000s (including strategic partnerships with France's Intermarche and Italy's Co-op Italia), the cooperative has become the second largest retail group in Spain (Carrefour is the largest) and one of the fifty biggest retailers in Europe.[45]

At the other end of the spectrum is the Weaver Street Market, a modestly sized worker–consumer cooperative in North Carolina that operates three retail stores specializing in organic produce and fair trade products.[46] The flagship in Carrboro, a community of approximately 21,000 residents bordering Chapel Hill and part of the larger Research Triangle Park area comprising the rapidly growing cities of Raleigh and Durham, opened in 1988. Initial funding came from a local credit union with an interest in community and locally owned businesses, the Carrboro municipal government, and a combination of individual loans and shareholder equity.[47] Success during the first several years prompted the opening of new outlets in the nearby town of Hillsborough and the Southern Village neighborhood of Chapel Hill. The expansion, however, was not without controversy as some owners became concerned that the cooperative was growing too large. At present, the Weaver Street Market is owned by 200 workers and 18,000 customer-households.[48]

Scaling up this model would entail establishment of worker–consumer cooperatives across a much wider range of activities.[49] For instance, a cooperative taxi service could provide reliable local transportation on a similar basis, circumventing firms in the ersatz sharing economy as well as proprietary providers. By joining up with other worker–consumer cooperatives across the country, indeed around the world, the business could become part of a wider Internet-facilitated consortium. Such collaboration would open up additional opportunities, for instance providing cooperators from afar with short-term travel accommodations as an alternative to ordinary hotels or Airbnb. By bridging the divide between production and consumption, and recognizing that we all produce and consume, the worker–consumer cooperative could facilitate seamless shifts between roles.

Realization of this vision would help to give birth to a sharing economy that was true to its promise and apportioned control to producers and consumers instead of platform investors. It could also contribute to bringing into view a more socially equitable and ecologically resilient future. Readers by this point should recognize that consumerist lifestyles in affluent countries are driven more by a quest for social distinction than a desire to satisfy biophysical needs (this does not discount the existence of perverse inequalities due to political circumstances). An emergent line of research suggests that cooperativism has the potential to orient people toward more solidaristic and other-regarding dispositions.[50] If correct, participation in firms of the kind described above could be a useful way to enhance social cohesion while more adequately meeting essential needs.

It also merits noting that to be successful, worker–consumer cooperatives would need to resist powerful impulses to expand simply by pushing the retail costs of goods and services down to unreasonable levels. While lower prices are definitely attractive from a consumer standpoint, in a cooperative structure they, as a general rule, undercut the livelihoods of workers, reduce resources for required investment, and weaken social sustainability. Such tensions will need to be managed by carefully constructed governance arrangements. From the angle of environmental sustainability, there is also the problem of perverse rebound effects as slashed prices in one product category almost always increase demand for other items by freeing up capacity in a household budget.[51] A worker–consumer cooperative where producers and consumers are equally empowered and, ideally, difficult to disentangle because they are regularly swapping roles, should help to discourage these untoward outcomes and enhance social inclusion and solidarity during the fading phases of consumer society. These businesses could also provide a measure of protection from technological unemployment because jobs will be predicated on reciprocity rather than simple tradeoffs between wage labor and digital technologies.

None of this is to suggest that bringing worker–consumer cooperatives into wider existence would be easy. At this preliminary stage, three obstacles in particular pose major challenges: the prospect of organizational degeneration, the impediments on access to capital, and the composition of institutional sponsorship.[52]

First, arrangements would need to be made to guard against one of the more common problems to which many cooperatives fall victim—passive engagement by cooperators leads either to structural deterioration or the supplanting of democratic processes by professional managers.[53] To address this situation, recent research has focused on wider deployment of several participatory models that have been applied across industries where worker ownership is relatively widespread.[54] These studies suggest that decision making in worker–consumer cooperatives could usefully range over a spectrum depending on the circumstances and the level of collective commitment. For example, some enterprises might operate on the basis of direct participation by all worker–consumers and others might delegate most responsibilities to an elected board of directors.[55] Another variant has been successfully operationalized in the United States by the thousands of ESOPs that currently exist in the country.

In these businesses it is increasingly common for worker–owners to participate in governance through so-called high performance systems that provide opportunities for input through functional teams (including teams that work with the board of directors and with customers).

Second, cooperative businesses—both worker-owned and consumer-owned—tend to suffer from undercapitalization because the founding sponsors, as well as the subsequent shareholders, of these initiatives lack substantial savings or assets and are thus attracted to commercial niches with low requirements for start-up capital. Firms are then typically required to rely on debt, secured on relatively unfavorable terms, to underwrite the cost of operations and to grow the enterprise.[56] In 2013, the Democracy at Work Institute identified approximately 300 worker cooperatives in the United States with 7,000 worker–owners, $367 million in total annual revenues, a median number of ten workers per firm, and an average of $300,000 in yearly sales.[57]

Consumer cooperatives are more numerous in the country, but because they face similar financial obstacles they have been confined primarily to a handful of sectors—notably retail trade, childcare, and allied health services—that do not require investment in expensive equipment and enable the funding of operations through regular cash flow.[58] Retail groceries are a particularly popular form of cooperative business in several parts of the United States and a survey conducted in 2005 by the National Cooperative Month Planning Committee counted 350 stores nationwide with $33 billion in total annual revenue and a yearly payroll of $1.8 billion.[59]

A potential way for worker–consumer cooperatives in the United States to overcome weaknesses due to undercapitalization might be to structure their operations as an ESOP. This mode of organization would make it possible to partially compensate worker–consumer cooperators by contributing shares to a trust maintained on their behalf. This arrangement would allow the enterprise to retain more cash for investment while at the same time accessing available tax benefits. Perhaps most importantly, the trust could borrow money from private lending institutions to purchase stock and use the proceeds to finance capital investments. As is the case for conventional ESOPs, the stock could then be distributed to member–owners as the loan is paid off.[60] Combining democratic participation with access to credit afforded by an ESOP could enhance the viability of worker–consumer cooperatives while demonstrating the effectiveness of this approach as an alternative business model.

Finally, relatively more prosperous communities with ample social capital should in many instances be able to raise the necessary resources to get modestly sized worker–consumer cooperatives off the ground and some of them might succeed over the longer term. However, less affluent locales would probably need to rely on philanthropic foundations or other outside assistance. Such circumstances raise significant risks because these sources of capital tend to evince vacillating and continuously evolving priorities and often engender outcomes that fly in the face of intentions.[61] In the absence of reliable organizational and financial support, worker–consumer cooperatives are liable to replicate (or even amplify) many of the inequities that are apparent in faltering consumer society. This raises the question of where nascent initiatives might turn for institutional assistance during an era when there is a conspicuous lack of civic support to advance the interests of working- and middle-class households.[62]

Two possible candidates for sponsorship of worker–consumer cooperatives are labor unions and municipal governments. Let us briefly examine each of these alternatives in turn. It is unarguable that organized labor in the United States has been in retreat for the last several decades and its membership ranks have experienced serious erosion.[63] At the same time, union leadership has over the years tended to keep its distance from the cooperative movement, preferring instead to focus on more traditional objectives such as collective bargaining.[64] Nonetheless, there are indications that this long-standing chasm may be starting to narrow. Especially significant is that at the height of the Great Recession in 2009, the United Steelworkers, the largest industrial union in North America with 1.2 million members and retirees, entered into an agreement with the Mondragón Corporation to encourage establishment of worker cooperatives.[65] One of the more salient developments to emerge out of this accord has been the Cincinnati Union Co-op Initiative (CUCI) launched in 2011.[66] By early 2016, CUCI was incubating three worker cooperatives—Our Harvest, Sustainergy, and Apple Street Market—with several other businesses under study.

Our Harvest is an urban farm and distribution hub for locally cultivated produce that operates in partnership with a local branch of the labor union representing food and commercial service workers.[67]

Sustainergy conducts energy audits and does residential retrofits in collaboration with Empower Gas and Electric, a Cincinnati-based utility company, and the area affiliate of the insulation workers union.[68] Perhaps most interesting for purposes of the current discussion, Apple Street Market is a retail grocery specifically constituted as a worker–consumer cooperative. The business is a partnership with the local branch of the food and commercial service workers union and has to date recruited more than 1,000 consumer–owners.[69] Initial experience from these projects demonstrates that unions can constructively enable the development of cooperatives with especially valued services being the provision of technical assistance, financing, and access to healthcare and retirement planning. These experiments also highlight the important role that organized labor can play in education and training as well as in mobilizing political support and conferring legitimacy.[70]

In assessing the future of union cooperatives it merits observing that the size of the businesses established to date remains extremely small, but it does seem possible to successfully manage the conflicts among different stakeholders. The real challenge will be how the relationship matures as these enterprises grow over time and establish more bureaucratic organizational structures. It furthermore is important to recognize that the union cooperatives created to date have only enlisted workers and have not—with the exception of Apple Street Market which is presently at the early stages of implementation—actively sought to encourage collaboration across the worker–consumer divide. Despite the practical inseparability of working, consuming, and owning, it remains to be clearly demonstrated whether a single organization can effectively harmonize the interests of all relevant constituencies.

Municipal governments with a history of progressive politics provide a second source of potential institutional sponsorship of worker–consumer cooperatives. For instance, New York City established the Worker Cooperative Business Development Initiative in 2014 with considerable fanfare and has to date allocated $3.3 million to support development of cooperative businesses and support services.[71] A broad coalition of economic justice and anti-poverty organizations, working under the leadership of the Federation of Protestant Welfare Agencies, spearheaded this effort to win municipal support. Momentum was jumpstarted with a widely circulated policy report highlighting the potential of worker cooperatives as a strategy for reducing income inequality.[72] The document attracted the support of key political figures including the newly elected mayor Bill de Blasio who campaigned for office on a platform of social inclusion. The public funding received to date has been allocated to establishing an array of activities including a legal assistance center and an incubator for development of cooperatively owned environmental businesses.

While New York City's steps are pacesetting, it is not the only municipality in the United States currently working along these lines.[73] Madison (Wisconsin) has created a loan fund to provide low- and no-interest loans to cooperative businesses, Minneapolis has—with public support—developed the highest density of retail food cooperatives of any city in the country, and Oakland is drafting model legislation.[74] While these undertakings are evidence of support among at least some municipal governments in the country, there is still much to learn about how best to develop effective business models and to successfully facilitate the fusion of workers and consumers into a single cooperative organization. It is, though, useful to keep in mind that recent action on the part of mayors and city councils has been in response to the growing scarcity of working- and middle-class jobs. This reflects the fact that among policymakers and the general public, the ongoing transition is presently framed in terms of inadequate employment, stagnating incomes, and economic inequality rather than increasingly inequitable consumption and the breakdown of conventional household routines. This understanding is likely to evolve as consumer society continues to wane.[75] As this process unfolds, and the implications of system failure become more visible with respect to provisioning practices, the notion of municipal sponsorship of worker–consumer cooperatives could acquire more salience.

Conclusion

Progress toward a sustainable future in the twenty-first century and beyond is generally construed as bringing outsized material throughput into alignment with the planet's biophysical limits and improving social equity at various geographic scales. As a new wave of digital automation dislocates increasing numbers of people from jobs that were, just a few short years ago, thought to provide a degree of economic security, we will need to expand our understanding of sustainability to also encompass workers upended by disruptive technological change. Just as we seem to be getting a grip—one that is admittedly very loose and highly uncertain—on our climate problems, a new source of instability is about to be unleashed. Affluent countries are prone to rapidly start shedding jobs as artificial intelligence and robotics become a common trait of our everyday landscape. Mainstay features of familiar production and consumption norms are likely to dissipate and recede from daily practices as the overall system continues to lose coherence.

There is no blueprint for how to approach this complex assemblage of conflicting and inconsistent developments, but we need to plan simultaneously for both the short and long terms. Transitions are rarely smooth and painless transformations and the persistent dissolution of established infrastructures and routines is sure to throw up no shortage of hardships. We should not proceed under false illusions. Worker, consumer, and worker–consumer cooperatives are not panaceas but the demands of a sustainable future require that we start to lay the groundwork for how to meet the provisioning needs of households while concurrently inculcating the democratic values and solidaristic social relations that will be essential for easing the overall process of innovating a new system of social organization.

7

Conclusion

Allusions to consumer society, for most people, typically bring to mind its most apparent features—advertising, marketing, television, and more recently, the Internet, smartphone apps, and social media. To understand consumerism as a system of social organization it is necessary to dig deeper and to expose its demographic, economic, social, and political underpinnings and to comprehend how it has become thoroughly embedded into cultural understandings and habitual practices. Such a perspective also brings to light the sequence of transitions that has occurred over the past three centuries, beginning with predominantly agrarian systems premised largely on subsistence provisioning. Industrialization overturned these arrangements and supplanted them with alternatives predicated on wage labor. Beginning in the late nineteenth century, and intensifying in the decades following World War II, consumer society was then constructed to ensure sufficient demand for the manufactured goods spilling forth from assembly lines and other production facilities.

We are presently at the point where the customary logic that upholds prevailing routines is beginning to break down due to demographic ageing, wage stagnation, infusion of new lifestyle priorities, political paralysis, and constrained resource availability (most notably atmospheric sinks in which to dispose of greenhouse gases, but also soil fertility, biodiversity, and toxic loading). At the same time, a recent study reports that 44 percent of Americans—a total of 90 million people—have participated in some aspect of the putative sharing economy over the last few years.[1] As noted in Chapter 4, another research report advises that 135 million people in the United States are Makers.[2] It is harder to grasp the scale of economic localization initiatives given their diversity and disparateness, but one analysis identifies eleven national organizations and a multitude of networks devoted to these efforts.[3]

While all surveys of this kind require careful interpretation, in combination they provide useful insights into changes taking place at the heart of consumer society. The advent of a new generation of digital technologies promises to make redundant a large cross-section of the labor force, potentially leading to protracted increases in economic insecurity and a cascade of consequences with respect to prevailing consumption practices.

Owing to the transitional circumstances in which we currently find ourselves, a new provisioning system is not yet fully apparent, but some of its contours are beginning to come into view. Most notably, customary jobs paying a living wage are likely to be less readily available in the future and the number of managerial positions that have supported middle-class lifestyles is going to contract as deployment of artificial intelligence and robotics picks up pace. People will need to develop a more diversified portfolio of earning activities: part-time salaried work, freelance gigs, and self- and collaborative-provisioning. In the absence of significant declines in the prices of basic goods and services—housing, food, education, transportation, and healthcare—it will become exceedingly difficult for households to maintain current standards of living and calls for supplemental sources of income are apt to grow louder in coming years.

History suggests that it will take time—perhaps a considerable amount—for favorable political conditions to emerge that would allow for the institutionalization of appropriate ameliorative policy responses and this is especially the case in the United States. In the meantime, it will be necessary to evolve new policy arrangements to safeguard the livelihoods of disparate and disorganized worker–consumers. The diminished status of the labor movement and the fact that trade unionism in the country never developed an enduring tradition of advocacy on behalf of consumers is a serious liability. The absence of widespread progressive political sensibilities among the American electorate is also a major disadvantage. The preconditions may be more favorable in Europe, but it would be a mistake to underestimate the fractiousness that exists on how to adapt the welfare state to new realities.[4]

The prospects for the major Asian countries, which have developed their own facsimiles—and sometimes caricatures—of American-style consumer society, are difficult to generalize. China, of course, is the workshop of global consumerism, and is immersed in its own efforts—

simultaneously aggressive and halting—to expand consumerist lifestyles at an unprecedented scale in the face of extremely volatile economic conditions. Japan, ridiculed for years for its underperformance, raises interesting possibilities because the country has demonstrated in the past a shrewd capacity to pivot rapidly when required to do so.[5] The nation is in the throes of pervasive, and probably irreversible, demographic contraction and the societal consensus constructed during the aftermath of World War II is to a large extent in tatters. The Fukushima nuclear accident in 2011 shook the country to its foundations and surfaced a number of existential questions regarding prevailing priorities and the complications of making a break with ordinary routines.[6] Inscrutable though Japan may be, there are indications that the country may be nearing a tipping point. Like a phase change in physics, the ultimate transitional moment may not be apparent until after it has occurred.

While Japan and parts of Europe raise some interesting questions about the prospects of consumer society, for the foreseeable future it is likely that most attention will continue to focus on the United States. To appreciate the impediments ahead, it is useful to realize that after more than two centuries the evolution of the country from an agricultural to an industrial system of social organization remains incomplete. For instance, vast sums are spent each year to mollify unresolved problems due to the partial and piecemeal transition from agrarianism. A walk among the ruins of any former manufacturing district reveals that we are also still working through the challenges raised by the fading of industrial society. And all of this is taking place at the same time that consumerist logic is starting to lose its capacity to deliver satisfactory livelihoods. Our reliance on familiar stage models poses a trap, one that suggests social change occurs in consecutive and orderly linear phases when actual developments are, of course, far messier and incoherent. Most affluent countries at present are simultaneously in the midst of three different, but overlapping, transitions. The most recent of these transformations, namely from consumerism to its successor, has only just begun to unfold and it may be necessary, at least for the time being, to acclimate ourselves to the admittedly awkward notion of "post-consumerism," an indefinite segue between the demise of consumer society and its longer-term aftermath. While we have yet to discern exactly where we are headed, it may be a source of consolation to recall that there was a period, before the industrial age crystalized, when something akin to "proto-industrialization" was predominant.[7] Moreover, it merits noting that the concept of post-industrialism has endured, at least among some social theorists, for several decades in a kind of suspended animation while waiting to apprehend what might come next.[8] Given this pattern, there is warrant in asking for some forbearance with respect to a worked-out blueprint of the future beyond consumer society.[9]

It may furthermore be useful to remind ourselves that there is no iron law that requires an incipient system of social organization to be available in preformed condition and able to assimilate the hollowed-out remains of its predecessor. Again, a historical analogy is appropriate. The contemporary situation may share some similarities with the earliest days of industrialism, when displaced farmworkers, as described in Chapter 4, toiled away in rural Lancashire cottages making crude fabrications. Few observers at the time were able to see past extant conditions of the day and to envision an eventual shift to the behemoth urban factories that would in due course become the engines of the Industrial Revolution. All that was known at that fluid juncture at the start of the nineteenth century was that farming was dissipating as a viable pursuit and growing numbers of people were making ends meet by haphazardly assimilating themselves to the "putting-out" system. It seems unavoidable that, at least for the next few decades, we are going to need to learn to live with some vexing uncertainty while waiting for the clouds to lift and our longer-term trajectory to become more readily discernible.

Unfortunately, preliminary outlines of that future are not especially propitious. Some prominent analysts contend that we are headed toward a post-consumer dystopia inhabited by millions of economically precarious neo-peasants.[10] Given today's widening chasm of income inequality and the seeming lack of political wherewithal to reverse the trend, such prognostications are ultimately hard to refute.[11] And the irony is that enthusiastic embrace of the goods and services provisioned by the likes of Google, Amazon, Uber, and Apple is complicitly contributing to this outcome by enabling these companies to both deepen and widen their market reach, further weakening what remains of the waning competition and rolling themselves up into impregnable monopolies. There seems to be little awareness of the end-game: once the paragons of digital automation have achieved absolute indispensability, and eliminated all practicable alternatives, the dividends will really begin to flow to their investor-stakeholders. Here, too, history offers lessons. During the formative years of consumer society, the economic landscape comprised hundreds of energy companies, electric utilities, automobile manufacturers, urban transportation providers, and so forth. It was not until a handful of companies—Standard Oil, Commonwealth Edison, Ford Motor Company—consolidated their positions and started to accumulate immense fortunes that calls for regulatory intervention began to gain any traction.

Opportunities that rely on the political system to steer toward a more sustainable future seem, once more, to be slipping through our fingers. The 2008 bailout of the financial industry and the 2009 rescue of General Motors were moments that could have marked symbolic departures beyond the flagging present, triggering a major crisis and creating some distance between ourselves and the faltering consumerist era. The United States seems instead to be heading toward circumstances where the vast majority of people encounter on a daily basis more rather than less economic insecurity. To ensure adequate livelihoods and dependable provisioning systems, households will likely need to rely on a combination of cultivated resourcefulness and social networks of mutual assistance built up and maintained by abiding institutions like labor unions and municipal governments. It is out of these organizational forms, we can hope, will emerge capacity to chart a path toward a sustainable future premised on the pursuit of social equity and resource sufficiency.

Notes

Preface

1. Michael Piore and Charles Sabel, *The Second Industrial Divide: Possibilities for Prosperity* (New York: Basic Books, 1984).
2. Stanley Aronowitz and William DiFazio, *The Jobless Future* (Minneapolis: University of Minnesota Press, 1994) and Jeremy Rifkin, *The End of Work: The Decline of the Global Labor Force and the Dawn of the Post-Market Era* (New York: G. P. Putnam's Sons, 1995).
3. See, for example, Erik Brynjolfsson and Andrew McAfee, *The Second Machine Age: Work, Progress, and Prosperity in a Time of Brilliant Technologies* (New York: W. W. Norton, 2014) and Martin Ford, *Rise of the Robots: Technology and the Threat of a Jobless Future* (New York: Basic Books, 2015).

Chapter 1. Introduction

1. The proclamation of Captive Nations Week seemed to be a source of particular annoyance for Khrushchev during the early part of his encounter with Nixon. The Soviet Premier unleashed a tirade at one point saying, "You have churned the water yourselves—why this was necessary God only knows. What happened? What black cat crossed your path and confused you? But that is your affair, we do not interfere with your problems." For more detailed discussion of the "kitchen debate," see Ruth Oldenzeil and Karin Zachmann, eds, *Cold War Kitchen: Americanization, Technology, and European Users* (Cambridge, MA: MIT Press, 2008) and Shane Hamilton and Sarah Phillips, *The Kitchen Debate and Cold War Consumer Politics: A Brief History with Documents* (New York: Bedford/St. Martin's, 2014).
2. These observations were informed by Khrushchev's personal experience. Prior to becoming Soviet Premier, he served as Party Director in Moscow and in this position was closely associated with the construction of so-called *Khrushchyovka*, multi-unit apartment blocks built from prefabricated concrete panels. The term is a portmanteau combining Khrushchev's name and the Russian word for slums. This mode of housing, typically rising to five stories (except in Moscow where they were built to greater height due to constraints on land availability) became a popular form of residential construction across the Soviet Union and Eastern Europe during the second half of the twentieth century. The upgrading of housing conditions, particularly with an emphasis

on the provision of privatized family-based units, was a priority for Khrushchev and represented a stark reversal of policies implemented first by Lenin and continued under Stalin. See Steven Harris, *Communism on Tomorrow Street: Mass Housing and Everyday Life After Stalin* (Baltimore: Johns Hopkins University Press, 2013) and Susan Reid, "Communist Comfort: Socialist Modernism and the Making of Cosy Homes in the Khrushchev Era," pp. 11–44 in K. H. Adler and Carrie Hamilton, eds, *Homes and Homecomings: Gendered Histories of Domesticity and Return* (Malden, MA: Wiley-Blackwell, 2010).

3. One of the major news reports of the "kitchen debate" appeared in *The New York Times*. See Harrison Salisbury, "Nixon and Khrushchev Argue in Public as US Exhibit Opens; Accuse Each Other of Threats," *The New York Times*, July 25, 1959. The newspaper also published an annotated transcript of the exchange on the same day under the title "The Two Worlds: A Day-Long Debate." For a useful historical retrospective on the fiftieth anniversary of the event, see William Safire, "The Cold War's Hot Kitchen," *The New York Times*, July 24, 2009. Safire, who would later became a presidential speechwriter for Nixon, was at the time of the exhibition a press agent for the American firm that constructed the model house. By further coincidence, he was responsible for taking the photograph of the two leaders at the event that became the iconic image of the extemporaneous debate.

4. The challenge that the Soviet Union faced in providing mass-consumption goods was a relatively new problem for the country. Often forgotten is that prior to the system of collectivization that Stalin introduced during the 1920s, Russia had a remarkably vibrant consumer culture with an extensive and modern retail sector. See, for example, Marjorie Hilton, *Selling to the Masses: Retailing in Russia, 1880–1930* (Pittsburgh: University of Pittsburgh Press, 2011) and Sally West, *I Shop in Moscow: Advertising and the Creation of Consumer Culture in Late Tsarist Russia* (Dekalb, IL: Northern Illinois University Press, 2011).

5. David Marples, *The Collapse of the Soviet Union, 1985–1991* (New York: Routledge, 2004) and Emily Rosenberg, "Consumer Capitalism and the End of the Cold War," pp. 489–512 in Melvyn Leffler and Odd Arne Westad, eds, *The Cambridge History of the Cold War, Volume 3: Endings* (New York: Cambridge University Press, 2010).

6. There is no question that the roots of consumer society run long and deep. In the first instance, consumption is a feature of all societies so the act of consuming cannot in any way be considered exceptional. More germane to the current discussion is the fact that historians variously trace the origin of consumerism back to thirteenth-century Venice, seventeenth-century Amsterdam, and elsewhere in medieval and early modern Europe. Imperial

China also maintained many practices generally consistent with contemporary consumption routines. See, for example, Peter Stearns, *Consumerism in World History: The Global Transformation of Desire* (New York: Routledge, 2001), Niall Ferguson, *Civilization: The West and the Rest* (New York: Penguin, 2011), and Frank Trentmann, ed., *The Oxford Handbook of the History of Consumption* (New York: Oxford University Press, 2012). Social scientists tend to rely for their point of departure either on the advent of the novel as a popular literary genre during the eighteenth century (because it conditioned the imagination to embrace fantasy) or the rise of the monumental department stores of the nineteenth century. Refer to Colin Campbell, *The Romantic Ethic and the Spirit of Modern Consumerism* (Malden, MA: Blackwell, 1987) and William Leach, *Land of Desire: Merchants, Power, and the Rise of a New American Culture* (New York: Vintage, 1994). However, mass consumption as the predominant system of social organization did not begin to take hold until the early decades of the twentieth century and then achieved unchallenged stature during the years following World War II, first in the United States and then more extensively.

7. This explanation is a somewhat abridged and admittedly stylized analysis of the reasons that prompted Ford to implement the five-dollar day and economic historians and others continue to debate the rationale behind this move. Importantly, this wage policy was not maintained over time. For more elaborate discussion of this important historical moment, refer to Stephen Mayer, *The Five Dollar Day: Labor Management and Social Control in the Ford Motor Company, 1908–1921* (Albany: State University of New York Press, 1981) and David Brinkley, *Wheels for the World: Henry Ford, His Company, and a Century of Progress* (New York: Penguin, 2004).

8. Robert Collins, *More: The Politics of Economic Growth in Postwar America* (New York: Oxford University Press, 2000).

9. Paul Krugman, "Walmart's Visible Hand," *The New York Times*, March 2, 2015.

10. Rick Perlstein, *The Invisible Bridge: The Fall of Nixon and the Rise of Reagan* (New York: Simon and Schuster, 2014).

11. For a videorecording of the speech, see http://millercenter.org/president/speeches/speech-3402 (accessed May 6, 2016).

12. Kevin Mattson, *"What the Heck Are You Up to, Mr. President?" Jimmy Carter, America's "Malaise," and the Speech that Should Have Changed the Country* (New York: Bloomsbury, 2009).

13. Sean Wilentz, *The Age of Reagan: A History, 1974–2008* (New York: Harper Perennial, 2009) and Bruce Schulman, *The Seventies: The Great Shift in American Culture, Society, and Politics* (Cambridge, MA: Da Capo Press, 2002).

14. Robert Collins, *Transforming America: Politics and Culture During the Reagan Years* (New York: Columbia University Press, 2006).

15. Robert Manning, *Credit Card Nation: The Consequences of America's Addiction to Credit* (New York: Basic Books, 2001).

16. Especially significant in the United States was the gradual reversal of the Glass-Steagall Act originally enacted in 1933. Among other things, this legislation required the separation of commercial and investment banking activities. Almost from the day it became law, an initiative was launched to undermine several of its key provisions (an effort ironically led by its chief sponsor and co-namesake, Carter Glass, a Democratic Senator from Virginia). These efforts continued and intensified during the 1970s and its eventual repeal in 1999 was more of a formality than a substantive undertaking because of the progressive weakening that had occurred over the years. See also Charles Geisst, *Collateral Damaged: The Marketing of Consumer Debt to America* (New York: Bloomberg Press, 2009).

17. Thomas Edsall, *The Age of Austerity: How Scarcity Will Remake American Politics* (New York: Anchor Press, 2012) and Thomas Mann and Norman Ornstein, *It's Even Worse Than It Looks: How the American Constitutional System Collided With the New Politics of Extremism* (New York: Basic Books, 2012).

18. Bethany McLean and Joe Nocera, *All the Devils Are Here: The Hidden History of the Financial Crisis* (New York: Portfolio, 2011) and Alan Blinder *After the Music Stopped: The Financial Crisis, the Response, and the Work Ahead* (New York: Penguin, 2013).

19. Daniel Bell, *The Coming of Post-Industrial Society: A Venture in Social Forecasting* (New York: Basic Books, 1973) and Alvin Toffler, *Future Shock* (New York: Random House, 1970).

20. Jacob Hacker, *The Great Risk Shift: The New Economic Insecurity and the Decline of the American Dream* (New York: Oxford University Press, 2008) and George Packer, *The Unwinding: An Inner History of the New America* (New York: Farrar, Straus and Giroux, 2013).

21. Todd Gitlin, *Occupy Nation: The Roots, the Spirit, and the Promise of Occupy Wall Street* (New York: It Books, 2012).

22. Walter Rostow, *The Stages of Economic Growth: A Non-Communist Manifesto* (New York: Cambridge University Press, 1960). See also Fernand Braudel, *A History of Civilizations*, Richard Mayne, trans. (New York: Penguin, 1995).

23. The term "demographic dividend" is usually applied to countries that realize a delayed economic benefit from a decline in the fertility rate. The reduction in births triggers an increase in the working-age population and a lowering in the size of the dependent population, and has been correlated with higher

rates of economic growth. This period of rising prosperity lasts for approximately twenty to thirty years and begins to taper off as the population ages and moves into retirement without a sufficiently large working-age cohort to generate the income to pay for pensions and healthcare costs. See, David Bloom, Jaypee Sevilla, and David Canning, *The Demographic Dividend: A New Perspective on the Economic Consequences of Population Change* (Santa Monica, CA: RAND, 2003), Milton Ezrati, *Thirty Tomorrows: The Next Three Decades of Globalization, Demographics, and How We Will Live* (New York: Thomas Dunne, 2014), and Clint Laurent, *Tomorrow's World: A Look at the Demographic and Socio-economic Structure of the World in 2032* (Hoboken, NJ: Wiley, 2013).

24. Kenneth Jackson, *Crabgrass Frontier: The Suburbanization of the United States* (New York: Oxford University Press, 1987).

25. Philip Stafford, *Elderburbia: Aging with a Sense of Place in America* (Santa Barbara, CA: Praeger, 2009), Laurence Kotlikoff and Scott Burns, *The Clash of Generations: Saving Ourselves, Our Kids, and Our Economy* (Cambridge, MA: MIT Press, 2012), and Jonathan Last, *What to Expect When No One's Expecting: America's Coming Demographic Disaster* (New York: Encounter Books, 2013).

26. Lawrence Glickman, *A Living Wage: American Workers and the Making of Consumer Society* (Ithaca, NY: Cornell University Press, 1997).

27. Teresa Sullivan, Elizabeth Warren, and Jay Westbrook, *The Fragile Middle Class: Americans in Debt* (New Haven, CT: Yale University Press, 2001).

28. Brian Cogan and Thom Gencarelli, *Baby Boomers and Popular Culture: An Inquiry into America's Most Powerful Generation* (Santa Barbara, CA: Praeger, 2014).

29. Dina ElBoghdady, "Student Debt May Hurt Housing Recovery by Hampering First-time Buyers," *The Washington Post*, February 17, 2014.

30. Maurie Cohen, "The Future of Automobile Society: A Socio-technical Transitions Perspective," *Technology Analysis and Strategic Management* 24(4):377–90 (2012). See also Sam Schwartz, *Street Smart: The Rise of Cities and the Fall of Cars* (New York: Public Affairs, 2015).

31. Tobias Kuhnimhof, Dirk Zumkeller, and Bastian Chlond, "Who Are the Drivers of Peak Car Use?" *Transportation Research Record* 2383:53–61 (2013) and Jenny Xie, "The Numbers Behind America's Mass Transit Resurgence," *Atlantic City Lab*, March 10, 2014 (http://www.citylab.com/commute/2014/03/numbers-behind-americas-mass-transit-resurgence/8600, accessed May 6, 2016).

32. The (re)urbanization of the United States is not only underway in frequently publicized places like the Northeast, parts of California, and the Pacific Northwest. According to the 2010 census, 80.7% of the population of the

country lives in urban areas. The five most heavily urbanized states in the country are California (95.0%), New Jersey (94.7%), Nevada (94.2%), Massachusetts (92.0%), and Hawaii (91.9%) and the five least urbanized states are Montana (55.9%), Mississippi (49.3%), West Virginia (48.7%), Vermont (38.9%), and Maine (38.7%). The western region of the country has the largest urban population as a percentage of total population (89.8%). See Patrick Doherty and Christopher Leinberger, "The Next Real Estate Boom," *Washington Monthly*, November/December, 2010, Edward Glaeser, *Triumph of the City: How Our Greatest Invention Makes Us Richer, Smarter, Greener, Healthier, and Happier* (New York: Penguin, 2012), and Alan Ehrenhalt, *The Great Inversion and the Future of the American City* (New York: Vintage, 2013). The extent to which prospective city dwellers will be able to act on this disposition remains to be seen because of the complications of affordably transitioning from suburban to urban housing. Refer to Halina Brown, "What Would Jane Jacobs Say?" *Great Transition Initiative*, May, 2014 (http://greattransition.org/publication/what-would-jane-jacobs-say, accessed May 6, 2016).

33. Michael Klare, *The Race for What's Left: The Global Scramble for the World's Last Resources* (New York: Metropolitan Books, 2012).

34. Kenneth Deffeyes, *Hubbert's Peak: The Impending World Oil Shortage* (Princeton, NJ: Princeton University Press, 2001).

35. Global oil discovery peaked in 1965 when approximately two new barrels were identified for each barrel consumed. See Colin Campbell, *Campbell's Atlas of Oil and Gas Depletion*, 2nd ed. (Dordrecht: Springer, 2013).

36. Fareed Zakaria, *Post-American World and Rise of the Rest* (New York: Penguin, 2009), Dambisa Moyo, *Winner Take All: China's Race for Resources and What It Means for the World* (New York: Basic Books, 2012), Aseem Shrivastava and Ashish Kothari, *Churning the Earth: The Making of Global India* (New York: Penguin, 2012), Sigfido Burgos Cáceres and Sophal Ear, *The Hungry Dragon: How China's Resource Quest Is Reshaping the World* (New York: Routledge, 2013), and Elizabeth Economy and Michael Levi, *By All Means Necessary: How China's Resource Quest is Changing the World* (New York: Oxford University Press, 2014).

37. Maggie Koerth-Baker, *Before the Lights Go Out: Conquering the Energy Crisis Before It Conquers Us* (Hoboken, NJ: Wiley, 2012).

38. Christopher Steiner, *$20 Per Gallon: How the Inevitable Rise in the Price of Gasoline Will Change Our Lives for the Better* (New York: Grand Central, 2010).

39. Evgeny Morozov, *To Save Everything, Click Here: The Folly of Technological Solutionism* (New York: Public Affairs, 2013) and Michael Huesemann and Joyce Huesemann, *Techno-Fix: Why Technology Won't Save Us or the Environment* (Gabriola Island, BC: New Society, 2011).

40. Clare Hinrichs and Thomas Lyson, *Remaking the North American Food System: Strategies for Sustainability* (Lincoln, NE: University of Nebraska Press, 2009).

41. Robert Gottlieb and Anupama Joshi, *Food Justice* (Cambridge, MA: MIT Press, 2013).

42. Jesse Rhodes, "Five Ways to See the Supermarket of the Future Today," *Smithsonian*, June 27, 2103 (http://www.smithsonianmag.com/arts-culture/five-ways-to-see-the-supermarket-of-the-future-today-3387065, accessed May 6, 2016).

43. Sabine Hielscher, Gill Seyfang, and Adrian Smith, "Grassroots Innovations for Sustainable Energy: Exploring Niche-development Processes among Community-energy Initiatives," pp. 133–58 in Maurie Cohen, Halina Szejnwald Brown, and Philip Vergragt, eds, *Innovations in Sustainable Consumption: New Economics, Socio-technical Transitions, and Social Practices* (Northampton, MA: Edward Elgar, 2013).

44. Yochai Benkler, *The Wealth of Networks: How Social Production Transforms Markets and Freedom* (New Haven, CT: Yale University Press, 2006).

45. Julian Agyeman, *Introducing Just Sustainabilities: Policy, Planning, and Practice* (Atlantic Highlands, NJ: Zed Books, 2013) and Juliet Schor and Craig Thompson, eds, *Sustainable Lifestyles and the Quest for Plenitude: Case Studies of the New Economy* (New Haven, CT: Yale University Press, 2014).

46. An important exception is research on the role of reduced working hours on consumptive throughput. See, for example, Martin Pullinger, "Working Time Reduction Policy in a Sustainable Economy: Criteria and Options for its Design," *Ecological Economics* 103:11–19 (2014), Kyle Knight, Eugene Rosa, and Juliet Schor, "Could Working Less Reduce Pressures on the Environment?" *Global Environmental Change* 23(4):691–700 (2013), and Giorgos Kallis, Michael Kalush, Hugh O'Flynn, Jack Rossiter, and Nicholas Ashford, "'Friday Off'": Reducing Working Hours in Europe," *Sustainability* 5(4):1545–67 (2013).

47. This conceptualization in fact comes quite close to what economists typically refer to as the "virtual cycle of economic activity" or the "circular flow of the economy."

48. Frank Geels, *Technological Transitions and System Innovations: A Co-evolutionary and Socio-technical Analysis* (Northampton, MA: Edward Elgar, 2005) and Cohen et al., *Innovations in Sustainable Consumption*.

49. See, for example, Frank Geels, "The Dynamics of Transitions in Socio-technical Systems: A Multi-level Analysis of the Transition Pathway from Horse-drawn Carriages to Automobiles (1860–1930)," *Technology Analysis and Strategic Management* 17(4):445–76 (2005).

50. John Gerzema and Michael D'Antonio, *Spend Shift: How the Post-Crisis Values Revolution Is Changing the Way We Buy, Sell, and Live* (San Francisco, CA: Jossey-Bass, 2010), Andrew Benett and Ann O'Reilly, *Consumed: Rethinking Business in the Era of Mindful Spending* (New York: Palgrave Macmillan, 2010), Shannon Hayes, *Radical Homemakers: Reclaiming Domesticity from a Consumer Culture* (Richmondville, NY: Left to Write Press, 2010), and Justin Lewis, *Beyond Consumer Capitalism: Media and the Limits to Imagination* (Malden, MA: Polity, 2013).

51. Duane Elgin, *Voluntary Simplicity: Toward a Way of Life that Is Outwardly Simple, Inwardly Rich* (New York: Morrow, 1981), David Shi, *The Simple Life: Plain Living and High Thinking in American Culture* (New York: Oxford University Press, 1985), Amitai Etzioni and Daniel Doherty, *Voluntary Simplicity: Responding to Consumer Culture* (Lanham, MD: Rowman and Littlefield, 2003), and Cecile Andrews and Wanda Urbanska, *Less Is More: Embracing Simplicity for a Healthy Planet, a Caring Economy, and Lasting Happiness* (Gabriola Island, BC: New Society, 2009).

52. See, for example, Caroline Bekin, Marylyn Carrigan, and Isabelle Szmigin, "Defying Marketing Sovereignty: Voluntary Simplicity at New Consumption Communities," *Qualitative Market Research* 8(4):413–29 (2005), Seonaidh McDonald, Caroline Oates, William Young, and Kumju Kwang, "Toward Sustainable Consumption: Researching Voluntary Simplifiers," *Psychology and Marketing* 23(6):515–34 (2006), and Marius De Geus, "The Transition to Green Lifestyles Based on Voluntary Simplicity: The Difficult Road towards Enjoyable, Graceful and Sustainable Lifestyles, *Advances in Sustainability and Environmental Justice* 13:31–49 (2013).

53. Thomas Princen, *The Logic of Sufficiency* (Cambridge, MA: MIT Press, 2005) and Diane Coyle, *The Economics of Enough: How to Run the Economy as if the Future Matters* (Princeton, NJ: Princeton University Press, 2011).

54. Douglas Holt, "Why the Sustainable Economy Movement Hasn't Scaled: Toward a Strategy that Empowers Main Street," pp. 202–32 in Schor and Thompson, *Sustainable Lifestyles and the Quest for Plenitude*. See also Guy Standing, *The Precariat: The New Dangerous Class* (New York: Bloomsbury, 2014).

Chapter 2. Fathoming Consumer Society

1. Kevin Mattson, *"What the Heck Are You Up to, Mr. President?" Jimmy Carter, America's "Malaise," and the Speech that Should Have Changed the Country* (New York: Bloomsbury, 2009).

2. Francis Fukuyama, *The End of History and the Last Man* (New York: Free Press, 1992).

3. Daniel Bell, *The Coming of Post-Industrial Society: A Venture in Social Forecasting* (New York: Basic Books, 1973), Wendell Bell and James Mau, eds, *The Sociology of the Future: Theory, Cases, and Annotated Bibliography* (New York: Russell Sage Foundation, 1971), and Edward Cornish, *The Study of the Future: An Introduction to the Art and Science of Understanding and Shaping Tomorrow's World* (New Brunswick, NJ: Transaction Publishers, 1977).

4. Exceptions to this characterization are the scenario methodologies and the notion of the learning organization developed by Royal Dutch Shell. See, for example, Kees van der Heijden, *Scenarios: The Art of Strategic Conversation* (Hoboken, NJ: Wiley, 1996), Peter Schwartz, *The Art of the Long View: Planning for the Future in an Uncertain World* (New York: Doubleday, 1996), and Arie de Geus, *The Living Company: Habits for Survival in a Turbulent Business Environment* (New York: Harvard Business Review Press, 2002). The general discourse surrounding sustainable development is another area where future-oriented analysis has continued to receive significant attention. I am grateful to Philip Vergragt for useful discussions on this point.

5. Tony Becher, *Academic Tribes and Territories: Intellectual Enquiry and the Cultures of Discipline*, 2nd ed. (Milton Keynes: Open University Press, 2001).

6. See, for example, Philip Abelson, "The Global 2000 Report," *Science* 209 (4458):761 (1980) and L. J. Carter, "Global 2000 Report: Vision of a Gloomy World," *Science* 209(445):575–6 (1980). The report also unleashed a vigorous response from some members of the scientific community who took issue with its pessimistic conclusions. Refer to Constance Holden, "Simon and Kahn versus Global 2000," *Science* 221(4608):341–3 (1983). For an overview and discussion of the resultant controversy, see James Gustave Speth, "The Global 2000 Report and its Aftermath," pp. 47–50 in Larry Rockwood, Ronald Stewart, and Thomas Dietz, eds, *Foundations of Environmental Sustainability: The Coevolution of Science and Policy* (New York: Oxford University Press, 2008) and Gerald Barney, "Incorporating Environment into Governance and National Planning: Lessons from the Global 2000 Project and the Threshold 21 Model," pp. 187–96 in Georg Frerks and Berma Goldewijk, eds, *Human Security and International Insecurity* (Wageningen: Wageningen Academic Publishers, 2007).

7. More than 1.5 million copies of the report were sold and it was translated into nine languages.

8. Viewed in a more positive light, the *Global 2000* report established some important intellectual foundations for work carried out during the 1980s that eventually led to establishment of the World Commission on Environment and Development and eventual publication of *Our Common Future*

which facilitated a political discourse around the notion of sustainable development. See Jeremy Caradonna, *Sustainability: A History* (New York: Oxford University Press, 2014).

9. This does not mean to suggest that the collapse of the housing market and the resultant financial crisis was a surprise. Among elite academic economists, Nouriel Roubini (dubbed by the media in the years leading up to 2008 as "Dr. Doom") is often credited with being out in front in anticipating the bursting of the financial bubble.

10. Stephen Roach, "Dying of Consumption," *The New York Times*, November 28, 2008.

11. Joseph Stiglitz, "Inequality Is Holding back the Recovery," *The New York Times*, January 19, 2013.

12. Robert Gordon, "Is US Economic Growth Over? Faltering Innovation Confronts the Six Headwinds," NBER Working Paper No. 18315. Boston, MA: National Bureau of Economic Research.

13. Stephen King, *When the Money Runs Out: The End of Western Affluence* (New Haven, CT: Yale University Press, 2014).

14. Ron Kaye, *Is This the End of the Consumer Society*, NBCLA.com, 2008 (http://www.nbclosangeles.com/news/local/Is-This-the-End-of-the-Consumer-Society.html, accessed May 6, 2016).

15. The 1920s especially brought forth a torrent of criticism of advertising, unsatisfactory product performance, and deceitful promotional practices. The Library of Congress in the United States provides a useful summary of these critiques at http://lcweb2.loc.gov:8081/ammem/amrlhtml/incritiq.html (accessed May 6, 2016). A small group of prominent economists took up several of these themes after World War II with perhaps the most notable contributions being by John Kenneth Galbraith, *The Affluent Society* (Boston: Houghton Mifflin, 1958), E. J. Mishan, *The Costs of Economic Growth* (London: Staples Press, 1967), and Tibor Scitovsky, *The Joyless Economy: An Inquiry into Human Satisfaction and Consumer Dissatisfaction* (New York: Oxford University Press, 1976). Journalist and social critic Vance Packard also covered some of this same ground in a series of books. See his *The Hidden Persuaders* (New York: D. McKay, 1957), *The Status Seekers* (New York: D. McKay, 1959), and *The Waste Makers* (New York: D. McKay, 1960). For a useful overview, see, Daniel Horowitz, *The Anxieties of Affluence: Critiques of American Consumer Culture, 1939–1979* (Amherst, MA: University of Massachusetts Press, 2005).

16. While advocacy groups like Adbusters or the firebrand actor who performs under the name Reverend Billy attract enthusiastic followings, they tend to appeal to decidedly countercultural audiences. Moreover, it is difficult to point to a recent popular indictment of consumer culture that has achieved

the resonance of, say, Galbraith's *The Affluent Society*. It also warrants observing that the earlier rebukes of consumerist lifestyles leveled by scholars of the Frankfurt School largely fell out of favor. In fact, the *zeitgeist* turned in the opposite direction, probably most visibly among scholars of consumer culture who unabashedly celebrate the allure of consumption goods as the means through which to express individual identity and to celebrate personal creativity. The eagerness with which the field of economics has credulously embraced consumer society is even more obvious.

17. See, for instance, Benjamin Barber, *Consumed: How Markets Corrupt Children, Infantilize Adults, and Swallow Citizens Whole* (New York: W. W. Norton, 2008), Amitai Etzioni, "Spent: America after Consumerism," *The New Republic*, June 17, 2009, and Michael Carolan, *Cheaponomics: The High Cost of Low Prices* (New York: Routledge, 2014).

18. Notable examples include Colin Beavan, *No Impact Man: The Adventures of a Guilty Liberal Who Attempts to Save the Planet, and the Discoveries He Makes About Himself and Our Way of Life in the Process* (New York: Picador, 2010) and Judith Levine, *Not Buying It: My Year Without Shopping* (New York: Pocket Books, 2007).

19. See, for example, Robert Wuthnow, *American Mythos: Why Our Best Efforts to Be a Better Nation Fall Short* (Princeton, NJ: Princeton University Press, 2006), Henrick Smith, *Who Stole the American Dream?* (New York: Random House, 2013), Donald Barlett and James Steele, *The Betrayal of the American Dream* (New York: Public Affairs, 2013), Morris Berman, *Why America Failed: The Roots of Imperial Decline* (Hoboken, NJ: Wiley, 2011), George Packer, *The Unwinding: An Inner History of the New America* (New York: Farrar, Straus and Giroux), and Slavoj Žižek, *Trouble in Paradise: From the End of History to the End of Capitalism* (New York: Melville House, 2015).

20. Robert Borosage and Katrina vanden Heuvel, "Can a Movement Save the American Dream?" *The Nation*, October 10, 2011.

21. See the comments of economist Kenneth Rogoff, "Celebrity Central Bankers," *Project Syndicate*, November 3, 2014 (https://www.project-syndicate.org/commentary/central-bankers-and-monetary-policy-by-kenneth-rogoff-2014-11, accessed May 6, 2016). Refer also to Anders Sörensen, "Superstar Technocrats: The Celebrity Central Banker," *Celebrity Studies* 5(3):364–7 (2014).

22. Paul Raskin, "Planetary Praxis: On Rhyming Hope and History," pp. 110–46 in Steven Keller and James Gustave Speth, eds, *The Coming Transformation: Values to Sustain Human and Natural Communities* (New Haven, CT: Yale School of Forestry and Environmental Studies, 2009).

23. Frank Trentmann, ed., *The Oxford Handbook of the History of Consumption* (New York: Oxford University Press, 2014).

24. World Bank, "Household Final Consumption Expenditures as % of GDP" (http://data.worldbank.org/indicator/NE.CON.PETC.ZS, accessed May 6, 2016). Some economists calculate a measure called "true consumption" which includes private consumption, government expenditures, and residential investment. On the basis of this metric, consumption is equal to more than 90 percent of GDP in the United States.

25. The figure for the United States in 1980 was 61.5 percent.

26. Ayalla Ruvio and Russell Belk, eds, *The Routledge Companion to Identity and Consumption* (New York: Routledge, 2012).

27. Roberta Sassatelli, *Consumer Culture: History, Theory, and Politics* (Thousand Oaks, CA: Sage, 2007).

28. The word "consume" derives from the Latin *consumere* formed from *con* meaning "altogether" and *sumere* "take up."

29. Anthony Giddens, *The Consequences of Modernity* (Palo Alto, CA: Stanford University Press, 1990); see also Mark Granovetter, "Economic Action and Social Structure: The Problem of Embeddedness," *American Journal of Sociology* 91(3):481–510 (1985).

30. Adam Smith, *The Wealth of Nations* (New York: Bantam Classics, 2003 [1776]).

31. Theodor Adorno, *The Culture Industry: Selected Essays on Mass Culture* (New York: Routledge, 2001).

32. David Gartman, *Auto Opium: A Social History of American Automobile Design* (New York: Routledge, 1994).

33. Karl Marx, *Capital* (New York: Penguin, 1992 [1867]).

34. Peter Gleick, *Bottled and Sold: The Story Behind Our Obsession with Bottled Water* (Washington, DC: Island Press, 2011).

35. Scott Bottles, *Los Angeles and the Automobile: The Making of the Modern City* (Berkeley, CA: University of California Press, 1991).

36. Daniel Slesnick, *Consumption and Social Welfare: Living Standards and their Distribution in the United States* (New York: Cambridge University Press, 2000), Paul Ransome, *Work, Consumption, and Culture: Affluence and Social Change in the Twenty-first Century* (Thousand Oaks, CA: Sage, 2005), and Branko Milanovic, *The Haves and the Have-Nots: A Brief and Idiosyncratic History of Global Inequality* (New York: Basic Books, 2012). Refer also to Norman Myers and Jennifer Kent, *The New Consumers: The Influence of Affluence on the Environment* (Washington, DC: Island Press, 2004).

37. See, for example, Johan Rockström, Will Steffen, Kevin Noone, Åsa Pesson, F. Stuart Chapin, Eric Lambin, Timothy Lenton, Marten Scheffer, Carl Folke, Hans Joachim Schellhuber, Björn Hykvist, Cynthia de Wit, Terry Hughes, Sander van der Leeuw, Henning Rodhe, Sverker Sörlin, Peter Snyder, Robert

Costanza, Uno Svedin, Malin Falkenmark, Louise Karlberg, Robert Corell, Victoria Fabry, James Hansen, Brian Walker, Diana Liverman, Katherine Richardson, Paul Crutzen, and Jonathan Foley, "A Safe Operating Space for Humanity," *Nature* 7263(461):472–5 (2009). On the tendency of increases in aggregate consumption to undermine efficiency improvements, refer to Horace Herring and Steve Sorrell, eds, *Energy Efficiency and Sustainable Consumption: The Rebound Effect* (New York: Palgrave Macmillan, 2009).

38. Tim Jackson, *Prosperity without Growth: Economics of a Finite Planet* (London: Earthscan, 2009).

39. Juliet Schor, *Born to Buy: The Commercialized Child and the New Consumer Culture* (New York: Scribner, 2005), Giles Slade, *Made to Break: Technology and Obsolescence in America* (Cambridge, MA: Harvard University Press, 2006), and Elizabeth Cline, *Overdressed: The Shockingly High Cost of Cheap Fashion* (New York: Portfolio, 2013).

40. Peter Whybrow, *American Mania: When More Is Not Enough* (New York: W. W. Norton, 2006), Avner Offer, *The Challenge of Affluence: Self-Control and Well-Being in the United States and Britain Since 1950* (New York: Oxford University Press, 2007), Alastair McIntosh, *Hell and High Water: Climate Change, Hope, and the Human Condition* (Edinburgh: Berlinn, 2008), Peter Tertzakian and Keith Hollihan, *The End of Energy Obesity: Breaking Today's Energy Addiction for a Prosperous and Secure Tomorrow* (Hoboken, NJ: Wiley, 2009), Leonard Nevarez, *Pursuing Quality of Life: From the Affluent Society to the Consumer Society* (New York: Routledge, 2011), and Miriam Tatzel, ed., *Consumption and Well-being in the Material World* (Berlin: Springer, 2013).

41. David Harvey, *A Brief History of Neoliberalism* (New York: Oxford University Press, 2007).

42. Robert Collins, *More: The Politics of Economic Growth in Postwar America* (New York: Oxford University Press, 2000), Daniel Béland, *Social Security: History and Politics from the New Deal to the Privatization Debate* (Lawrence, KS: University Press of Kansas, 2005), Alexander Field, *A Great Leap Forward: 1930s Depression and US Economic Growth* (New Haven, CT: Yale University Press, 2012), and Monica Prasad, *The Land of Too Much: American Abundance and the Paradox of Poverty* (Cambridge, MA: Harvard University Press, 2012).

43. Maurie Cohen, "The Emergent Environmental Policy Discourse on Sustainable Consumption," pp. 21–37 in Maurie Cohen and Joseph Murphy, eds, *Exploring Sustainable Consumption: Environmental Policy and the Social Sciences* (New York: Elsevier, 2001).

44. United Nations, *Agenda 21: Earth Summit—The United Nations Programme of Action from Rio* (New York: United Nations, 1992).

45. Norwegian Ministry of the Environment, *Oslo Roundtable on Sustainable Production and Consumption* (Oslo: Norwegian Ministry of the Environment, 1994).

46. The Organisation for Economic Co-operation and Development (OECD) played a particularly influential role in advancing the issue of sustainable consumption during these years. See, for example, OECD, *Sustainable Consumption and Production: Clarifying the Concepts* (Paris: OECD, 1997). Refer also to Joseph Murphy, "From Production to Consumption: Environmental Policy in the European Union," pp. 39–60 in Cohen and Murphy, *Exploring Sustainable Consumption*.

47. Lucia Reisch and Inge Røpke, eds, *The Ecological Economics of Consumption* (Northampton, MA: Edward Elgar, 2005), Gill Seyfang, *The New Economics of Sustainable Consumption: Seeds of Change* (New York: Macmillan Palgrave, 2009), and Maurie Cohen, Halina Szejnwald Brown, and Philip Vergragt, eds, *Innovations in Sustainable Consumption: New Economics, Socio-technical Transitions, and Social Practices* (Northampton, MA: Edward Elgar, 2014).

48. David Owen, *The Conundrum: How Scientific Innovation, Increased Efficiency, and Good Intentions Can Make our Energy and Climate Problems Worse* (New York: Riverhead Books, 2011). See also, Ozzie Zehner, *Green Illusions: The Dirty Secrets of Clean Energy and the Future of Environmentalism* (Lincoln, NE: University of Nebraska Press, 2012).

49. Arnold Toynbee, *Lectures on the Industrial Revolution* (Gloucester: Dodo Press, 2009 [1884]).

50. Numerous studies over the years are emblematic of this familiar approach. See, for example, Mikuláš Teich and Roy Porter, eds, *The Industrial Revolution in National Context: Europe and the USA* (New York: Cambridge University Press, 1996). For recent work that takes a more global view, refer to Jeff Horn, Leonard Rosenband, and Merritt Roe Smith, eds, *Reconceptualizing the Industrial Revolution* (Cambridge, MA: MIT Press, 2010).

51. To claim a weakening in the foundations of consumer society in the United States (and other advanced countries) is not meant to suggest that the widening and deepening of consumerist lifestyles in China, India, and elsewhere will not continue. On current global diffusion of consumer society, refer to Karl Gerth, *As China Goes, So Goes the World: How Chinese Consumers Are Transforming Everything* (New York: Hill and Wang, 2011), Christophe Jaffrelot and Peter van der Veer, eds, *Patterns of Middle Class Consumption in India and China* (Thousand Oaks, CA: Sage, 2008), Harold Wilhite, *Consumption and the Transformation of Everyday Life: A View from South India* (New York: Palgrave Macmillan, 2008), and Aseem Shrivastava and Ashish Kothari, *Churning the Earth: the Making of Global India* (New York: Penguin, 2012).

52. As noted earlier in this chapter, this is especially true of scholars anchored in the traditions of the Frankfurt School which in its day developed an expansive critique of consumer society. See, for example, Lauren Langman, "Bringing the Critical Back in: Toward the Resurrection of the Frankfurt School," *Current Perspectives in Social Theory* 32:195–227 (2014).

53. Maurie Cohen, "Collective Dissonance and the Transition to Post-consumerism," *Futures* 52:42–51 (2013), Maurie Cohen, "Toward a Post-consumerist Future? Social Innovation in an Era of Fading Economic Growth," pp. 426–39 in Lucia Reisch and John Thøgersen, eds, *Handbook of Research on Sustainable Consumption* (Northampton, MA: Edward Elgar, 2015), Maurie Cohen, "Transitioning to a Postconsumerist Future," *Green European Journal* 3:21–31 (2012), and Maurie Cohen, "The Decline and Fall of Consumer Society? Implications for Theories of Modernization," pp. 33–40 in Alberto Martinelli and Chuanqi He, eds, *Global Modernization Review: New Discoveries and Theories Revisited* (London: World Scientific Press, 2015). See also Justin Lewis, *Beyond Consumer Capitalism: Media and the Limits to Imagination* (Malden, MA: Polity, 2013), Anna Davies, Frances Fahy, and Henrike Rau, eds, *Challenging Consumption: Pathways to a More Sustainable Future* (New York: Routledge, 2014), Juliet Schor and Craig Thompson, eds, *Sustainable Lifestyles and the Quest for Plenitude: Case Studies of the New Economy* (New Haven, CT: Yale University Press, 2014), Karen Lykke Syse and Martin Lee Mueller, eds, *Sustainable Consumption and the Good Life: Interdisciplinary Perspectives* (New York: Routledge, 2014), Gerhard Scherhorn, "A Farewell to Consumer Society," *Journal of Consumer Policy* 29(3):319–28 (2006), Kate Soper, "The Other Pleasures of Post-consumerism," *Socialist Register* 36:115–32 (2000), Amitai Etzioni, "The Post-affluent Society," *Review of Social Economy* 62(3):407–20 (2004), Robert Frank, "Post-consumer Prosperity," *The American Prospect* 20(3): 12–15 (2009), Clive Hamilton, "Consumerism, Self-creation, and Prospects for a New Ecological Consciousness," *Journal of Cleaner Production* 18(6):1–5 (2009), Paul Gilding, *The Great Disruption: Why the Climate Crisis Will Bring on the End of Shopping and the Birth of a New World* (New York: Bloomsbury, 2011), and Diane Coyle, *The Economics of Enough: How to Run the Economy as if the Future Matters* (Princeton, NJ: Princeton University Press, 2011).

54. Joseph Tainter, *The Collapse of Complex Societies* (New York: Cambridge University Press, 1990) and Jared Diamond, *Collapse: How Societies Choose to Fail or Succeed* (New York: Penguin, 2005).

55. While the current discussion focuses on the United States, these factors have been present to varying degrees in other advanced countries as well.

56. Brink Lindsey, *The Age of Abundance: How Prosperity Transformed America's Politics and Culture* (New York: HarperCollins, 2007). See also Lizabeth Cohen, *A Consumers' Republic: The Politics of Mass Consumption in Postwar America* (New York: Vintage, 2003), Lawrence Glickman, *Consumer Society in American History: A Reader* (Ithaca, NY: Cornell University Press, 1999), and Michael Lind, *Land of Promise: An Economic History of the United States* (New York: Harper, 2012).

57. Robert Manning, *Credit Card Nation: The Consequences of America's Addiction to Credit* (New York: Basic Books, 2001) and Lendol Calder, *Financing the American Dream: A Cultural History of Consumer Credit* (Princeton, NJ: Princeton University Press, 2001).

58. Thom Gencarelli and Brian Cogan, eds, *Baby Boomers and Popular Culture: An Inquiry into America's Most Powerful Generation* (New York: Praeger, 2014).

59. Gordon, "Is US Economic Growth Over?"

60. Patrick Doherty and Chris Leinberger, "The Next Real Estate Boom," *Washington Monthly*, November/December, 2010. See also Paul Taylor, *The Next America: Boomers, Millennials, and the Looming Generational Showdown* (New York: PublicAffairs, 2014).

61. Paul Irving, *The Upside of Aging: How Long Life is Changing the World of Health, Work, Innovation, Policy and Purpose* (Hoboken, NJ: Wiley, 2014), Aimee Drolet, Norbert Schwarz, and Carolyn Yoon, eds, *The Aging Consumer: Perspectives from Psychology and Economics* (New York: Routledge, 2010), John Creedy and Ross Guest, *Population Ageing, Pensions and Growth: Intertemporal Trade-offs and Consumption Planning* (Northampton, MA: Edward Elgar, 2009). See also Chris Gilleard and Paul Higgs, *Ageing in a Consumer Society: From Passive to Active Consumption in Britain* (Bristol: Policy Press, 2008) and Theodore Roszak, *The Making of an Elder Culture: Reflections on the Future of America's Most Audacious Generation* (Gabriola Island, BC: New Society, 2009).

62. With 14.2 billion square feet of retail space (46.6 square feet per person), shopping capacity in the United States exceeds by a large margin the amount of space devoted to this purpose in other comparable countries. Even after considerable contraction over the last few years, the retail sector remains heavily overbuilt. The shift to online shopping (now approaching 10 percent of retail sales) is also contributing to retrenchment of customary establishments and over time will presumably free up land for reallocation to other purposes. The repurposing of former retail facilities is beginning to attract growing attention from architects and planners. See, for example, David Smiley, *Sprawl and Public Spaces: Redressing the Mall* (Princeton, NJ: Princeton University Press, 2002) and Julia Christensen, *Big Box Reuse* (Cambridge, MA: MIT Press, 2008).

63. Joseph Stiglitz, *The Great Divide: Unequal Societies and What We Can Do about Them* (New York: W. W. Norton, 2015), Thomas Piketty, *Capital in the Twenty-first Century* (Cambridge, MA: Belknap Press, 2014), John Brueggemann, *Inequality in the United States: A Reader* (New York: Routledge, 2015), and David Johnston, *Divided: The Perils of Our Growing Inequality* (New York: New Press, 2014).

64. United States Census Bureau, *Income, Poverty, and Health Insurance Coverage in the US: 2011* (Washington, DC: US Census Bureau, 2012).

65. Teresa Sullivan, Elizabeth Warren, and Jay Westbrook, *The Fragile Middle Class: Americans in Debt* (New Haven, CT: Yale University Press, 2001), Jacob Hacker, *The Great Risk Shift: The New Economic Insecurity and the Decline of the American Dream* (New York: Oxford University Press, 2008), Timothy Noah, *The Great Divergence: America's Growing Inequality Crisis and What We Can Do about It* (New York: Bloomsbury, 2012), and Alan Blinder, *After the Music Stopped: The Financial Crisis, the Response, and the Work Ahead* (New York: Penguin, 2013).

66. Robert Frank, *Richistan: A Journey through the American Wealth Boom and the Lives of the New Rich* (New York: Crown, 2008), Cynthia Freeland, *Plutocrats: The Rise of the New Global Super Rich and the Fall of Everyone Else* (New York: Penguin, 2012), Jeff Faux, *The Servant Economy: Where America's Elite is Sending the Middle Class* (Hoboken, NJ: Wiley, 2012). On the concept of positional goods see Fred Hirsch, *The Social Limits to Growth* (Cambridge, MA: Harvard University Press, 1976).

67. Ronald Inglehart, "Inequality and Modernization: Why Equality Is Likely to Make a Comeback," *Foreign Affairs* 95(1):2–10 (2016).

68. Stewart Lansley, "The Hourglass Society," *Los Angeles Review of Books*, May 28, 2010, Ellen Byron, "As Middle Class Shrinks, P&G Aims High and Low," *The Wall Street Journal*, September 12, 2011, and Nelson Schwartz, "The Middle Class Is Steadily Eroding. Just Ask the Business World," *The New York Times*, February 2, 2014. Recent developments in commercial air travel offer an especially evocative example of this phenomenon. First-class and business-class accommodation has become increasingly sumptuous, while space for passengers seated in the economy-class cabin is now more compressed and uncomfortable. See Jad Mouawad, "The Race to Build a Better Business Class," *The New York Times*, August 3, 2013 and Jad Mouawad and Martha White, "On Jammed Jets, Sardines Turn on One Another," *The New York Times*, December 22, 2013. A related development is the growing popularity of private aviation among especially affluent travelers. See Maurie Cohen, "Transition Management, Sustainable Systems Innovation, and the Challenge of Countervailing Trends: The Case of Personal Aeromobility," *Technology Analysis and Strategic Management* 21(2):249–65 (2009).

69. Andrew Benett and Ann O'Reilly, *Consumed: Rethinking Business in the Era of Mindful Spending* (New York: Palgrave Macmillan, 2010) and Alan Fairnington, *The Selfish Altruism: Why New Values are Killing Consumerism* (Hoboken, NJ: Wiley, 2010).

70. Determination of the extent to which the social practices of Generation Y-ers are cause or consequence of the more unstable and uncertain employment conditions in which they have come of age is methodologically difficult to discern. There is presumably a pattern of circular dependency at work. David Burstein, *Fast Future: How the Millennial Generation Is Shaping Our World* (Boston, MA: Beacon Press, 2013) and Morley Winograd and Michael Hais, *Millennial Momentum: How a New Generation Is Remaking America* (New Brunswick, NJ: Rutgers University Press, 2011).

71. Maurie Cohen, "The Future of Automobile Society: A Sociotechnical Transitions Perspective," *Technology Analysis and Strategic Management* 24(4) 377-90 (2012). Refer also to Alexa Delbosc and Graham Currie, "Causes of Youth Licensing Decline: A Synthesis of Evidence," *Transport Reviews* 33(3) 271-90 (2013).

72. David Metz, "Peak Car and Beyond: The Fourth Era of Travel," *Transport Reviews* 33(3):255-70 (2013), Derek Thompson and Jordan Weissmann, "The Cheapest Generation: Why Millennials Aren't Buying Cars or Houses and What that Means for the Economy," *The Atlantic*, September, 2012 and Tony Dutzik and Phineas Baxandall, *A New Direction: Our Changing Relationship with Driving and the Implications for America's Future* (Washington, DC: US PIRG Education Fund, 2013).

73. See, for example, Andreas Cornet, Detlev Mohr, Florian Weig, Benno Zerlin, and Arnt-Phillipp Hein, *Mobility of the Future: Opportunities for Automotive OEMs* (Munich: McKinsey and Company, Inc., 2012).

74. A common expression to describe this situation in Japan is *kuruma banare* which translates into "demotorization" but is more colloquially understood as "walking away from the car." See Akiko Kashiwagi, "A Post-car Society," *Newsweek*, February 16, 2008.

75. Eric Sanderson, *Terra Nova: The New World after Oil, Cars, and Suburbs* (New York: Harry N. Abrams, 2013), Alan Ehrenhalt, *The Great Inversion and the Future of the American City* (New York: Vintage, 2013), and Leigh Gallagher, *The End of the Suburbs: Where the American Dream Is Moving* (New York: Penguin, 2013).

76. National Commission on Fiscal Responsibility and Reform, *The Moment of Truth* (Washington, DC: The White House, 2010). See also Robert Pozen, "Heretic Reality: Mortgage Interest Deduction Needs to Be Slashed," *Forbes*, March 25, 2011. It merits noting that a number of countries have in recent years eliminated or substantially reduced allowable limits for the tax

deductibility of mortgage interest. For example, Finland instituted a major overall of this entitlement in 1993 and the UK did away with it in 2000. A lively debate on the issue has been taking place in the Netherlands for the past decade. For an overview, refer to Bruce Bartlett, "The Sacrosanct Mortgage Interest Deduction," *The New York Times*, August 6, 2013.

77. Roger Lowenstein, "Walk Away From Your Mortgage," *The New York Times*, January 10, 2010 and Tess Vigeland, "They Walked Away, and They're Glad They Did," *The New York Times*, November 8, 2011.

78. Michael Corkery, "Wall Street's New Housing Bonanza," *The Wall Street Journal*, February 29, 2014 and David Dayen, "Your New Landlord Works on Wall Street," *The New Republic*, February 12, 2013.

79. Shaila Dewan, "As Renters Move In, Some Homeowners Fret," *The New York Times*, August 28, 2013.

80. Benjamin Friedman, *The Moral Consequences of Economic Growth* (New York: Vintage, 2006), Annie Lowry, "Income Inequality May Take Toll on Growth," *The New York Times*, October 16, 2012, and Annie Lowry, "The Low Politics of Low Growth," *The New York Times*, January 12, 2013.

81. Umair Haque, "This Isn't Capitalism: It's Growthism, and It's Bad for Us, *Harvard Business Review*, October 28, 2013 (https://hbr.org/2013/10/this-isnt-capitalism-its-growthism-and-its-bad-for-us, accessed May 6, 2016).

82. Van Jones, "Working Together for a Green New Deal," *The Nation*, November 17, 2008 and Achim Steiner, "Global Green New Deal," *New Solutions* 19(2):185–93 (2009).

83. Larry Bartels, *Unequal Democracy: The Political Economy of the New Gilded Age* (Princeton, NJ: Princeton University Press, 2008), Robert Reich, *Beyond Outrage: What Has Gone Wrong with our Economy and our Democracy, and How to Fix It* (New York: Vintage, 2012), and Thomas Edsall, *The Age of Austerity: How Scarcity Will Remake American Politics* (New York: Doubleday, 2012).

84. Mark Blyth, *Austerity: The History of a Dangerous Idea* (New York: Oxford University Press, 2013), Robert Kuttner, *Debtors Prison: The Politics of Austerity versus Possibility* (New York: Knopf, 2013), and David Stucker and Sanjay Basu, *The Body Economic: Why Austerity Kills* (New York: Basic Books, 2013). See also, Amartya Sen, "The Economic Consequences of Austerity," *New Statesman*, June 4, 2015.

85. The issue becomes particularly salient when the OECD releases its triennial examination results of the Programme for International Student Assessment (PISA).

86. For further elaboration, see Thomas Frank, *What's the Matter with Kansas: How Conservatives Won the Heart of America* (New York: Metropolitan Books, 2004).

87. Michael Klare, *The Race for What's Left: The Global Scramble for the World's Last Resources* (New York: Metropolitan Books, 2012), Richard Heinberg,

The Party's Over: Oil, War, and the Fate of Industrial Societies (Gabriola Island, BC: New Society, 2005), David Goodstein, *Out of Gas: The End of the Age of Oil* (New York: W. W. Norton, 2005), James Howard Kunstler, *The Long Emergency: Surviving the End of Oil, Climate Change, and Other Converging Catastrophes of the Twenty-first Century* (New York: Grove Press, 2006), Christopher Steiner, *$20 per Gallon: How the Inevitable Rise in the Price of Gasoline Will Change our Lives for the Better* (New York: Grand Central, 2009), and Elizabeth Economy and Michael Levi, *By All Means Necessary: How China's Resource Quest Is Changing the World* (New York: Oxford University Press, 2014).

88. William Nel and Christopher Cooper, "Implications of Fossil Fuel Constraints on Economic Growth and Global Warming," *Energy Policy* 37(1):166–80 (2009), William Nel and Gerhardus van Zyl, "Defining Limits: Energy-constrained Economic Growth," *Applied Energy* 87(1):168–77 (2010), and Jeff Rubin, *The Big Flatline: Oil and the No-Growth Economy* (New York: Palgrave Macmillan, 2012).

89. David Murphy and Charles Hall, "Energy Return on Investment, Peak Oil, and the End of Economic Growth," *Annals of the New York Academy of Sciences* 1219(1):52–72 (2011). It merits noting that at present oil prices are, by historical standards, extremely low (approximately $37 per barrel in early 2016) because of slack demand in Europe and Asia, new domestic production in the United States (largely due to the advent of hydraulic fracturing) and intense competition among major exporters like Russia, Venezuela, Saudi Arabia, and Nigeria. See Clifford Krauss, "Oil Prices: What's Behind the Drop? Simple Economics," *The New York Times*, December 7, 2015.

90. Colin Campbell, *Campbell's Atlas of Oil and Gas Depletion*, 2nd ed. (Dordrecht: Springer, 2013).

91. For example, Royal Dutch Shell has invested $7 billion exploring for oil in the mostly ice-covered Chukchi Sea off the northern coast of Alaska and China is at present planning to open its fifth Antarctic research station.

92. Dambisa Moyo, *Winner Take All: China's Race for Resources and What It Means for the World* (New York: Basic Books, 2012).

93. Daniel Lipson, "Is the Great Recession only the Beginning? Economic Contraction in an Age of Fossil Fuel Depletion and Ecological Limits to Growth," *New Political Science* 33(4):555–75 (2011).

94. Ziauddin Sardar, "Welcome to Postnormal Times," *Futures* 42(5):435–44 (2010).

95. James Bullard, "Seven Faces of 'the Peril,'" *Federal Reserve Bank of St. Louis Review* 92(5):339–52 (2010) and Menzie Chen and Jeffry Frieden, *Lost Decades: The Making of America's Debt Crisis and the Long Recovery* (New York: W. W. Norton, 2011).

96. See, for example, Philip Vergragt and Halina Brown, "The Challenge of Energy Retrofitting the Residential Housing Stock: Grassroots Innovations and Socio-technical System Change in Worcester, MA, *Technology Analysis and Strategic Management* 24(4):407–20 (2012), James Kirwan, Brian Ilbery, Damian Maye, and Joy Carey, "Grassroots Social Innovations and Food Localisation: An Investigation of the Local Food Programme in England, *Global Environmental Change* 23(5):830–7 (2013), and Gabriella Dóci, Eleftheria Vasileiadou, and Arthur Petersen, "Exploring the Transition Potential of Renewable Energy Communities," *Futures* 66:85–95 (2015).

97. The most prominent case of top-down transition planning is the German *Energiewende* which involves an ambitious effort to shift the country's electricity-generation system from fossil fuels and nuclear power to renewable alternatives. The efforts underway in the United States are less renowned but nonetheless ongoing, especially in the electric utility sector which is experiencing extensive reorganization. Sanya Carley and Richard Andrews, "Creating a Sustainable U.S. Electricity Sector: The Question of Scale," *Policy Sciences* 45(2):97–121 (2012). It merits noting that there are also numerous countervailing forces in the country pushing to hold back or slow down this transition. Refer to David Hess, "Sustainability Transitions: A Political Coalition Perspective," *Research Policy* 43(2):278–83 (2014).

98. See, for example, James Gustave Speth, *America the Possible: Manifesto for a New Economy* (New Haven, CT: Yale University Press, 2012) and Michael Gerst, Paul Raskin, and Johan Rockström, "Contours of a Resilient Global Future," *Sustainability* 6(1):123–35 (2014).

99. Doug Stephens, *The Retail Revival: Reimagining Business for the New Age of Consumerism* (Hoboken, NJ: Wiley, 2013) and James Livingston, *Against Thrift: Why Consumer Culture is Good for the Economy, the Environment, and Your Soul* (New York: Basic Books, 2011).

100. Ben Schiller, "Brooklyn as a Lab to Amplify Urban Ideas," *Fast CoExist*, November 10, 2011 (http://www.fastcoexist.com/1678795/brooklyn-as-a-lab-to-amplify-urban-ideas, accessed May 6, 2016).

101. Jason Kaufman and Matthew Kaliner, "The Re-accomplishment of Place in Twentieth-century Vermont and New Hampshire: History Repeats Itself, until It Doesn't," *Theory and Society* 40(2):119–54 (2011).

102. The notion of agglomeration has to date been more commonly applied by economic geographers and urban economists to describe the economies of scale and other benefits that accrue when related businesses locate in close proximity.

103. Ian Whyte, *Scotland before the Industrial Revolution: An Economic and Social History, c.1050–c.1750* (New York: Longman, 1995), Christopher Hill, *The Penguin Economic History of Britain: Reformation to Industrial*

Revolution, 1530–1780 (New York: Penguin, 1999), Carlo Cipolla, *Before the Industrial Revolution: European Society and Economy, 1000–1700* (New York: W. W. Norton, 1994). See also David Landes, *The Unbound Prometheus: Technological Change and Industrial Development in Western Europe* (New York: Cambridge University Press, 1969).

104. Thomas Kelly, "The Origin of the Mechanics' Institutes," *British Journal of Educational Studies* 1(1):17–27 (1952).

105. Colin Campbell, *The Romantic Ethic and the Spirit of Modern Consumerism* (Malden, MA: Blackwell, 1987). For a useful review of historical research offering a complex view of pre-modern consumer practices, see Maryanne Kowaleski, "A Consumer Economy," pp. 238–59 in Rosemary Horrox and W. Mark Ormrod, *A Social History of England, 1200–1500* (New York: Cambridge University Press, 2006).

106. William Leach, *Land of Desire: Merchants, Power, and the Rise of a New American Culture* (New York: Vintage, 1994), William Lancaster, *The Department Store: A Social History* (Leicester: Leicester University Press, 2000), and Victoria de Grazia, *Irresistible Empire: America's Advance through 20th-Century Europe* (Cambridge, MA: Belknap Press, 2005).

107. Austrian economist Joseph Schumpeter coined the term "creative destruction" and referred to it as "the essential fact about capitalism." See his *Capitalism, Socialism, and Democracy* (New York: Harper and Brothers, 1942).

108. An especially notable example is Friedrich Engels, *The Condition of the Working Class in England* (New York: Penguin, (1987 [1845]).

109. Barry Bluestone and Bennett Harrison, *Deindustrialization of America: Plant Closings, Community Abandonment, and the Dismantling of Basic Industry* (New York: Basic Books, 1982) and William Julius Wilson, *When Work Disappears: The World of the New Urban Poor* (New York: Knopf, 1996).

110. Michael Porter and Mark Kramer, "Creating Shared Value," *Harvard Business Review* 89(1–2):62–87 (2011), Jagdish Sheth, Nirmal Sethia, and Shanthi Srinivas, "Mindful Consumption: A Customer-centric Approach to Sustainability," *Journal of the Academy of Marketing Science* 39(1):21–39 (2011), and Peter Wells, *Business Models for Sustainability* (Northampton, MA: Edward Elgar, 2013).

111. Hacker, *The Great Risk Shift*. See also Barbara Ehrenreich, *Bait and Switch: The (Futile) Pursuit of the American Dream* (New York: Holt, 2006) and Robert Putnam, *Our Kids: The American Dream in Crisis* (New York: Simon and Schuster, 2015).

112. Cohen, "Collective Dissonance and the Transition to Post-consumerism."

Chapter 3. The (Mostly) Empty Promise of the Sharing Economy

1. See, for example, Arianna Huffington, *Third World America: How Our Politicians Are Abandoning the Middle Class and Betraying the American Dream* (New York: Broadway Books, 2011), Maria Ivanova, "Consumerism and the Crisis: Whither 'the American Dream'?" *Critical Sociology* 37(3):329–50 (2011), and David Levering Lewis, "Exceptionalism's Exceptions: The Changing American Narrative," *Dædalus* 141(1):101–17 (2012). Refer also to New America Foundation, *What Will Replace the American Consumer?* (Washington, DC: New America Foundation, 2009).

2. Though the extent to which the "sharing economy" actually facilitates cooperative exchange is debatable, this chapter uses the terms "sharing economy," "sharing," and "shared access" (without quotation marks) in their now-common (but arguably mistaken) sense.

3. See, for example, "All Eyes on the Sharing Economy," *The Economist* 406 (8826), March 9, 2013 and Thomas Friedman, "Welcome to the 'Sharing Economy,'" *The New York Times*, July 20, 2013.

4. Jeremy Rifkin, *The Age of Access: The New Culture of Hypercapitalism, Where All of Life is a Paid-for Experience* (New York: Tarcher, 2001) and Kevin Kelly, "Better than Owning," *The Technium*, January 21, 2009 (http://kk.org/thetechnium/2009/01/better-than-own, accessed May 6, 2016).

5. Russell Belk, "Why Not Share Rather Than Own? *The Annals of the American Academy of Political and Social Science* 611:126–40 (2007) and Russell Belk, "You Are What You Can Access: Sharing and Collaborative Consumption Online," *Journal of Business Research* 67(8):1595–600 (2014).

6. Pia Albinsson and B. Ysanthi Perera, "Alternative Marketplaces in the 21st Century: Building Community through Sharing Eevents," *Journal of Consumer Behavior* 11(4):303–15 (2012).

7. Harald Heinrichs, "Sharing Economy: A Potential New Pathway to Sustainability," *GAIA* 22(4):228–31 (2013).

8. John Elkington, *Cannibals with Forks: The Triple Bottom Line of 21st Century Business* (London: Capstone, 1997).

9. The classic treatment of this point is Jane Jacobs, *The Death and Life of Great American Cities* (New York: Random House, 1961). See also James Howard Kunstler, *The Geography of Nowhere: The Rise and Decline of America's Man-Made Landscape* (New York: Free Press, 1994).

10. The social science literature speaks about this phenomenon in terms of diminished "social capital." See Robert Putnam, *Bowling Alone: The Collapse and Revival of American Community* (New York: Simon & Schuster, 2001).

11. Juliet Schor, *The Overspent American: Why We Want What We Don't Need* (New York: Harper Perrenial, 1999), Kim Humphery, *Excess: Anti-consumerism*

in the West (Malden, MA: Polity Press, 2009), and John de Graaf, David Wann, and Thomas Naylor, *Affluenza: How Overconsumption Is Killing Us—and How to Fight Back* (San Francisco, CA: Berrett-Koehler, 2014).

12. David Owen, *The Conundrum: How Scientific Innovation, Increased Efficiency, and Good Intentions Can Make our Energy and Climate Problems Worse* (New York: Riverhead Books, 2011).

13. Michael Huesemann and Joyce Huesemann, *Techno-Fix: Why Technology Won't Save Us or the Environment* (Gabriola Island, BC: New Society, 2011).

14. David Brooks, "The Evolution of Trust," *The New York Times*, June 30, 2014.

15. See, for example, Craig Shapiro, "What's the Future of the Sharing Economy?" *Fast Company* (http://www.fastcoexist.com/1681009/whats-the-future-of-the-sharing-economy, accessed May 6, 2016).

16. David Rose, *Enchanted Objects: Design, Human Desire, and the Internet of Things* (New York: Scribner's, 2014).

17. Susie Cagle, "The Case Against Sharing: On Access, Scarcity, and Trust," *The Medium* (https://medium.com/the-nib/the-case-against-sharing-9ea5ba3d216d, accessed May 6, 2016).

18. Based on financing deals, Uber was estimated in December 2015 to have a market capitalization of $68 billion. See Liyan Chen, "At $68 Billion Valuation, Uber Will Be Bigger than GM, Ford, and Honda," *Forbes*, December 4, 2015. Airbnb has been appraised during the same timeframe at $24 billion. See Rolfe Winkler and Douglas Macmillan, "The Secret Math of Airbnb's $24 Billion Valuation," *The Wall Street Journal*, June 17, 2015.

19. David Beito, *From Mutual Aid to the Welfare State: Fraternal Societies and Social Services, 1890–1967* (Chapel Hill, NC: University of North Carolina Press, 2000).

20. Graham Russell and Gao Hodges, *Taxi! A Social History of the New York City Cabdriver* (Baltimore: Johns Hopkins University Press, 2007).

21. Andrew Andoval-Strausz, *Hotel: An American History* (New Haven, CT: Yale University Press, 2007).

22. Warren Belasco, *Americans on the Road: From Autocamp to Motel, 1910–1945* (Baltimore: Johns Hopkins University Press, 1997).

23. Antony Sammarco, *A History of Howard Johnson's: How a Massachusetts Soda Fountain Became an American Icon* (New York: History Press, 2013). See also, Victor Luckerson, "How Holiday Inn Changed the Way We Travel," *Time*, August 1, 2012.

24. Randall Upchurch and Kurt Gruber, "The Evolution of a Sleeping Giant: Resort Timesharing," *International Journal of Hospitality Management* 21(3):211–55 (2002).

25. "Car Renting . . . its Development . . . and Future," *Automotive Fleet*, December, 1962 (http://www.automotive-fleet.com/channel/operations/article/story/

1962/12/car-renting-its-development-and-future.aspx, accessed May 6, 2016). Refer also to the historical overview available on the Hertz website (https://www.hertz.com/rentacar/abouthertz/index.jsp?targetPage=CorporateProfile.jsp&c=aboutHertzHistoryView, accessed May 6, 2016).

26. Miles Lambert, "Death and Memory: Clothing Bequests in English Wills 1650–1830," *Costume* 48(1):46–59 (2014).

27. Victoria Barahona and José Sánchez, "Dressing the Poor: The Provision of Clothing among the Lower Classes in Eighteenth-century Madrid," *Textile History* 43(1):23–42 (2012), Miles Lambert, "'Cast-off Wearing Apparell': The Consumption and Distribution of Second-hand Clothing in Northern England during the Long Eighteenth Century," *Textile History* 35(1):1–26 (2004), Patricia Allerston, "Reconstructing the Second-hand Trade in Sixteenth- and Seventeenth-century Venice," *Costume* 33 (1):46–56 (1997), Elizabeth Sanderson, "Nearly New: The Second-hand Clothing Trade in Eighteenth-century Edinburgh," *Costume* 31(1):38–48 (1997), John Styles, "Clothing the North: The Supply of Non-elite Clothing in the Eighteenth-century North of England," *Textile History* 25 (2):139–66 (1994), and Madeleine Ginsburg, "Rags to Riches: The Second-hand Clothes Trade 1700–1978," *Costume* 14(1):121–35 (1980). A factor in the eventual decline of repurposed clothing was concern among public health officials that it was unsanitary to trade used garments. See, for example, G. W. N. Joseph, "Some Remarks on Second-hand Clothing and the Spread of Infectious Disease," *Public Health* 28 (4–12):267–70 (1915).

28. Kenneth Jackson, *Crabgrass Frontier: The Suburbanization of the United States* (New York: Oxford University Press, 1987) and Lizabeth Cohen, *A Consumers' Republic: The Politics of Mass Consumption in Postwar America* (New York: Vintage, 2003).

29. Victor Lebow, "The Real Meaning of Consumer Demand," *Journal of Retailing*, Spring, 1955.

30. Jim Cullen, *The American Dream: A Short History of an Idea that Shaped a Nation* (New York: Oxford University Press, 2004).

31. Susan Shaheen, Daniel Sperling, and Conrad Wagner, "Carsharing in Europe and North America: Past, Present, and Future," *Transportation Quarterly* 52(3):35–52 (1998).

32. Micheline Maynard. *Curbing Cars: America's Independence from the Auto Industry* (New York: Forbes Media, 2014).

33. Despite the achievements of the most prominent sharing initiatives, a significant number of these efforts have not succeeded. For an overview of some of them, refer to Sarah Needleman and Angus Loten, "Startups Want to Be the Next Airbnb, Uber," *The Wall Street Journal*, May 7, 2014.

34. Rachel Botsman and Roo Rogers, *What's Mine Is Yours: The Rise of Collaborative Consumption* (New York: HarperBusiness, 2010) and Lisa Gansky, *The Mesh: Why the Future of Business Is Sharing* (New York: Portfolio Penguin, 2012).

35. A more customary example of the sharing of aircraft involves airplanes that are owned on a fractional share basis in which individual owners hold partial title and are allocated a proportional number of flying hours per month. For a more detailed discussion, refer to Maurie Cohen, "Destination Unknown: Pursuing Sustainable Mobility in the Face of Rival Societal Aspirations," *Research Policy* 39(4):459–70 (2010).

36. Harvey Molotch and Laura Noren, *Toilet: Public Restrooms and the Politics of Sharing* (New York: New York University Press, 2010).

37. The notion of usership is related to the concept of usufruct which derives from Roman law. The *Encyclopedia Britannica* defines usufruct as "the temporary right to the use and enjoyment of the property of another, without changing the character of the property."

38. Christian Fuchs, "The Implications of New Information and Communication Technologies for Sustainability," *Environment, Development, and Sustainability* 10(3):291–309 (2008).

39. While complementary to some extent, it is useful to differentiate "car-sharing" (as outlined in the main discussion) from "ride-sharing." The latter activity is associated with platforms like Uber and Lyft and involves a car and driver providing taxi-like services. In all of the cases described in the subsequent typology, the user operates the car so they are not specifically relevant to car-sharing but could be alternatively applied to this type of mobility service.

40. Relay Rides previously offered an hourly rental option, but the transaction costs associated with such short periods of time were excessive and in 2013 the company discontinued this alternative.

41. But see Tom Slee, "Sharing and Caring," *Jacobin*, January 24, 2014 (https://www.jacobinmag.com/2014/01/sharing-and-caring, accessed May 6, 2016).

42. Mark Scott, "BlaBlaCar, a Ride-sharing Start-up in Europe, Looks to Expand its Map," *The New York Times*, July 2, 2014.

43. Mathew Yglesias, "There Is No 'Sharing Economy,'" *Slate*, December 23, 2016 (http://www.slate.com/blogs/moneybox/2013/12/26/myth_of_the_sharing_economy_there_s_no_such_thing.html, accessed May 7, 2016).

44. An interesting measure of the scale of outsized consumption is that the disposal of excess consumer goods has become a source of popular entertainment in the form of reality television shows like *Storage Wars*, *Pawn Stars*, and *Hoarders*. See Charmaine Eddy, "The Art of Consumption: Capital Excess and Individual Psychosis in Hoarders," *Canadian Review of American Studies* 44(1):1–24 (2014) and Susan Lepselter, "The Disorder of Things:

Hoarding Narratives in Popular Media," *Anthropological Quarterly* 84(4): 919–48 (2011).

45. Frederick Winslow Taylor, *The Principles of Scientific Management* (New York: Harper and Row, 1911). See also Robert Kanigel, *One Best Way: Frederick Winslow Taylor and the Enigma of Efficiency* (New York: Viking, 1997) and Jane Lancaster, *Making Time: Lillian Moller Gilbreth—A Life Beyond "Cheaper by the Dozen"* (Boston: Northeastern University Press, 2006). Other seminal figures in the development of the field of domestic science were Ellen Richards (the first woman to attend MIT) and Christine Frederick (head of the Associated Clubs of Domestic Science).

46. Janice Rutherford, *Selling Mrs. Consumer: Christine Frederick and the Rise of Household Efficiency* (Athens: University of Georgia Press, 2003) and Carolyn Goldstein, *Creating Consumers: Home Economists in Twentieth-Century America* (Chapel Hill, NC: University of North Carolina Press, 2012). The films *Cheaper by the Dozen* and *Belles on their Toes* (adapted from books with the same titles) provide comic treatment of these efforts to enhance household efficiency.

47. Dick Vestbro and Liisa Horelli, "Design for Gender Equality: The History of Co-housing Ideas and Realities," *Built Environment* 38(3):315–35 (2012).

48. Elizabeth Shove, *Comfort, Cleanliness, and Convenience: The Social Organization of Normality* (New York: Berg, 2004). See also Helen Zoe Veit, "Time to Revive Home Ec," *The New York Times*, September 2, 2011.

49. Robin Chase, "Remixing Excess Capacity," *Journal of Urban Regeneration and Renewal* 4(4):354–7 (2011). Efforts to enhance the resource efficiency of household operations are generally consistent with environmental social scientific perspectives advanced by advocates of ecological modernization. See, for example, Gert Spaargaren, "Ecological Modernization Theory and Domestic Consumption," *Journal of Environmental Policy and Planning* 2(4):323–35 (2000).

50. Thomas Princen, *The Logic of Sufficiency* (Cambridge, MA: MIT Press, 2005).

51. Ernst von Weizsacker, Amory Lovins, and L. Hunter Lovins, *Factor Four: Doubling Wealth, Halving Resource Use* (London: Earthscan, 1998).

52. William Stanley Jevons, *The Coal Question: An Inquiry Concerning the Progress of the Nation, and the Probable Exhaustion of our Coal Mines* (London: Macmillan, 1865).

53. There is an expansive body of literature on Jevons Paradox and related issues. For an introduction, refer to John Polimeni, Kozo Mayumi, Mario Giampietro, and Blake Alcott, *The Jevons Paradox and the Myth of Resource Efficiency Improvements* (London: Earthscan, 2007) and Horace Herring and Steve

Sorrell, eds, *Energy Efficiency and Sustainable Consumption: The Rebound Effect* (New York: Palgrave Macmillan, 2009).

54. Keith Bradsher, *High and Mighty—SUVs: The World's Most Dangerous Vehicles and How They Got That Way* (New York: Public Affairs, 2002).

55. In addition, when American households purchase a more energy-efficient refrigerator the previous unit is typically not decommissioned. Instead, a common practice is to move the old appliance to the basement or garage where it provides overflow capacity. The household that relied in a prior time on one refrigerator now consumes energy to operate two units.

56. I am reminded of a university colleague who purchased a Toyota Prius on the eve of his retirement and announced that he would be using the car to drive across the United States on vacation. All things considered, this is not an inappropriate way to usher in one's departure from regular academic life, but he may have been less inclined to take the trip if he had to pay the costs of driving a conventional gasoline-powered car.

57. Ken Belson, "Car-sharing Services Cut Cost of Ownership," *The New York Times*, October 22, 2009.

58. I recently received a poignant email from one of my students thanking me for having introduced her to Airbnb. She was appreciative of the fact that without access to this service she would not have been able to afford the month-long trip to Florida from which she had just returned.

59. Johan Rockström, Will Steffen, Kevin Noone, Åsa Pesson, F. Stuart Chapin, Eric Lambin, Timothy Lenton, Marten Scheffer, Carl Folke, Hans Joachim Schellhuber, Björn Hykvist, Cynthia de Wit, Terry Hughes, Sander van der Leeuw, Henning Rodhe, Sverker Sörlin, Peter Snyder, Robert Costanza, Uno Svedin, Malin Falkenmark, Louise Karlberg, Robert Corell, Victoria Fabry, James Hansen, Brian Walker, Diana Liverman, Katherine Richardson, Paul Crutzen, and Jonathan Foley, "A Safe Operating Space for Humanity," *Nature* 461(7263):472–5 (2009).

60. James Meadowcroft, "Reaching the Limits? Developed Country Engagement with Sustainable Development in a Challenging Conjuncture," *Environment and Planning C (Government and Policy)* 31(6):988–1002 (2013).

61. The term "solutionism" is from Evgeny Morozov, *To Save Everything Click Here: The Folly of Technological Solutionism* (New York: Public Affairs, 2014). On the limits of technology more generally refer to Marc Pratarelli, "When Human Nature Confronts the Need for a Global Environmental Ethics," *Journal of Social, Evolutionary, and Cultural Psychology* 6(3):384–403 (2012).

62. Rockström et al., "A Safe Operating Space for Humanity."

63. Joe Peach, "Why the Sharing Economy Is a Big Opportunity for Cities," *Sustainable Cities Collective* (http://sustainablecitiescollective.com/big-city/

183761/why-sharing-economy-big-opportunity-cities, accessed May 7, 2016).

64. Donella Meadows, *Thinking in Systems: A Primer* (White River Junction, VT: Chelsea Green, 2008).

65. John Sterman, "Sustaining Sustainability: Creating a Systems Science in a Fragmented Academy and Polarized World," pp. 21–58 in Michael Weinstein and R. Eugene Turner, eds, *Sustainability Science: The Emerging Paradigm and the Urban Environment* (New York: Springer, 2012).

66. Peter Victor, *Managing without Growth: Slower by Design, Not Disaster* (Northampton, MA: Edward Elgar, 2008).

67. In response to this situation, the platform is introducing a new smartphone app for organizing carpools that it calls Lyft Line. Carpooling in the United States peaked in the 1970s at approximately 20 percent of commuters and is currently down to 10 percent. Among analysts there is considerable skepticism whether Lyft's service will be able to overcome prevailing cultural barriers to traveling to work with a previously unknown companion. See Farhad Manjoo, "Coaxing Commuters to Leave their Cars," *The New York Times*, August 7, 2014.

68. The management of Zipcar (which was acquired by the Avis Budget Group in 2013) evinces ambivalence about whether the company is rightfully part of the sharing economy and is even uncertain about whether "car-sharing" appropriately describes its business model. The company makes an explicit point in its public communications to differentiate its short-term rental approach from what it describes as "peer-to-peer" sharing. See http://www. zipcar.com/ziptopia/around-the-bend/mark-norman/how-do-you-sustain-a-good-idea (accessed May 7, 2016).

69. The extent to which these positive outcomes might be achieved has been explored though life-cycle analysis and consumer surveys. See, for example, Laura Farrant, Stig Olsson, and Arne Wangel, "Environmental Benefits from Reusing Clothes," *International Journal of Life Cycle Assessment* 15(7):726–36 (2010) and Costanza Bianchi and Grete Birtwistle, "Consumer Clothing Disposal Behaviour: A Comparative Study," *International Journal of Consumer Studies* 36(3):335–41 (2012).

70. Kristine Wong, "Lessons from Airbnb about Business in the Sharing Economy," GreenBiz.com, (http://www.greenbiz.com/news/2013/02/15/les sons-airbnb-about-business-sharing-economy, accessed May 7, 2016).

71. It is necessary to be careful not to overstate the positive equity impacts of Airbnb. It has been repeatedly demonstrated that a significant number of its properties are listed by owners of second homes and by landlords of multiple units.

72. Ian Yeoman, *2050: Tomorrow's Tourism* (Bristol: Channel View Publications, 2012).

73. Daniel Carpenter and David Moss, eds, *Preventing Regulatory Capture: Special Interest Influence and How to Limit It* (New York: Cambridge University Press, 2014).

74. David Streitfeld, "Companies Built on Sharing Balk When It Comes to Regulators," *The New York Times*, April 21, 2014.

75. For example, Uber has been engaged in widely publicized regulatory battles in Berlin, Barcelona, London, and other cities. Seoul banned the platform from operating despite an initiative by municipal authorities to declare the city a "Sharing City."

76. Richard Florida, *Who's Your City? How the Creative Economy Is Making Where to Live the Most Important Decision of Your Life* (New York: Basic Books, 2008).

77. San Francisco Supervisor David Chiu effectively captured this sensibility when he said, "I believe we are becoming the capital of the sharing economy. We've been a city of innovation since the Gold Rush." See also Cat Johnson, "Is Seoul the Next Great Sharing City?" *Shareable*, July 16, 2013 (http://www.shareable.net/blog/is-seoul-the-next-great-sharing-city, accessed May 7, 2016) and Cagle, "The Case against Sharing."

78. Robert Kuttner, "The Task Rabbit Economy," *American Prospect*, October 10, 2103 (http://prospect.org/article/task-rabbit-economy, accessed May 7, 2016) and Sarah Kessler, "Pixel & Dimed: On (Not) Getting by in the Gig Economy," *Fast Company*, March 18, 2014 (http://www.fastcompany.com/3027355/pixel-and-dimed-on-not-getting-by-in-the-gig-economy, accessed May 7, 2016).

79. Natasha Singer, "Check App. Accept Job. Repeat," *The New York Times*, August 17, 2014.

80. Alison Griswold, "The Problem with Jobs in the Sharing Economy," *Slate*, May 29, 2014 (http://www.slate.com/blogs/moneybox/2014/05/29/uber_and_driverless_cars_the_sharing_economy_is_not_the_future_of_labor.html, accessed May 7, 2016).

81. Gideon Lewis-Kraus, "Su Casa Es Mi Casa," *The New York Times*, May 5, 2013 (http://tmagazine.blogs.nytimes.com/2013/05/05/su-casa-es-mi-casa, accessed May 7, 2016).

82. Evgeny Morozov writes that "the sharing economy amplifies the worst excesses of the dominant economic model: it is 'neoliberalism on steroids.'" See his article "The 'Sharing Economy' Undermines Workers' Rights," *Financial Times*, October 14, 2013. Refer also to Kessler, "Pixel & Dimed" and Cagle, "The Case against Sharing." The term the "1099 economy" refers to a tax document with this numerical designation issued in the United States to report annual compensation paid to non-employee workers.

83. This is a point of discussion on social media focused on offering advice to individuals seeking to overcome burdensome levels of financial debt. See, for

example, http://blog.readyforzero.com/feeling-a-need-to-maintain-appearances (accessed May 7, 2016).

84. Guy Standing, *The Precariat: The New Dangerous Class* (New York: Blooms-bury, 2011). See also, Kuttner, "The Task Rabbit Economy."

85. Jacob Hacker, *The Great Risk Shift: The New Economic Insecurity and the Decline of the American Dream* (New York: Oxford University Press, 2008).

86. This point touches on the fact that participation in the sharing economy generally requires some wealth in terms of asset ownership. In addition, success as a service provider entails significant cultural capital. Cagle quotes Nikki Silvestri, Executive Director of Green for All, as remarking, "African Americans had to share because white folks ain't give us nothin'. One of my fears is that with the sharing economy, the same things will happen. The best performers in Airbnb are white women and the worst performers are black men. There's an inherent difference in lived experience. We ignore people of color and low income people." See also Benjamin Edelman and Michael Luca, "Digital Discrimination: The Case of Airbnb.com," Harvard Business School, Working Paper 14-054, January 10, 2014.

87. See http://blog.airbnb.com/belong-anywhere (accessed May 7, 2016). This strategy of linking a commercial offering to a transcendent value is remin-iscent of the Coca-Cola Company's pioneering "I'd Like to Buy the World a Coke" campaign from the early 1970s that situated its eponymous product in a narrative of global peace. Benetton has successfully used evocative imagery of racial and ethnic diversity to similar effect and Starbuck's has linked itself to ideals celebrating communal association. The aim of these efforts is to poignantly connect an otherwise mundane product with an aspirational social mission. Refer to Fredrik Nordin, "Transcendental Marketing: A Conceptual Framework and Empirical Examples," *Management Decision* 47(10):1652–64 (2009).

88. Cagle, "The Case against Sharing."

89. See, for example, Farhad Manjoo, "Grocery Deliveries in Sharing Economy," *The New York Times*, May 21, 2014.

90. Farhad Manjoo, "Instacart's Bet on Online Grocery Shopping," *The New York Times*, April 29, 2015.

91. William Freudenburg and Robert Gramling, "Mid-range Theory and Cutting-edge Sociology: A Call for Culmination," *Newsletter of the Environment, Technology, and Society Section of the American Sociological Association* 76(1):3–6 (1994). This discussion is further developed in Naomi Krogman, "Frame Disputes in Environmental Controversies: The Case of Wetland Regulations in Louisiana," *Sociological Spectrum* 16(4):371–400 (1996). See also William Freudenburg and Margarita Alario, "Weapons of Mass Distraction: Magicianship, Misdirection, and the Dark Side of Legitimation," *Sociological Forum* 22(2):146–73 (2007).

Chapter 4. The Mass-Market Maker Movement

1. "The Art and Craft of Business," *The Economist*, January 4, 2014 (http://www.economist.com/news/business/21592656-etsy-starting-show-how-maker-movement-can-make-money-art-and-craft-business, accessed May 7, 2016).

2. Neil Gershenfeld, *Fab: The Coming Revolution on Your Desktop: From Personal Computers to Personal Fabrication* (New York: Basic Books, 2007), Chris Anderson, *Makers: The New Industrial Revolution* (New York: Crown Business, 2012), and Mark Hatch, *The Maker Movement Manifesto: Rules for Innovation in the New World of Crafters, Hackers, and Tinkerers* (New York: McGraw Hill, 2014).

3. Charles Howard, Andrea Gerosa, Maria Mejuto, and Gregor Giannella, "The Maker Movement: A New Avenue for Competition in the EU," *European View* 13(2):333–40 (2014) and Stephen Fox, "Third Wave Do-it-Yourself (DIY): Potential for Prosumption, Innovation, and Entrepreneurship by Local Populations in Regions without Industrial Manufacturing Infrastructure," *Technology in Society* 39:18–30 (2014).

4. Dane Strangler and Kate Maxwell, "DIY Producer Society," *Innovations* 7(3):3–10 (2012). See also Peter Diamandis and Steven Kotler, *Abundance: The Future Is Better than You Think* (New York: Free Press, 2012).

5. Celeste LeCompte, "Made in China 2.0," *Selamta Magazine*, July/August, 2013. See also Silvia Lindtner, "Hackerspaces and the Internet of Things in China: How Makers Are Reinventing Industrial Production, Innovation, and the Self," *China Information* 28(2):145–67 (2014), Silvia Lindtner and David Li, "Created in China: The Makings of China's Hackerspace Community," *Interactions* 19(6):18–22 (2012), and Emily Parker, "In China, Lessons of a Hackerspace," *The Wall Street Journal*, October 4, 2013.

6. Louise Stewart, "Maker Movement Reinvents Education," *Newsweek*, September 8, 2014, Tim Bajarin, "Why the Maker Movement Is Important to America's Future, *Time*, May 9, 2014, and Noelle Swan, "The 'Maker Movement' Creates D.I.Y. Revolution," *The Christian Science Monitor*, July 6, 2014.

7. Kylie Peppler and Sophia Bender, "Maker Movement Spreads Innovation One Project at a Time," *Phi Delta Kappan Magazine* 95(3):22–7 (2013) and Patrick Colegrove, "Libraries as Makerspaces?" *Information Technology and Libraries* 32(1):2–5 (2013). See also Margaret Honey and David Kanter, eds, *Design, Make, Play: Growing the Next Generation of STEM Innovators* (New York: Routledge, 2013).

8. Mark Hatch, the CEO of TechShop, a network of commercial makerspaces, is one of the more effusive champions of the Maker Movement. Borrowing unabashedly from the technology visionary Ray Kurzweil, he writes, "We are standing on the foundation of the largest explosion of creativity, knowledge

creation, and innovation in all of human history . . . Call it what you will, the next industrial revolution, the Maker Movement, the creative revolution, the third industrial revolution, whatever you like. History will name it once it is over . . . I'm confident that nothing is going to get in its way and that eventually it will become the massive force for creativity around the globe it deserves to become." Hatch, *The Maker Movement Manifesto*, p. 199.

9. This estimate is from Atmel (a producer of touchscreen controllers, microcontrollers, and other computer components) and reported in *Time* magazine where the firm is described as a "major backer" of the Maker Movement. The same article goes on to note that the market for 3D printers and allied equipment was $2.2 billion in 2012 and projected to reach $6 billion by 2017 and $8.4 billion by 2020. See Bajarin, "Why the Maker Movement Is Important to America's Future."

10. The term "prosumption" was originally coined by Alvin Toffler in 1980 as a portmanteau for "proactive consumer" or "professional consumer" and as a way to capture then-emergent developments that were seen as dissolving the barriers between customary production and consumption activities. See Alvin Toffler, *The Third Wave* (New York: Morrow, 1980). Archetypal examples of prosumption at the time included technology enthusiasts who would customize standardized products like video cameras. The concept also captured more long-standing practices such as keeping a backyard garden or carrying out maintenance and repair on one's home. The term today is generally interpreted as the conflation of "production" and "consumption" and describes, for example, the assembly of IKEA furniture, the management of personal bank accounts via an automatic teller machine or online platform, and the making of beer for individual consumption. For an example of more recent work on prosumption, refer to George Ritzer, Paul Dean, and Nathan Jurgenson, "The Coming Age of the Prosumer," *American Behavioral Scientist*, 56(4):379–98 (2012).

11. Office of the Press Secretary, Presidential Proclamation—National Day of Making, 2014 (Washington, DC: The White House, 2014) (http://www.whitehouse.gov/the-press-office/2014/06/17/presidential-proclamation-national-day-making-2014, accessed May 7, 2016).

12. See, for example, Tyler Lynch, "The Maker Movement Makes its Mark," *USA Today*, August 8, 2014.

13. Jackson Lears, *No Place of Grace: Antimodernism and the Transformation of American Culture, 1880–1920* (New York: Pantheon, 1981).

14. The last few years have seen publication of a series of notable books describing the personal satisfaction that comes with handwork. See Richard Sennett, *The Craftsman* (New Haven, CT: Yale University Press, 2008), Matthew Crawford, *Shop Class as Soulcraft: An Inquiry into the Value of Work*

(New York: Penguin, 2010), and Peter Korn, *Why We Make Things and Why It Matters: The Education of a Craftsman* (Boston: David Godine, 2013).

15. See Dale Dougherty, "The Maker Movement," *Innovations*, 7(3):11–14 (2012), p. 12.

16. Colin Campbell, "The Craft Consumer: Culture, Craft and Consumption in a Postmodern Society," *Journal of Consumer Culture*, 5(1):23–42 (2005), p. 36.

17. Campbell, "The Craft Consumer," p. 37. Daniela Rosner and Jonathan Bean advance a similar argument that suggests engagement in making activities enables participants to adopt the more heroic persona of an active and creative producer rather than the less appealing identity of a passive and indoctrinated consumer. See Daniela Rosner and Jonathan Bean, "Making: Movement or Brand?" *Interactions*, 21(1):26–7 (2014).

18. Barry Bluestone and Bennett Harrison, *The Deindustrialization of America: Plant Closings, Community Abandonment, and the Dismantling of Basic Industry* (New York: Basic Books, 1984).

19. Judith Stein, *Pivotal Decade: How the United States Traded Factories for Finance in the Seventies* (New Haven, CT: Yale University Press, 2011).

20. Thomas Friedman, *The World Is Flat: A Brief History of the Twenty-first Century* (New York: Farrar, Straus and Giroux, 2005). See also Steven Greenhouse, *The Big Squeeze: Tough Times for the American Worker* (New York: Anchor, 2009).

21. Don Peck, *Pinched: How the Great Recession Has Narrowed our Futures and What We Can Do About It* (New York: Broadway Books, 2012).

22. John Urry, *Offshoring* (Malden, MA: Polity, 2014).

23. Campbell, "The Craft Consumer," p. 38.

24. Several formerly middle-class occupations have experienced notable processes of deprofessionalization over the past twenty years including medicine, social work, education, and, most recently, law and accounting (see Chapter 6). Refer also to Robert Brooks, *Cheaper by the Hour: Temporary Lawyers and the Deprofessionalization of the Law* (Philadelphia: Temple University Press, 2011), Richard Epstein, "Big Law and Big Med: The Deprofessionalization of Legal and Medical Services," *International Review of Law and Economics* 38(S):64–76 (2013), James Lampe and Andy Garcia, "The History of Deprofessionalization in US Public Accountancy," *Research on Professional Responsibility and Ethics in Accounting*, 17:1–45 (2013), and Ruby Mendehall, Ariel Kalil, Laurel Spindel, and Cassandra Hart, "Job Loss at Mid-life: Managers and Executives Face the "New Risk Economy," *Social Forces* 87(1):185–210.

25. Korn, *Why We Make Things and Why It Matters*, p. 52.

26. In merits observing that this interpretation stands in stark contrast to the explanations that Maker Movement proponents have formulated to explain

the rise of making and which tend to rely on relatively uncritical assimilation of Richard Florida's concept of the "creative class." See, in particular, Hatch, *The Maker Movement Manifesto*, pp. 52–3. For an incisive critique of the "creative class" argument, see Neil Brenner, Peter Marcuse, and Margit Mayer, eds, *Cities for People, Not for Profit: Critical Urban Theory and the Right to the City* (New York: Routledge, 2011).

27. Campbell, "The Craft Consumer," p. 38.

28. In Mark Hatch's words, "You won't be a very good welder at the end of our two-hour safety and basic use class, but you'll know the basics of welding and how to operate the equipment safely, and you will weld something. The odds are very high that you will be able to produce useful things with even this little bit of welding experience. And with some practice—well, lots of practice—you can get good at it." Hatch, *The Maker Movement Manifesto*, p. 80.

29. This is the case for the for-profit organizations that comprise the Maker Movement. By contrast, Kickstarter is a popular Internet platform of upfront financing for aspirational micro-entrepreneurs seeking a foothold in the market for maker-produced goods. The website does not facilitate equity investing, but rather provides a way for small-scale enterprises to raise money to refine a prototype and manufacture a few demonstration models. "Investors" (though more accurately understood to be "customers") of sufficient scale become eligible to receive an early version when the item becomes available. Kickstarter has proven to be an effective strategy to raise sums in the range of a few thousand dollars and a small handful of ideas have been sufficiently captivating to generate substantially more. Most of these campaigns are for next-generation consumer products rather than groundbreaking industrial innovations.

30. See, for example, Lears, *No Place of Grace* and Steven Levy, *Hackers: Heroes of the Computer Revolution* (New York: Anchor, 1984).

31. Dale Dougherty, the founder of *Make:* a widely read magazine for the Maker Movement originally published by O'Reilly Media, remarks that he avoids using the term "inventor" and claims that "most people just don't identify themselves that way." He relies instead on less daunting terms like "making" and "tinkering," presumably because such phrasing is more effective as a recruitment strategy. See Dougherty, "The Maker Movement."

32. Hatch, *The Maker Movement Manifesto*, p. 79. He goes on to observe that "at our shop, we impart the minimum amount of information learners need to operate a machine safely and move their projects to the next step. It's a focus on adequacy rather than mastery."

33. Fox, "Third Wave Do-it-Yourself," p. 30.

34. Sennett, *The Craftsman*, pp. 42–4.

35. Scott Timberg, *Culture Crash: The Killing of the Creative Class* (New Haven, CT: Yale University Press, 2015).
36. Jathan Sadowski and Paul Manson, "3D Print your Way to Freedom and Prosperity," *Al Jazeera America*, May 17, 2014.
37. Hatch, *The Maker Movement Manifesto* and Anderson, *Makers*.
38. Anderson, *Makers*, p. 50.
39. See, for example, Peter Kriedte, Hans Medick, and Jürgen Schlumbohm, *Industrialization before Industrialization* (New York: Cambridge University Press, 1981).
40. For a dissenting view of the relationship between cottage and factory production, see Rab Houston and K. D. M. Snell, "Proto-industrialization? Cottage Industry, Social Change, and Industrial Revolution," *The Historical Journal*, 27(2):473–92 (1984).
41. David Landes, *The Unbound Prometheus: Technological Change and Industrial Development in Western Europe from 1750 to the Present* (New York: Cambridge University Press, 1969) and Michael Žmolek, *Rethinking the Industrial Revolution* (New York: Brill, 2013).
42. Kriedte et al., *Industrialization before Industrialization*.
43. Duncan Bythell, "Cottage Industry and the Factory System," *History Today*, April: 17–23 (1983).
44. Anderson, *Makers*, pp. 48–9.
45. Bythell, "Cottage Industry and the Factory System," p. 21.
46. Bythell, "Cottage Industry and the Factory System," p. 23.
47. See also Kirkpatrick Sale, *Rebels Against the Future: The Luddites and Their War on the Industrial Revolution—Lessons for the Computer Age* (New York: Basic Books, 1996).
48. E. P. Thompson, *The Making of the English Working Class* (New York: Pantheon, 1964). Michael Žmolek further observes, "The eighteenth century was effectively the golden age of cottage industry. E. P. Thompson has cautioned against making such a claim, for the conditions of cottage weavers and other domestic manufacturers in the eighteenth century were not exactly enviable. However, when set against the sufferings of the early nineteenth century and the rise of industrial factories to replace cottage industry in a rapid and bloody transformation, the idealized memories of an eighteenth-century cottage life have survived." Michael Žmolek, "Further Thoughts on Agrarian Capitalism: A Reply to Albritton," *Journal of Peasant Studies* 29(1):129–54 (2001).
49. David Weil, *The Fissured Workplace: Why Work Became So Bad for So Many and What Can Be Done to Improve It* (Cambridge, MA: Harvard University Press, 2014). See also Crawford, *The Case for Working with your Hands*, Korn, *Why We Make Things and Why It Matters*, and Sennett, *The Craftsman*.

50. Anderson, *Makers*, pp. 46–7.

51. Levy, *Hackers*.

52. Heidi Ledford, "The Printed Organs Coming to a Body Near You," *Nature* 520(7457):273.

53. Hatch, *The Maker Movement Manifesto*, p. 98. Within the Maker Movement there is confusion about the role that cost-effective production in China might play over the longer term. It is instructive to contrast Hatch's comments cited here with other remarks where he observes, "I prefer to see manufacturing closer to the market. But the reality of international commerce and economics is such that it is often just plain cheaper to get a product made overseas." Contract manufacturing more generally has been an extremely contentious issue for the Maker Movement. Toward the end of 2013, the Internet marketplace Etsy revamped (and then subsequently further revised) its guidelines requiring that sellers personally handcraft the products sold on the website. The new standards allow for various modes of contract manufacturing. See https://blog.etsy.com/news/2014/clarifying-our-guidelines-on-outside-manufacturing (accessed May 7, 2016).

54. David Rotman, "The Difference between Makers and Manufacturers," *MIT Technology Review*, January 2, 2013.

55. Rotman, "The Difference between Makers and Manufacturers."

56. Rotman, "The Difference between Makers and Manufacturers."

57. Sennett, *The Craftsman*, p. 44.

58. Doreen Jakob, "Crafting Your Way Out of the Recession? New Craft Entrepreneurs and the Global Economic Downturn," *Cambridge Journal of Regions, Economy and Society*, 6(1):127–40 (2013).

59. Jakob, "Crafting Your Way Out of the Recession?" pp. 137–8.

60. See, for example, Benjamin Wallace, "The Twee Party," *New York Magazine*, April 15, 2012 and Hanna Raskin, "The Artisanal Irony: The Mass-produced Hand-crafted Food Dilemma," *SF Weekly*, June 27, 2012. Refer also to Andrew Potter, *The Authenticity Hoax: Why the "Real" Things We Seek Don't Make Us Happy* (New York: HarperPerennial, 2011).

61. For an interesting case study of how debates over authenticity emerge, see Matteo Corciolani, "How Do Authenticity Dramas Develop? An Analysis of Afterhours Fans' Responses to the Band's Participation in the San Remo Music Festival," *Marketing Theory*, 14(2):185–206 (2014).

62. Chris Zelov, Phil Cousineau, and Brian Danitz, *Design Outlaws on the Ecological Frontier* (Hellertown, PA: Knossus Project, 2001) and L. Steven Sieden, *Buckminster Fuller's Universe: His Life and Work* (New York: Basic Books, 2000).

63. Fred Turner, *From Counterculture to Cyberculture: Stewart Brand, the Whole Earth Network, and the Rise of Digital Utopianism* (Chicago: University of

Chicago Press, 2008) and Andrew Kirk, *Counterculture Green: The Whole Earth Catalog and American Environmentalism* (Lawrence, KS: University of Kansas Press, 2007). See also Mark Dowie, *Losing Ground: American Environmentalism at the Close of the Twentieth Century* (Cambridge, MA: MIT Press, 1996).

64. Allison Artieff, "Yes We Can. But Should We?" *Medium*, September 15, 2014   (https://medium.com/re-form/just-because-you-can-doesnt-mean-you-should-252fdbcf76c8, accessed May 7, 2016).

65. Anderson, *Makers*, p. 83.

66. Hatch, *The Maker Movement Manifesto*, p. 38. Though the performance of a 3D printed gun is contested, the problems that it raises usefully highlight the challenges that ensue when there are few constraints on technologies with potentially pervasive social consequences.

67. There is little question that Anderson, and most certainly Hecht, would disagree with this contention. For example, Hecht writes that "Lowering the bar to entrepreneurialism is the most liberating, democratizing, and just thing that can be done for those who are creative, bold, and daring enough to trust their talents and try." See Hecht, *The Maker Movement Manifesto*, p. 110.

68. Jeremy Rifkin, *The Zero Marginal Cost Society: The Internet of Things, the Collaborative Commons, and the Eclipse of Capitalism* (New York: Palgrave Macmillan, 2014).

69. Anderson especially is quite explicit about this point and observes that "digital fabrication inverts the economics of traditional manufacturing. In mass production, most of the costs are in up-front tooling, and the more complicated the product is the more changes you make, the more it costs. But with digital fabrication, it's the reverse: the things that are expensive in traditional manufacturing become free." He identifies three areas where this phenomenon is at work: *variety* (it costs no more to make every product different than to make them all the same), *complexity* (a minutely detailed product, with many fiddly components, can be 3D printed as cheaply as a plain block of plastic), and *flexibility* (changing a product after production has started just means changing the instruction code). To this list we could also add the lowering of barriers to entry which means that today's successful maker-entrepreneur is likely to be supplanted by tomorrow's nascent upstart. This situation suggests a future of continuous churn and upending that will, if realized, be very different from the twentieth-century industrial model where often insurmountable obstacles to new entrants ensured relatively stable market shares. See Anderson, *Makers*, pp. 88–9.

70. David Owen, *The Conundrum: How Scientific Innovation, Increased Efficiency, and Good Intentions Can Make our Energy and Climate Problems*

Worse (New York: Riverhead Books, 2011). Some manifestations of this problem are referred to as Jevons Paradox on which there is a large body of literature. See, for example, John Polimeni, Kozo Mayumi, Mario Giampietro, and Blake Alcott, *The Jevons Paradox and the Myth of Resource Efficiency Improvements* (London: Earthscan, 2007) and Horace Herring and Steve Sorrell, *Energy Efficiency and Sustainable Consumption: The Rebound Effect* (New York: Palgrave Macmillan, 2009).

71. For an interesting statistical portrait of the sociodemographic attributes of the Maker Movement, see the video presentation by Leah Buechley at http://vimeo.com/110616469 (accessed May 7, 2016).

72. Rosner and Bean, "Making: Movement or Brand?" See also Joan Voight, "Which Big Brands Are Courting the Maker Movement, and Why: From Levi's to Home Depot," *Adweek*, March 17, 2014.

73. On the apolitical character of the Maker Movement, see Evgeny Morozov, "Making It," *The New Yorker*, January 13, 2014.

74. Kelvin Willoughby, *Technology Choice: A Critique of the Appropriate Technology Movement* (Boulder, CO: Westview Press, 1990) and Richard Sclove, *Democracy and Technology* (New York: Guilford Press, 1995). See also Adrian Smith, "Technology Networks for Socially Useful Production," *Journal of Peer Production* May 13, 2015 (http://peerproduction.net/issues/issue-5-shared-machine-shops/peer-reviewed-articles/technology-networks-for-socially-useful-production/, accessed May 22, 2016).

75. Sadowski and Manson, "3D Print your Way to Freedom and Prosperity."

76. On the distinction between ruptural transformation and ameliorative reform, see Erik Olin Wright, "Transforming Capitalism through Real Utopias," *American Sociological Review*, 78(1):1–25 (2013).

77. Jane Margolies, "Can a Pop-up Service Fix It? Probably," *The New York Times*, April 11, 2014. See also the website iFixit (http://www.ifixit.com, accessed May 7, 2016) which advocates for the "right to repair" and serves as a crowd-sourced compilation of repair manuals and technical advice.

78. Jenna Wortham, "Skillshare Raises $3.1 Million to Turn Everyone into Teachers," *The New York Times*, August 16, 2011. A leader in the field of community-based skill-sharing is the Brooklyn Brainery. See Amanda Petrusich, "You're Never Too Old to Learn Shoemaking," *The New York Times*, May 12, 2011 and Joshua Stein, "The Make-your-own Schoolhouse," *The New York Times*, April 4, 2012.

79. Jennifer Lioy, "Skills Factory," *Bellwethr Magazine* (http://bellwethrmag.com/connect/skills-factory, accessed May 7, 2016).

80. Helen Zoe Veit, "Time to Revive Home Ec," and Crawford, *Shop Class as Soulcraft*.

Chapter 5. Localization Fallacies

1. See, for example, Rob Hopkins, *The Transition Handbook: From Oil Dependency to Local Resilience* (Cambridge, MA: UIT Cambridge, 2014), John Stanton, *Democratic Sustainability in a New Era of Localism* (New York: Routledge, 2014), and David Hess, *Localist Movements in a Global Economy: Sustainability, Justice, and Urban Development in the United States* (Cambridge, MA: MIT Press, 2009).

2. One could stock a modestly sized library with the books published in recent years documenting the deeply seated problems of present-day industrial agriculture. See, for example, Michael Pollen, *The Omnivore's Dilemma: A Natural History of Four Meals* (New York: Penguin, 2007), Marion Nestle, *Food Politics: How the Food Industry Influences Nutrition and Health* (Berkeley, CA: University of California Press, 2007), Eric Schlosser, *Fast Food Nation* (New York: Harper Perennial 2005), and Gary Nabhan, *Coming Home to Eat: The Pleasures and Politics of Local Foods* (New York: Norton, 2002).

3. Lucy Jarosz, "The City in the Country: Growing Alternative Food Networks in Metropolitan Areas," *Journal of Rural Studies*, 24(3):231–44 (2008) and Elizabeth Henderson and Robyn Van En, *Sharing the Harvest: A Citizen's Guide to Community Supported Agriculture*, 2nd ed. (White River Junction, VT: Chelsea Green, 2007).

4. Claire Nettle, *Community Gardening as Social Action* (Farnham: Ashgate, 2014).

5. Roberta Sonnino, "Escaping the Local Trap: Insights on Re-localization from School Food Reform," *Journal of Environmental Policy and Planning*, 12(1):23–40 (2010) and Patricia Allen and Julie Guthman, "From 'Old School' to 'Farm-to-School': Neoliberalization from the Ground Up," *Agriculture and Human Values*, 23(4):401–15 (2006).

6. Peter Ladner, *The Urban Food Revolution: Changing the Way We Feed Cities* (Gabriola Island, BC: New Society, 2011).

7. Dickson Despommier, *The Vertical Farm: Feeding the World in the 21st Century* (New York: Picador, 2011) and Alisa Smith and J. B. Mackinnon, *The 100-Mile Diet: A Year of Eating Locally* (New York: Random House, 2007). For details on yardfarming, refer to http://yardfarmers.us (accessed May 7, 2016).

8. Sabine Hielscher, Gill Seyfang, and Adrian Smith, "Grassroots Innovations for Sustainable Energy: Exploring Niche-development Processes among Community-energy Initiatives," pp. 133–58 in Maurie Cohen, Halina Szejnwald Brown, and Philip Vergragt, eds, *Innovations in Sustainable Consumption: New Economics, Socio-technical Transitions, and Social Practices* (Northampton, MA: Edward Elgar, 2013) and Gill Seyfang and Alex Haxeltine, "Growing

Grassroots Innovations: Exploring the Role of Community-based Initiatives in Governing Sustainable Energy Transitions," *Environment and Planning C (Government and Policy)*, 30(3):381–400 (2012).

9. See, for example, Ian Bailey, Rob Hopkins, and Geoff Wilson, "Some Things Old, Some Things New: The Spatial Representations and Politics of Change of the Peak Oil Relocalisation Movement," *Geoforum*, 41(4):595–605 (2010).

10. Emilie Dubois, Juliet Schor, and Lindsey Carfagna, "New Cultures of Connection in a Boston Time Bank," pp. 95–124 in Juliet Schor and Craig Thompson, eds, *Sustainable Lifestyles and the Quest for Plenitude* (New Haven, CT: Yale University Press, 2014).

11. On the sourcing of local building materials, the Architecture Foundation of British Columbia has hosted the 100-Mile House Competition where all building materials must be obtained from within 100 miles of the city of Vancouver. See http://100mh.architecturefoundationbc.ca (accessed May 7, 2016). Regarding local eco-industrialism, see Gillian Bristow and Peter Wells, "Innovative Discourse for Sustainable Local Development: A Critical Analysis of Eco-industrialism," *International Journal of Innovation and Sustainable Development*, 1(1–2):168–79 (2005), Peter Wells and Paul Nieuwenhuis, "Business Models for Relocalisation to Deliver Sustainability," *Greener Management International*, 47:88–98 (2006), and Peter Wells and Gillian Bristow, "Embedding Eco-industrialism into Local Economies: The Search for Sustainable Business and Policy Paradigms," *Progress in Industrial Ecology*, 4(3–4):205–18 (2007). See also Allison Arieff, "The Future of Manufacturing Is Local," *The New York Times*, March 27, 2011.

12. For a discussion of localism in antiquity, see Kirkpatrick Sale, *Human Scale* (New York: Perigee Books, 1980). More recent precursors of current interest are described in, for example, Jonathan Beecher, *Charles Fourier: The Visionary and his World* (Berkeley, CA: University of California Press, 1990) and Caroline Cahm, *Kropotkin: And the Rise of Revolutionary Anarchism, 1872–1886* (New York: Cambridge University Press, 2002).

13. Sale, *Human Scale*, p. 445.

14. J. F. C. Harrison, *Robert Owen and the Owenites in Britain and America: The Quest for the New Moral World* (New York: Routledge, 2009).

15. Peter Hall and Colin Ward, *Sociable Cities: The 21st Century Reinvention of the Garden City*, 2nd ed. (New York: Routledge, 2014).

16. Helen Meller, *Patrick Geddes: Social Evolutionist and City Planner* (New York: Routledge, 1994) and Donald Miller, *Lewis Mumford: A Life* (New York: Grove Press, 2002).

17. Janet Biehl, *Ecology of Catastrophe: The Life of Murray Bookchin* (New York: Oxford University Press, 2015), Andy Price, *Recovering Bookchin* (Porsgrunn, Norway: New Compass Press, 2012), Ivan Illich, *Tools for Conviviality*

(New York: Harper and Row, 1973), Jerry Mander and Edward Goldsmith, eds, *The Case Against the Global Economy: And a Turn Toward the Local* (San Francisco, CA: Sierra Club Books, 1997), and Freddie Whitefield and Satish Kumar, eds., *Visionaries of the 20th Century: A Resurgence Anthology* (White River Junction, VT: Chelsea Green, 2006).

18. E. F. Schumacher, *Small Is Beautiful: Economics as if People Mattered* (New York: Harper Collins, 1973). See also, Barbara Wood, *Alias Papa: A Life of Fritz Schumacher* (New York: Harper and Row, 1984).

19. Karen Litfin, "Localism," pp. 156–64 in Carl Death, ed., *Critical Environmental Politics* (New York: Routledge, 2013) and Roli Varma, "E. F. Schumacher: Changing the Paradigm of Bigger Is Better," *Bulletin of Science, Technology, and Society*, 23(2):114–24 (2003).

20. Many of the points raised in the Schumacher critique were foreshadowed by Jane Jacobs in *The Death and Life of Great American Cities* (New York: Random House, 1961), Jacques Ellul, *The Technological Society* (New York: Knopf, 1964), and Donella Meadows, Dennis Meadows, Jorgen Randers, and William Behrens, *The Limits to Growth* (New York: Universe Books, 1972).

21. John Dryzek, *The Politics of the Earth: Environmental Discourses* (New York: Oxford University Press, 1997) and John Hannigan, *Environmental Sociology: A Social Constructivist Perspective* (New York: Routledge, 1995).

22. Bill McKibben, *Deep Economy: The Wealth of Communities and the Durable Future* (New York: Times Books, 2007), Richard Heinberg, *The Party's Over: Oil, War, and the Fate of Industrial Societies* (Gabriola Island, BC: New Society, 2005), and David Korten, *Change the Story, Change the Future: A Living Economy for a Living Earth* (San Francisco, CA: Berrett-Koehler, 2015).

23. Barbara Kingsolver, *Animal, Vegetable, Miracle: A Year of Food Life* (New York: Harper Collins, 2007).

24. For a discussion of the institutionalization of Schumacher's work beyond the range of these organizations, refer to John Toye, "The World Improvement Plans of Fritz Schumacher," *Cambridge Journal of Economics*, 36(2):387–403 (2012).

25. See, for example, Raymond De Young and Thomas Princen, eds, *The Localization Reader: Adapting to the Coming Downshift* (Cambridge, MA: MIT Press, 2012), Rhonda Phillips, Bruce Seifer, and Ed Antczak, *Sustainable Communities: Creating Durable Local Economy* (New York: Routledge, 2013), and Gill Seyfang, *The New Economics of Sustainable Consumption: Seeds of Change* (New York: Palgrave Macmillan, 2011).

26. The United States Department of Agriculture observes that "though 'local' has a geographic connotation, there is no consensus on a definition in terms of the distance between production and consumption. Definitions related to

geographic distance between production and sales vary by regions, companies, consumers, and local food markets." See Stephen Martinez, Michael Hand, Michelle Da Pra, Susan Pollack, Katherine Ralston, Travis Smith, Stephen Vogel, Shellye Clark, Luanne Lohr, Sarah Low, and Constance Newman, "Local Food Systems: Concepts, Impacts, and Issues," Economic Research Report EER–97 (Washington, DC: Economic Research Service, United States Department of Agriculture, 2010).

27. Michael Shuman, *Going Local: Creating Self-Reliant Communities in a Global Age* (New York: Routledge, 2000). Though commercial localization is often treated as a novel strategy for economic development this is not the case. For an illuminating discussion of the use of local spending to spur revival during the Great Depression, see Sarah Elvins, "Shopping for Recovery: Local Spending Initiatives and the Great Depression in Buffalo and Rochester, New York," *Urban History*, 29(6):670–93 (2003).

28. "Social licensing" is a common psychological feature of ostensibly "green" consumer practices and arises out of the ethical affirmation that consumers experience when purchasing an environmentally or socially ascribed product and which is then used to excuse—or give social license—to actions that are more questionable in terms of their moral valence. See, for example, Nina Mazar and Chen-Bo Zhong, "Do Green Products Make Us Better People?" *Psychological Science*, 21(4):494–8 (2010).

29. This topic has been extensively developed in the field of human geography. Refer to Sallie Marston, "The Social Construction of Scale," *Progress in Human Geography*, 24(2):219–42 (2000) and Donna Sundbo, "Local Food: The Social Construction of a Concept," *Acta Agriculturae Scandinavica (Section B: Soil and Plant Science)*, 63(S1):66–77 (2013).

30. Marston, "The Social Construction of Scale," p. 222.

31. Marston, "The Social Construction of Scale," p. 222.

32. Sundbo, "Local Food."

33. Brídín Carroll and Frances Fahy, "Locating the Locale of Local Food: The Importance of Context, Space, and Social Relations," *Renewable Agriculture and Food Systems*, 30(6):563–76 (2015).

34. The 100-mile threshold is derived from Smith and Mackinnon, *The 100-Mile Diet*. This distance apparently owes its salience to the fact that one hundred is a round number but, notably, has nothing to do with soils, watersheds, transportation infrastructure, or other arguably more consequential criteria. See Sarah DeWeerdt, "Is Local Food Better?" *World Watch Magazine*, 22(3):6–10 (2009).

35. Sundbo, "Local Food." See also Benjamin Campbell, Saneliso Mhlanga, and Isabelle Lesschaeve, "Perception versus Reality: Canadian Consumer Views of Local and Organic," *Canadian Journal of Agricultural Economics*,

61(4):531–58 (2013) and Corinna Feldmann and Ulrich Hamm, "Consumers' Perceptions and Preferences for Local Food: A Review," *Food Quality and Preference*, 40 (Part A):152–64 (2015).

36. William Lafferty, "The Politics of Sustainable Development: Global Norms for National Implementation," *Environmental Politics*, 5(2):185–208 (1996).

37. Angela Meah and Matt Watson, "Cooking up Consumer Anxieties about 'Provenance' and 'Ethics,'" *Food, Culture, and Society*, 16(3):495–512 (2013).

38. In a widely disseminated study by Christopher Weber and H. Scott Matthews, transportation was found to account for 11 percent of the carbon emissions associated with an average American diet and 83 percent of associated releases occur before shipment from the farm. See Christopher Weber and H. Scott Matthews, "Food-miles and the Relative Climate Impacts of Food Choices in the United States," *Environmental Science and Technology*, 42(10):3508–13 (2008).

39. While most LCAs are expensive to produce and require expert assistance to interpret, researchers at the University of California at Berkeley have developed an easy-to-use tool called the GoodGuide that can be downloaded to a smartphone for free and used to access data and rankings on thousands of consumer products. See http://www.goodguide.com (accessed May 7, 2016).

40. Tom Waas, Jean Hugé, Thomas Block, Tarah Wright, Francisco Benitez-Capistros, and Aviel Verbruggen, "Sustainability Assessment and Indicators: Tools in a Decision-making Strategy for Sustainable Development," *Sustainability*, 6(9):5512–34 (2014). See also Maurie Cohen and Jeff Howard, "Success and its Price: The Institutionalization and Political Relevance of Industrial Ecology," *Journal of Industrial Ecology*, 10(2):1–2 (2006).

41. Annika Carlsson-Kanyama, "Food Consumption Patterns and their Influence on Climate Change," *Ambio*, 27(7):528–34. For an especially ambitious project, see Kirk Johnson, "Closing the Farm-to-table Gap in Alaska," *The New York Times*, January 3, 2016.

42. See, for example, Elinor Hallström, Elin Röös, and Pal Börjesson, "Sustainable Meat Consumption: A Quantitative Analysis of Nutritional Intake, Greenhouse Gas Emissions, and Land Use from a Swedish Perspective," *Food Policy*, 47:81–90 (2014) and Fredrik Hedenus, Stefan Wirsenius, and Daniel Johansson, "The Importance of Reduced Meat and Dairy Consumption for Meeting Stringent Climate Change Targets," *Climatic Change*, 124(1–2):79–91 (2014). Refer also to Denis Hayes and Gail Boyer Hayes, *Cowed: The Hidden Impact of 93 Million Cows on America's Health, Economy, Politics, Culture, and Environment* (New York: W. W. Norton, 2015).

43. See, for example, Charles Levkoe, "Towards a Transformative Food Politics," *Local Environment*, 16(7):687–705 (2011) and Brian Obach and Kathleen

Tobin, "Civic Agriculture and Community Engagement," *Agriculture and Human Values*, 31(2):307–22 (2014).

44. For a useful critique of localism that echoes much of what is described here, see Mi Park, "Imagining a Just and Sustainable Society: A Critique of Alternative Economic Models in the Global Justice Movement," *Critical Sociology*, 39(1):65–85 (2013).

45. It is important to note that for small farms direct-to-consumer sales can be a significant share of total annual income. See Sarah Low and Stephen Vogel, "Direct and Intermediated Marketing of Local Foods in the United States," EER Report No. 128 (Washington, DC: Economic Research Service, United States Department of Agriculture, 2011).

46. J. Christopher Brown and Mark Purcell, "There's Nothing Inherent about Scale: Political Ecology, the Local Trap, and the Politics of Development in the Brazilian Amazon," *Geoforum*, 36(5):607–24 (2005), p. 608. See also Branden Born and Mark Purcell, "Avoiding the Local Trap: Scale and Food Systems in Planning Research," *Journal of Planning Education and Research*, 26(2):195–207 (2006).

47. Brown and Purcell, "There's Nothing Inherent about Scale," p. 609.

48. Prior to the popularization of this term, Clare Hinrichs coined the expression the "perilous trap of the local" and Marcia Campbell wrote about "defensive localization." See Claire Hinrichs, "The Practice and Politics of Food System Localization," *Journal of Rural Studies*, 19(1):33–45 (2003) and Marcia Campbell, "Building a Common Table: The Role of Planning in Community Food Systems," *Journal of Planning Education and Research*, 23(4):341–55 (2004).

49. Born and Purcell, "Avoiding the Local Trap," pp. 195–6.

50. See, for example, E. Melanie DuPuis and David Goodman, "Should We Go 'Home' to Eat? Toward a Reflexive Politics of Localism," *Journal of Rural Studies*, 21(3):359–71 (2005).

51. Hinrichs, "The Practice and Politics of Food System Localization."

52. See, for example, Julie Guthman, "Neoliberalism and the Making of Food Politics in California," *Geoforum*, 39(3):1171–83 (2008) and Allen and Guthman, "From 'Old School' to 'Farm-to-School.'"

53. Sonnino, "Escaping the Local Trap," p. 24.

54. Born and Purcell, "Avoiding the Local Trap," p. 196.

55. Richard Andrews. *Managing the Environment, Managing Ourselves: A History of American Environmental Policy*, 2nd ed. (New Haven, CT: Yale University Press, 2006).

56. Hess, *Localist Movements in the Global Economy*.

57. Jeffrey Ayres and Michael Bosia, "Beyond Global Summitry: Food Sovereignty as Localized Resistance to Globalization," *Globalizations*, 8(1):47–63 (2011).

58. Craig Thompson and Gokcen Coskuner-Balli, "Enchanting Ethical Consumerism: The Case of Community Supported Agriculture," *Journal of Consumer Culture*, 7(3):275–303 (2007).

59. Simin Davoudi and Ali Madanipour, "Introduction," pp. 1–4 in Simon Davoudi and Ali Madanipour, eds, *Reconsidering Localism* (New York: Routledge, 2015). It is also useful to acknowledge the modes of libertarian-anarchist localism (sometimes termed "negative localism") that are mobilized by, for instance, the "Prepper Movement" in the United States which envisions social decline brought on by various environmental and resource emergencies and emphasizes military-like readiness, survivalism, and stockpiling of food provisions and gasoline. Refer to Keith O'Brien, "How to Survive Societal Collapse in Suburbia," *The New York Times Magazine*, November 16, 2012.

60. See, for example, Kenneth MacDonald, "The Morality of Cheese: A Paradox of Defensive Localism in a Transnational Cultural Economy," *Geoforum*, 44:93–102 (2013).

61. Greg Sharzer, *No Local: Why Small-Scale Alternatives Won't Change the World* (Alresford, Hants: Zero Books, 2011). See also Robin Hahnel, "Eco-localism: A Constructive Critique," *Capitalism Nature Socialism*, 18(2):62–78 (2007) and Gregory Albo, "The Limits of Eco-localism: Scale, Strategy, Socialism," *Socialist Register*, 43:1–27 (2007).

62. Sharzer, *No Local*, p. 2.

63. Sharzer, *No Local*, p. 3.

64. Sharzer, *No Local*, p. 24.

65. Sharzer, *No Local*, p. 24.

66. Sharzer, *No Local*, p. 39.

67. Sharzer, *No Local*, p. 55.

68. Sharzer, *No Local*, p. 73.

69. Sharzer, *No Local*, p. 89.

70. Pierre Bourdieu, *Distinction: A Social Critique of Judgement of Taste* (Cambridge, MA: Harvard University Press, 1984).

71. Sharzer, *No Local*, pp. 91–3.

72. Michael Maniates, "Individualization: Plant a Tree, Buy a Bike, Save the World?," pp. 43–66 in Thomas Princen, Michael Maniates, and Ken Conca, eds, *Confronting Consumption* (Cambridge, MA: MIT Press, 2002), p. 45.

73. Maniates, "Individualization: Plant a Tree, Buy a Bike, Save the World?," p. 45.

74. For a discussion of how this process is operationalized in the Slow Food movement, see Luca Simonetti, "The Ideology of Slow Food," *Journal of European Studies*, 42(2):168–89 (2012) and Sam Binkley, "Liquid Consumption: Anti-consumerism and the Fetishized De-fetishization of Commodities," *Cultural Studies*, 22(5):599–623 (2008).

75. Sharzer, *No Local*, pp. 99–100.

76. For example, Sharzer writes that "industrial towns were often centers of intense class struggle between owners and workers. Not coincidentally, industrial towns created close community networks forged in that struggle. These close-knit communities of workers also demonstrated all the values of collective self-sacrifice, yet localists never mention them, preferring fuzzy invocations of consumerist fantasy." Sharzer, *No Local*, p. 100.

77. Nicholas Iuviene and Lily Song, "Leveraging Rooted Institutions: A Strategy for Cooperative Economic Development in Cleveland, Ohio," pp. 58–92 in Lorlene Hoyt, ed., *Transforming Cities and Minds through the Scholarship of Engagement: Economy, Equity, and Environment* (Nashville, TN: Vanderbilt University Press, 2013), Jennie Stephens and Stephen McCauley, "Clusters in Transition: Analysis of a Sustainable Energy-cluster Initiative in Worcester, Massachusetts, USA," pp. 179–205 in Maurie Cohen, Halina Szejnwald Brown, and Philip Vergragt, eds, *Innovations in Sustainable Consumption: New Economics, Socio-technical Transitions, and Social Practices* (Northampton, MA: Edward Elgar, 2013), and Francesca Forno, Cristina Grasseni, and Silvana Signori, "Italy's Solidarity Purchase Groups as "Citizenship Labs," pp. 67–88 in Emily Huddart Kennedy, Maurie Cohen, and Naomi Krogman, eds, *Putting Sustainability into Practice: Applications and Advances in Research on Sustainable Consumption* (Northampton, MA: Edward Elgar, 2016).

78. Forno et al., "Italy's Solidarity Purchase Groups as "Citizenship Labs," pp. 84–5.

79. See, for example, René Kemp, Johan Schot, and Remco Hoogma, "Regime Shifts to Sustainability through Processes of Niche Formation: The Approach of Strategic Niche Management," *Technology Analysis and Strategic Management*, 10(2):175–95 (1998) and Frank Geels, *Technological Transitions and Systems Innovation: A Co-evolutionary and Socio-technical Analysis* (Northampton, MA: Edward Elgar, 2005).

80. As Peter North contends, the contemporary economy is far more imperfect than most Marxist analysis allows. He observes that "arguing that all productive or economic units are inevitably capitalist or growth-oriented 'businesses' is like assuming all women are maternal or child-oriented. Some 'businesses' do focus on growth, but there is a much greater diversity in economic forms." See Peter North, "Eco-localisation as a Progressive Response to Peak Oil and Climate Change: A Sympathetic Critique," *Geoforum*, 41(4):585–94 (2010).

81. Peter Hall and David Soskice, eds., *Varieties of Capitalism: The Institutional Foundations of Comparative Advantage* (New York: Oxford University Press, 2001). See also Erik Olin Wright, "Transforming Capitalism through Real Utopias," *American Sociological Review*, 78(1):1–25 (2013) and J. K. Gibson-Graham, *The*

End of Capitalism (As We Knew It): A Feminist Critique of Political Economy (Minneapolis: University of Minnesota Press, 2006).

82. William Rees, *Avoiding Collapse: An Agenda for Sustainable Degrowth and Relocalizing the Economy* (Vancouver: Canadian Centre for Policy Alternatives, 2014).

83. For instance, Karen Liftin contends that localization "might arguably be the only viable game in town" for reconfiguring affluent consumer society in accordance with biophysical limits, but also observes that it is an efficacious strategy only if it is pursued under the umbrella of global solidarity. Litfin, "Localism," pp. 159–61.

84. John Friedman and Clyde Weaver, *Territory and Function: The Evolution of Regional Planning* (Berkeley, CA: University of California Press, 1979).

85. Quoted in Robert Dorman, *Revolt of the Provinces: The Regionalist Movement in America, 1920–1945* (Chapel Hill, NC: University of North Carolina Press, 2003), p. 53. See also Mark Luccarelli, *Lewis Mumford and the Ecological Region: The Politics of Planning* (New York: Guilford Press, 1995).

86. James Howard Kunstler, *The Long Emergency: Surviving the End of Oil, Climate Change, and Other Converging Catastrophes of the Twenty-First Century* (New York: Grove Press, 2006), Christopher Steiner, *$20 Per Gallon: How the Inevitable Rise in the Price of Gasoline Will Change our Lives for the Better* (New York: Grand Central, 2010), Richard Heinberg, *Peak Everything: Waking up to the Century of Declines* (Gabriola Island, BC: New Society, 2010), and Stan Cox, *Any Way You Slice It: The Past, Present, and Future of Rationing* (New York: New Press, 2013).

87. Sharzer, *No Local*, pp. 76–9.

88. For discussions of neolocalism and local-living economies, see Julian Lamb and Karen Leach, "The Credit Crisis: A Golden Opportunity to Extend Localisation and Stimulate Genuinely Sustainable Local Economic Development," *International Journal of Green Economics*, 5(2):204–12 (2011), Steven Schnell, "Deliberate Identities: Becoming Local in America in a Global Age," *Journal of Cultural Geography*, 30(1):55–89 (2013), James Gustave Speth, "Beyond the Growth Paradigm: Creating a Unified Progressive Politics," *Development*, 56(2):202–7 (2013), and Korten, *Change the Story, Change the Future*.

Chapter 6. Consumption in the Era of Digital Automation

1. Karl Polanyi, *The Great Transformation: The Political and Economic Origins of Our Time* (Boston, MA: Beacon Press, 2001 [1944]), Daniel Bell, *The Coming of Post-industrial Society: A Venture in Social Forecasting* (New York: Basic

Books, 1976), and Krishan Kumar, *From Post-industrial to Post-modern Society: New Theories of the Contemporary World* (Malden, MA: Blackwell, 1995).

2. Notable exceptions include Paul Ransome, *Work, Consumption, and Culture: Affluence and Social Change in the Twenty-first Century* (Thousand Oaks, CA: Sage, 2005), George Ritzer, *Enchanting a Disenchanted World: Continuity and Change in the Cathedrals of Consumption*, 3rd ed. (Thousand Oaks, CA: Sage, 2009), and Justin Lewis, *Beyond Consumer Capitalism: Media and the Limits to Imagination* (Malden, MA: Polity, 2013).

3. David Harvey, *A Brief History of Neoliberalism* (New York: Oxford University Press, 2007).

4. For overviews of theories of social change, see Trevor Noble, *Social Theory and Social Change* (New York: Palgrave Macmillan, 2000), Jay Weinstein, *Social Change*, 3rd ed. (Lanham, MD: Rowman and Littlfield, 2010), and Garth Massey, *Ways of Social Change: Making Sense of Modern Times*, 2nd ed. (Thousand Oaks, CA: Sage, 2015).

5. It also merits noting that the boundaries between unalloyed forms of production and consumption have been shifting over time and becoming more and more difficult to distinguish. This fusing between the two domains is captured by the notion of prosumption originally coined in the 1970s. See Alvin Toffler, *Future Shock* (New York: Random House, 1970).

6. Thomas Friedman, "If I Had a Hammer," *The New York Times*, January 11, 2014 and Erik Brynnjolfson and Andrew McAfee, *The Second Machine Age: Work, Progress, and Prosperity in a Time of Brilliant Technologies* (New York: W. W. Norton, 2014). See also Jaron Lanier, *Who Owns the Future?* (New York: Simon and Schuster, 2013), James Barrat, *Our Final Invention: Artificial Intelligence and the End of the Human Era* (New York: St. Martin's, 2013), and Nick Bostrom, *Superintelligence: Paths, Dangers, Strategies* (New York: Oxford University Press, 2014).

7. The challenges raised by this wave of technologies were first highlighted by futures-oriented social theorists during the mid-1990s. See, for example, Stanley Aronowitz and William DiFazio, *The Jobless Future* (Minneapolis: University of Minnesota Press, 1994) and Jeremy Rifkin, *The End of Work: The Decline of the Global Labor Force and the Dawn of the Post-Market Era* (New York: G. P. Putnam's Sons, 1995).

8. Brynnjolfson and McAfee, *The Second Machine Age*, pp. 7–8.

9. Jerry Kaplan, *Humans Need Not Apply: A Guide to Wealth and Work in the Age of Artificial Intelligence* (New Haven, CT: Yale University Press, 2015), pp. 39–40.

10. The number of certified public accountants in the United States has declined by an estimated 17 percent over the past decade, a development that is largely attributed to the advent of automated tax-preparation software. See also

William Dennis Huber, "The History of the Decline and Fall of the American Accounting Profession," *International Journal of Economics and Accounting* 4(4):365–88 (2013). In a related development, the number of students applying to law school has fallen by 40 percent over the same period. Jacob Gershman, "Law School Applicant Pool Still Shrinking," *The Wall Street Journal*, April 23, 2015.

11. Martin Ford, *Rise of the Robots: Technology and the Threat of a Jobless Future* (New York: Basic Books, 2015), p. 95.

12. Carl Benedikt Frey and Michael Osborne, "The Future of Employment: How Susceptible Are Jobs to Computerisation?" Oxford: Programme on the Impacts of Future Technology, Oxford Martin School.

13. Ford writes that "the idea that technology might someday truly transform the job market and ultimately demand fundamental changes to both our economic system and the social contract remains either completely unacknowledged or at the very fringes of public discourse ... among practitioners of economics and finance there is often almost reflexive tendency to dismiss anyone who argues that this time might be different." The general understanding among economists is, briefly stated, that technology creates new jobs at more or less the same rate that it destroys old ones. While there may be a lag over the long term, the orthodox view across the discipline is that technology does not induce structural unemployment. Over the last couple of years, several prominent economists have broken from this interpretation. See, in particular, Lawrence Summers, "Lawrence H. Summers on the Economic Challenge of the Future: Jobs," *The Wall Street Journal*, July 7, 2014 and Paul Krugman, "Sympathy for the Luddites," *The New York Times*, June 13, 2013.

14. John Maynard Keynes, *Essays in Persuasion* (New York: W. W. Norton, 1963), pp. 358–73.

15. Kirkpatrick Sale, *Rebels Against the Future: The Luddites and Their War on the Industrial Revolution—Lessons for the Computer Age* (New York: Basic Books, 1996).

16. It is important not to lose sight of already institutionalized ways to supplement incomes, most notably through partial or fully subsidized provision of public goods and services such as education, transportation, and healthcare.

17. All of the concepts discussed below are traceable to the foundational insights of former law professor, political economist, and investment banker Lewis Kelso who advocated for giving workers greater opportunity to accumulate wealth derived from the improving productivity of technology. See Louis Kelso and Mortimer Adler, *The Capitalist Manifesto* (New York: Random House, 1958). See also Robert Ashford, Ralph Hall, and Nicholas Ashford, "Broadening Capital Acquisition with Earnings of Capital as a Means of

Sustainable Growth and Environmental Sustainability," *The European Financial Review*, October/November: 70–4 (2012).

18. Authors and other policy proponents deploy a variety of terms to describe the same fundamental idea including unconditional basic income, guaranteed basic income, guaranteed minimum income, and citizen's wage. The notion of a negative income tax is a similar strategy but does not entail a direct cash payment.

19. Brian Steensland, *The Failed Welfare Revolution: America's Struggle over Guaranteed Income Policy* (Princeton, NJ: Princeton University Press, 2007) and Allan Sheahen, *Basic Income Guarantee: Your Right to Economic Security* (New York: Palgrave Macmillan, 2012).

20. Philippe Van Parijs, *Arguing for Basic Income: Ethical Foundations for a Radical Reform* (New York: Verso, 1992) and Bruce Ackerman and Anne Alstott, *The Stakeholder Society* (New Haven, CT: Yale University Press, 1999).

21. David Wheeler, "What if Everybody Didn't Have to Work to Get Paid?" *The Atlantic*, May 18, 2015.

22. On the progressive side in the United States, UBI is championed by organizations like the U.S. Basic Income Guarantee Network (http://www.usbig. net, accessed May 9, 2016). The concept has also received the support of David Frum, former speechwriter for George W. Bush. See David Frum, "A Rule for Conservative Anti-poverty Plans: Keep It Simple," *The Atlantic*, July 31, 2014. Refer also to Charles Murray, *In Our Hands: A Plan to Replace the Welfare State* (Washington, DC: AEI Press, 2006) and Yuval Levin, "A Conservative Governing Vision," pp. 15–21 in *Room to Grow* (Washington, DC: YG Network, 2014) (http://conservativereform.com/wp-content/uploads/2014/05/Room-To-Grow.pdf, accessed May 9, 2016).

23. Jon Stone, "British Parliament to Consider Motion on Universal Basic Income," *Independent*, January 20, 2016 and Judith Shulevitz, "It's Payback Time for Women," *The New York Times*, January 8, 2016. At the international level, the leading campaign organization is the Basic Income Earth Network (formerly the Basic Income European Network). See http://www. basicincome.org (accessed May 9, 2016).

24. Philippe Van Parijs, "Basic Income: A Simple and Powerful Idea for the Twenty-first Century," *Politics and Society*, 32(1):7–39 (2004).

25. Peter Barnes, *With Liberty and Dividends for All: How to Save Our Middle Class When Jobs Don't Pay Enough* (San Francisco, CA: Berrett-Koehler, 2014).

26. See http://www.apfc.org/home/Content/dividend/dividendamounts.cfm (accessed May 9, 2016) for a record of annual APF disbursements since 1982.

27. The concept of the citizen's dividend was initially formulated over a half a century ago by the aforementioned Louis Kelso who developed a plan for a general stock ownership trust in the 1980s for Alaska that nearly became the model used instead of APF. For the general theory, see Kelso and Adler, *The Capitalist Manifesto*. The details of the plan are set out in Louis Kelso and Patricia Hetter Kelso, *Democracy and Economic Power* (Cambridge, MA: Ballinger, 1986).

28. Matthew Riddle, "Cap and Dividend: Carbon Revenue as Common Wealth," pp. 73-91 in James Boyce, ed., *Economics, the Environment, and Our Common Wealth* (Northampton, MA: Edward Elgar, 2012).

29. Peter Barnes, Robert Costanza, Paul Hawken, David Orr, Elinor Ostrom, Alvaro Umaña, and Oran Young, "Creating an Earth Atmospheric Trust," *Science*, 319(5864):724 (2008).

30. Barnes explains how California's cap-and-trade initiative for reducing greenhouse-gas emissions has effectively evolved into a "climate dividend" program. See, *With Liberty and Dividends for All*, pp. 117-18. He also describes several other schemes in the United States and elsewhere that achieve similar ends (pp. 128-9). Refer also to Joshua Farley, Robert Costanza, Gary Flomenhoft, and Daniel Kirk, "The Vermont Common Assets Trust: An Institution for Sustainable, Just and Efficient Resource Allocation," *Ecological Economics* 109:71-9 (2015).

31. Joseph Blasi, Richard Freeman, and Douglas Kruse, *The Citizen's Share: Reducing Inequality in the 21st Century* (New Haven, CT: Yale University Press, 2013). Blasi and colleagues demonstrate that broad-based stock (or property) ownership is not a new idea in the United States but such a policy has been endorsed by national leaders since the earliest days of the country as well as during the nineteenth and twentieth century by several renowned industrialists including John Rockefeller, George Eastman, William Cooper Procter, and Henry Ford. Earlier proponents expressed concern about the perverse effects of wealth concentration on democratic governance while latter supporters were attracted to the idea out of a desire to ensure sufficient consumer-purchasing capacity for manufactured outputs.

32. Emmanuel Saez, "Striking it Richer: The Evolution of Top Incomes in the United States (Updated with 2011 Estimates)," Berkeley, CA: Department of Economics, University of California Berkeley, 2013 (http://eml.berkeley.edu//~saez/saez-UStopincomes-2011.pdf, accessed May 9, 2016).

33. Richard Freeman and Joseph Blasi, "What the Founding Fathers Believed: Stock Ownership for All," *PBS Newshour*, November 15, 2013 (http://www pbs.org/newshour/making-sense/what-the-founding-fathers-beli,   accessed May 9, 2016).

34. The ESOP was another idea originally developed by Lewis Kelso. See Blasi et al., *The Citizen's Share*, pp. 167–94.

35. The Georgetown study reports that there were 149.9 million jobs in the United States at the end of 2015. In the absence of the Great Recession, the authors estimate that the American economy would have developed to support 155.3 million jobs. The figure of 6.4 million is calculated as the difference between these two figures. Anthony Carnevale, Tamara Jayasundera, and Artem Gulish, "Six Million Missing Jobs: The Lingering Pain of the Great Recession," Washington, DC: Georgetown University, Center on Education and the Workforce, 2015.

36. Amy Scott, "A Degree in Hand, but a Slow Start up the Career Ladder," *The New York Times*, March 24, 2014. It furthermore warrants mentioning that the official unemployment rate also does not count former workers who have ceased to actively seek a new job.

37. Thomas Geoghegan, *Only One Thing Can Save Us: Why America Needs a New Kind of Labor Movement* (New York: New Press, 2014) and Kim Phillips-Fein, "Why Workers Won't Unite," *The Atlantic*, April, 2015. In addition, much has been written about the tendency of the millennial generation to shun politics. The United States, though, faces more pervasive problems of political disengagement that are attributable to restrictions on electoral participation (both through intimidation and voting access) and the gerrymandering of electoral districts, as well as to self-imposed withdrawal due to disaffection and alienation. For a recent profile of the situation in one part of the country, see Alec MacGillis, "Who Turned my Blue State Red?" *The New York Times*, November 20, 2015.

38. Nathan Schneider, "Owning Is the New Sharing," *Shareable*, December 21, 2014 (http://www.shareable.net/blog/owning-is-the-new-sharing, accessed May 9, 2016), Trebor Scholz, "Platform Cooperativism vs. the Sharing Economy," *Medium*, December 5, 2014 (https://medium.com/@trebors/platform-cooperativism-vs-the-sharing-economy-2ea737f1b5ad#.dj2j99i3m, accessed May 9, 2016), and Trebor Scholz, *Platform Cooperativism: Challenging the Corporate Sharing Economy* (New York: Rosa Luxemburg Stiftung–New York Office, 2016) (http://www.rosalux-nyc.org/wp-content/files_mf/scholz_platformcooperativism_2016.pdf, accessed May 9, 2016). See also Neal Gorenflo, "How Platform Coops Can Beat Death Stars," *Shareable*, November 3, 2015 (http://www.shareable.net/blog/how-platform-coops-can-beat-death-stars-like-uber-to-create-a-real-sharing-economy, accessed May 9, 2016).

39. An example of open-source software to support the establishment of sharing networks is Sharetribe (https://www.sharetribe.com, accessed May 9, 2016). See also Nina Misuraca Ignaczak, "3 Platforms to Start your Own Sharing Service," *Shareable*, April 22, 2014 (http://www.

shareable.net/blog/3-platforms-to-start-your-own-sharing-service, accessed May 9, 2016).

40. Cooperativism over the last few years has attracted a growing number of people associated with sustainability scholarship and advocacy. See Sonja Novkovic and Tom Webb, eds, *Co-operatives in a Post-Growth Era* (London: Zed Books, 2014). Refer also to John Restakis, *Co-operatives in the Age of Capital* (Garbiola Island, BC: New Society, 2010), John Curl, *For All the People: Uncovering the Hidden History of Cooperation, Cooperative Movements, and Communalism in America*, 2nd ed. (Oakland, CA: PM Press, 2012), and Tom Malleson, *After Occupy: Economic Democracy for the 21st Century* (New York: Oxford University Press, 2014).

41. Victor Pestoff, "Local Economic Democracy and Multi-stakeholder Cooperatives," *Journal of Rural Cooperation*, 23(2):151–67 (1995), p. 158. Pestoff is critical of consumer cooperatives because the financial stake on the part of members is typically quite nominal and insufficient to engender a sustained ownership commitment.

42. Pestoff traces this polarization within the cooperative movement to the conference of the International Cooperative Alliance held in 1895. He describes how the French delegation argued at the conclave for the practice of "co-partnership" between producers and consumers as a requirement for membership. However, the so-called "Anglo-Saxon view" of single-stakeholder cooperativism prevailed and continues to be dominant today. See Pestoff, "Local Economic Democracy and Multi-stakeholder Cooperatives," p. 158.

43. Multi-stakeholder cooperatives have management structures that allow for the direct participation of more than one category of stakeholder and the specific model referred to here is sometimes known as a "worker–consumer hybrid." Other types could include some or all of the following that contribute to the co-production of the organization: suppliers, professional managers, investors, local community members, and government representatives. Some commentators also conceive of the full range of stakeholders as comprising society at large and both past and future generations. See Yair Levi, "Beyond Traditional Models: Multi-stakeholder Cooperatives and their Differential Roles," *Journal of Rural Cooperation*, 26(1–2):49–64 (1998), Yair Levi, "From the 'Double Nature' of Cooperation to the Social Economy: Fifty Years of Associationalism," *International Review of Sociology*, 16(1):149–63 (2006), and Martine Vézina and Jean-Pierre Girard, "Multi-stakeholder Co-operative Model as a Flexible Sustainable Framework for Collective Entrepreneurship: An International Perspective," pp. 64–78 in Caroline Guselinckx, Li Zhao, and Sonja Novkovic, eds, *Co-operative Innovations in China and the West* (New York: Palgrave Macmillan, 2014).

44. Mondragón is a large corporation that encompasses numerous worker-owned cooperatives and some businesses, notably Eroski, which is owned by both workers and consumers. For further discussion of the firm see David Thompson, "Mondragon's Eroski as a Mass Retailer," *Cooperative Grocer*, 97: November/December, 2001 (http://www.grocer.coop/articles/mondragons-eroski-mass-retailer, accessed May 9, 2016). For case studies, see Giamcomo Manetti and Simone Toccafondi, "The Contribution of Network Governance to Preventing Opportunistic Behaviour by Managers and to Increasing Stakeholder Involvement: The Eroski Case," *International Journal of Business Governance and Ethics*, 7(3):252–78 (2012), John Storey, Imanol Basterretxea, and Graeme Salaman, "Managing the Resisting 'Degeneration' in Employee-owned Businesses: A Comparative Study of Two Large Retailers in Spain and the United Kingdom," *Organization*, 21(5):626–44 (2014), and Saioa Arando, Monica Gago, Derek Jones, and Takao Kato, "Efficiency in Employee-owned Enterprises: An Econometric Case Study of Mondragón," *Industrial and Labor Relations Review*, 68(2):398–425 (2015). On Mondragón more generally, see William Foote Whyte and Kathleen King Whyte, *Making Mondragón: The Growth and Dynamics of the Worker Cooperative Complex* (Ithaca, NY: ILR Press, 2014).

45. Grupo Eroski: Company Profile, Information, Business Description, History, Background Information on Grupo Eroski, Reference for Business (http://www.referenceforbusiness.com/history2/84/Grupo-Eroski.html, accessed May 9, 2016).

46. See http://www.weaverstreetmarket.coop (accessed May 9, 2016). The cooperative also ran a restaurant until it was closed in 2013.

47. Chris Quinn, "Weaver Street Market: A Modern Day Co-op Story," *Cooperative Grocer*, 21 (February/March) (1989) (http://www.grocer.coop/articles/weaver-street-market-modern-day-co-op-story, accessed May 9, 2016).

48. Another example of a successful worker–consumer cooperative is the Black Star Co-op, a "neighborhood beer bar" in Austin, Texas. According to its website, at the end of 2013, the cooperative had 27 staff workers (17 of whom had voting rights) and 3,200 member–owners. See http://www.blackstar.coop/cooperate/#/history (accessed May 9, 2016).

49. A useful resource on the myriad details of establishing worker–consumer cooperatives is Margaret Lund, *Solidarity as a Business Model: A Multi-Stakeholder Cooperatives Manual* (Kent, OH: Kent State University, Cooperative Development Center, 2011).

50. For example, Luigi Mittone and Matteo Ploner, "Cooperative Attitudes among Workers in Social Cooperatives: Evidence from an Artefactual Field Experiment," *Voluntas*, 26(2):510–30 (2015).

51. Ways to circumvent this problem would be to work less, deposit the difference in a non-lending financial institution, or destroy the surplus cash. On rebound

effects more generally, see for example, David Owen, *The Conundrum: How Scientific Innovation, Increased Efficiency, and Good Intentions Can Make our Energy and Climate Problems Worse* (New York: Riverhead Books, 2011).

52. Some scholars of the cooperative movement also point to cultural barriers that make more solidarisitic organizational forms difficult to establish and maintain in the United States in comparison to, say, the Basque region of Spain. A contrasting perspective suggests that the relatively low rate of formation in the country reflects a generally low level of familiarity with cooperative modes of business organization.

53. Storey et al., "Managing and Resisting 'Degeneration' in Employee-owned Businesses." See also Philip Whyman, "Cooperative Principles and the Evolution of the 'Dismal Science': The Historical Interaction between Co-operative and Mainstream Economics," *Business History*, 54(6):833–54 (2012) and Baleren Bakaikoa, Anjel Errasti, and Agurtzane Begiristain, "Governance of the Mondragón Corporación Cooperativa," *Annals of Public and Cooperative Economics*, 75(1):61–87 (2004). For a more optimistic appraisal of the success of worker cooperatives, refer to Erik Olsen, "The Relative Survival of Worker Cooperatives and Barriers to their Creation," *Advances in the Economic Analysis of Participatory and Labor-Managed Firms*, 14:84–107 (2013).

54. See, for example, Frank Shipper, *Shared Entrepreneurship: A Path to Engaged Employee Ownership* (New York: Palgrave Macmillan, 2014).

55. An instance of the direct decision-making model applied to a worker coopera-tive, is Isthmus Engineering & Manufacturing, a Wisconsin-based company with several hundred worker–owners that designs and builds custom automa-tion equipment. For details on the company see http://www.isthmuseng.com (accessed May 9, 2016). Refer also to Michael Billeaux, Anne Reynolds, Trevor Young-Hyman, Ayca Zayim, "Worker Cooperative Case Study: Isthmus Engineering & Manufacturing," Madison, WI: University of Wisconsin Center for Cooperatives, 2011. Some worker cooperatives actively encourage extensive participation with all worker–owners voting on the admission of new members because democratic socialization is deemed essential to ensure a high level of expected performance. An example is Equal Exchange, a worker-owned cooperative that specializes in the sourcing and distribution of fair trade products. This case is described in Benita Harris, Frank Shipper, Karen Manz, and Charles Manz, "Equal Exchange: Doing Well by Doing Good," pp. 119–32 in Michael Hitt, R. Duane Ireland, and Robert Hoskisson, eds, *Strategic Management: Competitiveness and Globalization (Concepts and Cases)*, 11th ed. (Stamford, CT: Cengage Learning, 2015). See also http://equalexchange.coop (accessed May 9, 2016). The representative democracy model is exemplified by Amsted Industries, a Chicago-headquartered

federation of worker-owned companies that manufactures railroad and vehicular equipment and construction and industrial products. See http://www.amsted.com (accessed May 9, 2016). It is also a feature of the Mondragón Corporation as detailed in Whyte and Whyte, *Making Mondragón*.

56. The Mondragón Corporation was able to overcome the credit problem by establishing its own cooperative bank at an early point in its development and in the United States the National Cooperative Bank has played a similar role.

57. Tim Palmer, *Democratic Workplace Ownership after the Great Recession* (San Francisco, CA: Democracy at Work Institute, 2013).

58. This characterization excludes consumer cooperatives in the utility sector (especially electricity), housing, and banking, which in the United States are either heavily subsidized by the federal government or receive special regulatory treatment. A 2005 survey identified 9,346 credit unions (86 million members), 930 electric utility cooperatives (37 million members), and 7,500 housing cooperatives (1.2 million households) (http://www.uwcc.wisc.edu/info/stats/uscoopbus05.pdf, accessed May 9, 2016).

59. See http://www.uwcc.wisc.edu/info/stats/uscoopbus05.pdf (accessed May 22, 2016). The largest consumer cooperative in the United States is Seattle-based Recreational Equipment, Inc., a retailer of outdoor equipment and related supplies, with more than two million members.

60. Blasi et al., *The Citizen's Share*, p. 162. This strategy does not provide any special advantage to the consumption side of worker–consumer cooperatives. One possibility is that the federal government could offer financial assistance as has historically been the case for utility and housing cooperatives in the United States.

61. David Stroh, *Systems Thinking for Social Change: A Practical Guide to Solving Complex Problems, Avoiding Unintended Consequences, and Achieving Lasting Results* (White River Junction, VT: Chelsea Green, 2015).

62. Hilary Abell, "Worker Cooperatives: Pathways to Scale," Takoma Park, MD: Democracy Collaborative, 2014 (http://community-wealth.org/sites/clone.community-wealth.org/files/downloads/WorkerCoops-PathwaysToScale.pdf, accessed May 9, 2016). Peter Barnes characterizes the problem in incisive terms when he writes, "The middle class as a whole lacks a sense of identity. It's split into subgroups—workers in various industries, seniors, students, farmers, minorities, and so on—each of which identifies more with its own agenda than with a unifying goal. This makes the middle class extremely difficult to organize." Quoted in Barnes, *With Liberty and Dividends for All*, p. 132.

63. Union membership in the United States has declined from 20.1 percent of all waged and salaried workers in 2004 to 11.1 percent in 2014. See http://www.

bls.gov/opub/ted/2015/union-membership-rate-in-private-industry-and-public-sector-in-2014.htm (accessed May 9, 2016). There are, though, notable differences in the extent of unionization in the United States between workers in the private and public sectors. While the rate of union membership among private sector workers was 6.6 percent in 2014, among public sector employees it was 35.7 percent.

64. For a useful review of the historical relationship between labor unions and cooperatives in the United States, refer to Dan Bell, "Worker–Owners and Unions," *Dollars & Sense*, September/October, 2006 (http://www.dollarsandsense.org/archives/2006/0906bell.html, accessed May 9, 2016).

65. Rob Witherell, "An Emerging Solidarity: Worker Cooperatives, Unions, and the New Union Cooperative Model in the United States," *International Journal of Labour Research*, 5(2):251–68 (2013) and John Clay, "Can Union Co-ops Help Save Democracy?" *Truthout*, July 4, 2013 (http://truthout.org/news/item/17381-can-union-co-ops-help-save-democracy, May 9, 2016).

66. This initiative grew out of a long process of research and organizing dating back to the 1980s. For a valuable review of this history, see Laura Hanson Schlachter, "Stronger Together? The USW-Mondragón Union Co-op Model," Paper presented at the Mid-Year Fellows Workshop in Honor of Louis O. Kelso, New Brunswick, NJ: Rutgers University, School of Management and Labor Relations, 2016. The following discussion about union cooperatives draws extensively on this work and I am grateful for the extremely useful input.

67. http://ourharvest.coop (accessed May 22, 2016).

68. http://www.sustainergy.coop (accessed May 9, 2016).

69. https://applestreetmarket.coop (accessed May 9, 2016).

70. Complementing these locally cultivated initiatives, CUCI is also involved in efforts to catalyze union-cooperatives across the United States and a recent compilation assembled by Laura Hanson Schlachter identifies ongoing projects in eleven cities including Chicago, Denver, Los Angeles, Pittsburgh, and San Francisco.

71. The New York City Council allocated $1.2 million in 2014 to this purpose and a further $2.1 million in 2015. See Ajowa Nzinga Ifateyo, "A Co-op State of Mind," *In These Times*, August 18, 2014 and Michelle Stearn, "From New York to Oakland, CA, City Governments Support Worker Coops," Cleveland, OH: Democracy Collaborative, 2015 (http://community-wealth.org/content/new-york-oakland-ca-city-governments-support-worker-coops, accessed May 9, 2016).

72. Jennifer Jones Austin, "Worker Cooperatives for New York City: A Vision for Addressing Income Inequality," New York: Federation of Protestant

Welfare Agencies, 2014 (http://institute.coop/resources/worker-cooperatives-new-york-city-vision-addressing-income-inequality, accessed May 9, 2016).

73. Camille Kerr, "Local Government Support for Cooperatives," Oakland, CA: Democracy at Work Institute, 2015 (http://www.uwcc.wisc.edu/pdf/local%20govt%20support.pdf, accessed May 9, 2016).

74. Stearn, "From New York to Oakland, CA, City Governments Support Worker Co-ops" and Kerr, "Local Government Support for Cooperatives."

75. For an instructive step in this direction, see Mark Rank, Thomas Hirschl, and Kirk Foster, *Chasing the American Dream: Understanding What Shapes Our Fortunes* (New York: Oxford University Press, 2014).

Chapter 7. Conclusion

1. The study was carried out by the communications consultancy Burson-Marsteller and the Aspen Institute's Future of Work Initiative in collaboration with *Time* magazine. The number of "users" (42 percent) in the national population was greater than the number of "offerers" (22 percent). The most popular activity was ride-sharing followed in declining order by accommodation-sharing (22 percent users/10 percent offerers), service platforms (19 percent users/9 percent offerers), car rental (14 percent users/6 percent offerers), and food and goods delivery (11 percent users/7 percent offerers). Katy Steinmetz, "See How Big the Gig Economy Really Is," *Time*, January 6, 2016. For other estimates, see "Smooth Operators: A New Report Reveals the Scale and Purpose of App-based Earnings," *The Economist*, February 20, 2016.

2. This research should be interpreted with a little skepticism as it was carried out by Atmel, a microcontroller manufacturer that is heavily vested in the Maker Movement. See "DIY by the Numbers: Why the Maker Movement Is Here to Stay" (http://blog.atmel.com/2014/09/15/diy-by-the-numbers-why-the-maker-movement-is-here-to-stay, accessed May 9, 2016) and Tim Bajarin, "Why the Maker Movement Is Important to America's Future," *Time*, May 19, 2014.

3. Nancy Kurland, Sara Jane McCaffrey, and Douglas Hill, "The Localism Movement: Shared and Emergent Values," *Journal of Environmental Sustainability*, 2(2):45–57 (2012).

4. Stefan Svallfors, ed., *Contested Welfare State: Welfare Attitudes in Europe and Beyond* (Palo Alto, CA: Stanford University Press, 2012).

5. David Pilling, *Bending Adversity: Japan and Art of Survival* (New York: Penguin, 2014), R. Taggart Murphy, *Japan and the Shackles of the Past* (New York: Oxford University Press, 2014), and Morris Berman, *Neurotic Beauty: An Outsider Looks at Japan* (Portland, OR: Water Street Press, 2015).

6. Norihiro Kato, "Japan in a Post-growth Age," *The New York Times*, December 2, 2013.

7. Sheilagh Ogilvie and Markus Cerman, eds, *European Proto-industrialization: An Introductory Handbook* (New York: Cambridge University Press, 1996). The notion of "proto-industrialization" was obviously formulated in retrospect; an alternative term might be "post-agrarianism."

8. Krishan Kumar, *From Post-industrial to Post-modern Society: New Theories of the Contemporary World* (Cambridge, MA: Blackwell, 1995).

9. For other recent efforts to grapple with some of these same questions, see David Korten, *The Post-Corporate World: Life after Capitalism* (San Francisco, CA: Berrett-Koehler, 2000), Raphael Sassower, *Postcapitalism: Moving beyond Ideology in America's Economic Crises* (Boulder, CO: Paradigm, 2009), J. K. Gibson-Graham, *A Postcapitalist Politics* (Minneapolis: University of Minnesota Press, 2006), J. K. Gibson-Graham, *The End of Capitalism (As We Knew It): A Feminist Critique of Political Economy* (Minneapolis: University of Minnesota Press, 2006), Gerda Roelvink, Kevin St. Martin, and J. K. Gibson-Graham, eds, *Making Other Worlds Possible: Performing Diverse Economies* (Minneapolis: University of Minnesota Press, 2015), and Paul Mason, *Post-Capitalism: A Guide to Our Future* (New York: Farrar, Straus and Giroux, 2015).

10. A notable example of this vision is Guy Standing, *The Precariat: The New Dangerous Class* (New York: Bloomsbury, 2011).

11. Martin Ford describes an even more unsettling dystopian scenario where "the vast majority of humanity would effectively be disenfranchised. Economic mobility would become nonexistent. The plutocracy would shut itself away in gated communities or in elite cities, perhaps guarded by autonomous military robots and drones. In other words, we would see a return to something like the feudal system that prevailed during the Middle Ages. There would be one very important difference, however: medieval serfs were essential to the system since they provided the agricultural labor. In a futuristic world governed by automated feudalism the peasants would be largely superfluous." Martin Ford, *Rise of the Robots: Technology and the Threat of a Jobless Future* (New York: Basic Books, 2015), p. 219.

Index